CONDUCTING TECHNICAL RESEARCH

CONDUCTING TECHNICAL RESEARCH

EDITORS:
Everett N. Israel
Department of Industrial Technology
Eastern Michigan University
Ypsilanti, Michigan

R. Thomas Wright
Department of Industry and Technology
Ball State University
Muncie, Indiana

36th Yearbook, 1987

Council on Technology Teacher Education

Glencoe Publishing Company
15319 Chatsworth Street
Mission Hills, CA 91345

Printed in the United States of America

Orders and requests for information about cost and availability of yearbooks should be addressed to the company.

Requests to quote portions of yearbooks should be addressed to the Secretary, Council on Technology Education, in care of the publisher, for forwarding to the current Secretary.

This publication is available in microform.

University Microfilms International

300 North Zeeb Road
Dept. P.R.
Ann Arbor, MI 48106

ISBN 0-02-677113-6

Foreword

The Council on Technology Teacher Education, formerly called the American Council on Industrial Arts Teacher Education, is pleased to present its 36th Yearbook. This Yearbook, Conducting Technical Research, is different in that it will prove highly useful for teacher educators and those involved in technical research in business/industry.

Drs. Everett N. Israel and R. Thomas Wright have provided us with a reference to help us conceptualize the process of conducting technical research. This work covers the entire spectrum from the role of technology and science to the steps involved in designing, conducting, evaluating and reporting technical research. The book closes with a refreshing look at specific inventors in the areas of manufacturing, construction, communication and transportation.

All of us in Technology Education should realize the value of developing that creative spark in our students. The processes of invention and innovation have been with us since the human first utilized technical means for survival. It is imperative that we work with young people so that they comprehend the processes involved, whether it be solving technical problems in our personal lives, or in our roles as productive employees today and in the future. The authors have identified traits, techniques and guiding principles which will be of value to all of us.

The council commends Everett Israel and Thomas Wright for their contribution to the discipline of Technology Education and to inventors and innovators in today's business/industry. The Council also recognizes the Glencoe Publishing Company for its continued support of the Council, this Yearbook, and the discipline as a whole.

March 1987   Donald P. Lauda
                               President, CTTE

Yearbook Planning Committee

Terms Expiring in 1987:
Ervin A. Dennis
University of Northern Iowa
Paul W. DeVore
West Virginia University

Terms Expiring in 1988:
Donald P. Lauda
California State University—Long Beach
Donald F. Smith
Ball State University

Terms Expiring in 1989:
M. James Bensen
University of Wisconsin-Stout
Franzie L. Loepp
Illinois State University

Terms Expiring in 1990:
William E. Dugger
Virginia Polytechnic Institute and State University
Jack Kirby
University of Wisconsin-Platteville

Terms Expiring in 1991:
Leonard Sterry
University of Wisconsin-Stout
John R. Wright
California University of Pennsylvania

Chairperson:
R. Thomas Wright
Ball State University

Officers of the Council

Yearbook Proposals

Each year, at the ITEA International conference, the CTTE Yearbook Committee reviews the progress of yearbooks in preparation and evaluates proposals for additional yearbooks. Any member is welcome to submit a yearbook proposal. It should be written in sufficient detail for the committee to be able to understand the proposed substance and format. Fifteen copies of the proposal should be sent to the committee chairperson by February 1 of the year in which the conference is held. Below are the criteria employed by the committee in making yearbook selections.

CTTE Yearbook Committee

CTTE Yearbook Guidelines

A. Purpose:

The CTTE Yearbook Series is intended as a vehicle for communicating education subject matter in a structured, formal series that does not duplicate commercial textbook publishing activities.

B. Yearbook topic selection criteria:

An appropriate Yearbook topic should:
1. Make a direct contribution to the understanding and improvement of technology teacher education.
2. Add to the accumulated body of knowledge of the field.
3. Not duplicate publishing activities of commercial publishers or other professional groups.
4. Provide a balanced view of the theme and not promote a single individual's or institution's philosophy or practices.
5. Actively seek to upgrade and modernize professional practice in technology teacher education.
6. Lend itself to team authorship as opposed to single authorship.

Proper yearbook themes *may* also be structured to:
1. Discuss and critique points of view which have gained a degree of acceptance by the profession.
2. Raise controversial questions in an effort to obtain a national hearing.
3. Consider and evaluate a variety of seemingly conflicting trends and statements emanating from several sources.

C. The yearbook proposal:

1. The Yearbook Proposal should provide adequate detail for the Yearbook Planning Committee to evaluate its merits.
2. The Yearbook Proposal should include:
   (a) An introduction to the topic
   (b) A listing of chapter titles
   (c) A brief description of the content or purpose of each chapter
   (d) A tentative list of authors for the various chapters
   (e) An estimate of the length of each chapter

Previously Published Yearbooks

*1. Inventory Analysis of Industrial Arts Teacher Education Facilities, Personnel and Programs, 1952.

*2. Who's Who in Industrial Arts Teacher Education, 1953.

*3. Some Components of Current Leadership: Techniques of Selection and Guidance of Graduate Students; An Analysis of Textbook Emphases; 1954, three studies.

*4. Superior Practices in Industrial Arts Teacher Education, 1955.

*5. Problems and Issues in Industrial Arts Teacher Education, 1956.

*6. A Sourcebook of Reading in Education for Use in Industrial Arts and Industrial Arts Teacher Education, 1957.

*7. The Accreditation of Industrial Arts Teacher Education, 1958.

*8. Planning Industrial Arts Facilities, 1959, Ralph K. Nair, ed.

*9. Research in Industrial Arts Education, 1960. Raymond Van Tassel, ed.

*10. Graduate Study in Industrial Arts, 1961. R. P. Norman and R. C. Bohn, eds.

*11. Essentials of Preservice Preparation, 1962. Donald G. Lux, ed.

*12. Action and Thought in Industrial Arts Education, 1963. E. A. T. Svendsen, ed.

*13. Classroom Research in Industrial Arts, 1964. Charles B. Porter, ed.

14. Approaches and Procedures in Industrial Arts, 1965. G. S. Wall, ed.

15. Status of Research in Industrial Arts, 1966. John D. Rowlett, ed.

16. Evaluation Guidelines for Contemporary Industrial Arts Programs, 1967. Lloyd P. Nelson and William T. Sargent, eds.

17. A Historical Perspective of Industry, 1968. Joseph F. Luetkemeyer, Jr., ed.

18. Industrial Technology Education, 1969. C. Thomas Dean and N.A. Hauer, eds. Who's Who in Industrial Arts Teacher Education, 1969. John M. Pollock and Charles A. Bunten, eds.

19. Industrial Arts for Disadvantaged Youth, 1970. Ralph O. Gallington, ed.

20. Components of Teacher Education, 1971. W. E. Ray and J. Streichler, eds.

21. Industrial Arts for the Early Adolescent, 1972. Daniel L. Householder, ed.

*22. Industrial Arts in Senior High Schools, 1973. Rutherford E. Lockette, ed.

23. Industrial Arts for the Elementary School, 1974. Robert G. Thrower and Robert D. Weber, eds.

24. A Guide to the Planning of Industrial Arts Facilities, 1975. D. E. Moon, ed.

25. Future Alternatives for Industrial Arts, 1976. Lee H. Smalley, ed.

26. Competency-Based Industrial Arts Teacher Education, 1977. Jack C. Brueckman and Stanley E. Brooks, eds.

27. Industrial Arts in the Open Access Curriculum, 1978. L. D. Anderson, ed.

28. Industrial Arts Education: Retrospect, Prospect, 1979. G. Eugene Martin, ed.

29. Technology and Society: Interfaces with Industrial Arts, 1980. Herbert A. Anderson and M. James Benson, eds.

30. An Interpretive History of Industrial Arts, 1981. Richard Barella and Thomas Wright, eds.

31. The Contributions of Industrial Arts to Selected Areas of Education, 1982. Donald Maley and Kendall N. Starkweather, eds.

32. The Dynamics of Creative Leadership for Industrial Arts Education, 1983. Robert E. Wenig and John I. Mathews, eds.

33. Affective Learning in Industrial Arts, 1984. Gerald L. Jennings, ed.

34. Perceptual and Psychomotor Learning in Industrial Arts Education, 1985. John M. Shemick, ed.

35. Implementing Technology Education, 1986. Ronald E. Jones and John R. Wright, eds.

---

*Out-of-print yearbooks can be obtained in microfilm and in Xerox copies. For information on price and delivery, write to Xerox University Microfilms, 300 North Zeeb Road, Ann Arbor, Michigan, 48106.

Contents

Chapter 1

Paul W. DeVore
West Virginia University

Chapter 2

Paul W. DeVore
West Virginia University

Chapter 3

Richard D. Seymour
Ball State University

Chapter 4

Gary D. Weede
Illinois State University

Chapter 5

Michael R. White
University of Northern Iowa

Chapter 6

Harold H. Halfin
Orville W. Nelson
University of Wisconsin-Stout

Chapter 7

Donald L. Clark
Texas A&M University

Chapter 8

Chapter 9

Chapter 10

Chapter 11

Chapter 12

Preface

Technology is a subject discussed almost daily in the popular press. It has been the force that has allowed humankind to have an ever increasing standard of living. "Technology turned the United States from a wilderness which few suspected could be held together into one of the greatest nations on Earth" (*Technology: the lightening rod* . . . p. 12). Over a hundred years ago most people could not conceive of a world in which the horse was not the major form of transportation. (*Technology: Mongols on horseback* . . . p. 12). However, today few people in the Western world have used animal power for anything other than recreation.

Some years ago, Theobald (1967, p. 9) suggested that those who study technology agree that humans must invent their future if the future is to have any meaning. This invention of the future will be based on research. New methods of communication and transportation, improved materials, more efficient manufacturing and construction techniques are being developed and introduced to project this new future.

For example, a recent issue of *Scientific American* focused on advanced materials. Clark and Flemings (1986) suggest in the lead article "A fundamental reversal in the relationship between human beings and materials is taking place . . . Historically humans have adapted such natural materials as stone, clay, vegetable fiber and animal tissue to economic uses. The smelting of metals and the production of glass represented a refinement in this relationship" (p. 51). Yet, these authors suggest that recent advances in the understanding of matter have made it possible to start with a need, then, develop a material to meet it.

Likewise communications have advanced from pairs of wires connecting telephone sets to fiber optic guideways that are measured by their ability to carry "encyclopedias of information" per second. It is through this type of communication advance "that knowledge will be universally available and accessible. [These] advanced information systems will enable each individual to be better informed and to pursue his interests in his own way at his own speed" (*Technology: not enough information* . . . p. 12).

"Research in the service of free enterprise has worked wonders for our economy and our personal wants" (*Technology: Adam Smith* . . . p. 12). In this light, this yearbook addresses the topic of *Technical Research* through a study of a systematic structure. The editors and authors are fully aware that research activities often seem to be "unstructured". This appearance often comes from the researcher internalizing the research process and, therefore, seemingly omits steps or fails to carefully complete each step outlined in this book. However, it is the considered opinion of the various participants in this writing effort, that research is easier to conduct and is more likely to bear fruit, when the research is totally familiar with a systematic approach to the activity.

With this view as a guide, this yearbook was developed with four major sections. Chapters 1 and 2 introduce the reader to technology and the role research plays in its development. Chapter 3 presents a general model for technical research. The following chapters more fully describe each step in the research process. The last chapter presents a series of technical research case studies.

Each chapter is written as a general presentation of the topic. Specific information, such as statistical treatment formula and tables, are not presented. This information is best obtained from books which provide a narrow, in-depth presentation of one aspect of technical research.

It is the hope of the entire writing and editing team that this yearbook will help each reader to better understand and conduct technical research.

Everett N. Israel
R. Thomas Wright

REFERENCES

Clark, J.P. and Flemings, M.C. Advanced Materials and the Economy. *Scientific American.* Vol. 255, October 1986, pp. 51-57.

Technology: Adam Smith, Uncle Sam and Big Brother. Rolling Meadows, IL: Gould, Inc., n.d.

Technology: Mongols on horseback, planes without jets, and a plant that grows gas. Rolling Meadows, IL: Gould, Inc., n.d.

Technology: Not enough information, too much information and the information democracy. Rolling Meadows, IL: Gould, Inc., n.d.

Technology: The lightning rod, Ben Franklin and the American Revolution. Rolling Meadows, IL: Gould Inc., n.d.

Theobald, R. (ed.) *Dialogue on Technology.* Indianapolis: Bobbs-Merrill Company, 1967.

Acknowledgments

We would like to express our sincere appreciation to the many people who helped make this yearbook a reality.

The critical element in all successful yearbooks is the author team. The editors have had the distinct pleasure of working with a group of true professionals. Each author produced chapter manuscripts which were insightful and clearly written. Additionally, the authors graciously accepted the extensive editing that was necessary to make this yearbook an integrated whole rather than a book of readings. We thank each author individually for their scholarship and understanding.

Supporting the production of each yearbook are a number of people whose names do not appear formally in the text of the book. We would like to single out four individuals who worked tirelessly behind the scenes to make the editors' tasks easier. A special thank you is extended to Wes Stephens and Ronald Baird for reviewing and reacting to each chapter manuscript. Also, warm appreciation is extended to Virginia Ridenour from Illinois State University and Becky Liskey from Eastern Michigan University who word processed the edited manuscript. Without their help this project would not have been completed.

Both editors are always appreciative of the support and encouragement given by their wives. Thank you Julie Israel and Phyllis Wright for your understanding and for alternately hosting us during our five editing sessions.

Also, we would like to thank Joe Carrel and Purdue University for making meeting sites available for our early meeting with the author team. Additionally, we sincerely extend our appreciation to Ball State, Illinois State, and Eastern Michigan Universities for absorbing so many "hidden" costs associated with producing this yearbook.

Last, and certainly not least, we thank the staff at Glencoe Publishing Company's Bennett and McKnight Division for their help in producing this yearbook and for continuing to support the Council for Technology Teacher Education's Yearbook Series.

Everett N. Israel
R. Thomas Wright

CHAPTER 1

A Perspective for Technical Research

by Paul W. DeVore

Sub-Topics:
- Overview of the Chapter
- A Prospect
- Technical Creativity
- The Technical Process
- The Context of Technical Research
- Summary

Developing new and alternative technical means involves human creativity of the highest order. Internal combustion engines, instrument landing systems, space frames and heart pacers are not found in nature; they are invented, developed and produced by humans. Fundamental to bringing these new and alternative technical means into being are intellectual processes. Over the centuries, as the technical means have become more complex, human beings have recognized that the intellectual processes associated with the creation of new technical means could be enhanced if the process was better understood. Numerous investigations have been conducted by individuals, committees, associations, corporation task groups and students of creativity. Each has contributed a better understanding of the intellectual processes and helped the development of procedures, structures and environments to enhance creativity in the technologies.

OVERVIEW OF THE CHAPTER

The purpose of this chapter is to provide a background and setting for the study of technical research and to explore the process of creativity in the technologies. This chapter will identify the role of technical research in invention-innovation and innovation-development.

Today, more than ever before, there is a concern by people throughout the world about the nature and direction of our technical means. More people are realizing that there is a direct relationship between the type of technical means we create and adopt and the nature of our societies. We are asking:

What is the relationship between human beings, their societies and technical means?

What is the essence of technical means?

What are the fundamental human problems and political issues related to various types of technical means?

What are the implications for the preparation of citizens?

In what direction shall we proceed in our evolutions?

What kind of technical means should we create that will contribute toward our future direction?

How can we improve and enhance our abilities to create the appropriate technical means?

The focus of this yearbook is the structured procedures used to help answer the last question.

A PROSPECT

The process of becoming human began at least three million years ago. Throughout this period of human cultural evolution, the creation and use of technical means (tools, technics, techniques and technical systems) played a significant role. They not only enhanced the survival potential of humans, but a direct relationship has existed between the intellectual and social evolution of the human species and the creation and use of tools.

The creation of new technical means has changed the perceptions of human beings about themselves and their relation to others and the natural environment. Our perceptions of time, space, distance and the future have all been altered by the creation of technical means ranging from food preservation processes to space flight.

Technical Research and Human Potential

The creation and use of technical means have served as the processes through which basic human needs and social purposes are met and human potential enhanced. When the technical means have been *appropriate* to the natural and social environments and the needs of the people, standards of living have been enhanced, health improved, life lengthened, laborious toil reduced, time for leisure increased, status improved and, in many instances, political choice enhanced.

The *most* appropriate technical means required to meet human needs and to enhance human potential have not been created. Only recently have we begun to understand the great potential for creativity in the technologies and in the relationship to the creation of a better social order for all. Directly related to this goal is the use of technical research for creating and developing appropriate technical means compatible with agreed-upon social purposes. A better understanding of the creative process will contribute to a new potential and new choices for a better society.

The survival of the human species continues to be augmented by new technical means which enable the repair, restoration and replacement of organic organs with bio-technical tools, such as plastic valves, external life support systems and communication devices. Through the invention and development of tools humans have altered the process of evolution by externalizing and amplifying the organic functions of seeing, recording, lifting, moving, holding and hearing. Human muscles have been augmented and amplified through the use of power in manufacturing, construction and transportation systems. Developments in the storage, transmission and use of information have significantly enhanced the human senses of seeing, hearing, smelling and memory. Examples include electron microscopes, tape recordings, pollution monitoring devices, heat sensing devices, and telecommunication devices. Amplifiers of thought processes include mathematical tables, chemical formulas, slide rules, computers and information processing systems. The latter are new *intellectual technologies* which add new dimension to human potential and the behavior of technical and social systems.

Technical Research—Key to the Future

There are many reasons for investigating the technical research process. The sustainability and enhancement of human societies and potential are related directly to creating and using appropriate technical means.

Unfortunately, not all technical means that have been created are appropriate. A number of problems have emerged. These range from resource depletion to the demise of single-industry communities. This range includes problems associated with energy conversion systems, food supplies, toxic wastes, adequate housing and social problems such as employment and the quality of natural and social environments.

Future technical and related research will focus on both the creation of new tools and technical systems, and the appropriateness of these new technical means. The research will focus on the behavior of the technical elements and the impact they have on humans, their social systems and the natural environment. The challenge will be to determine the variables and relationships so that humans can control, for human purposes, their social/technological systems.

Technological and Social Change

Throughout recorded history many social changes have resulted from the creation and introduction of a new tool, technical device or technical system. The destruction of the indigo dye industry in India during the latter part of the 19th century was a result of the creation of synthetic coal-tar dyes by the Englishman Henry Perkins. The loss of jobs in the automotive and steel industries in Britain and the United States during the last quarter of the 20th century are examples of social change and problems brought about by the creation, use or control of new technical means.

Problems of employment and meaningful work roles are world- wide problems. Countries that are becoming more industrialized provide significant competition to developed countries in the manufacture of products, automobiles and telecommunication equipment.

The economies of various nations have been altered constantly by the creation of new products and manufacturing processes. Many of these developments have revolutionized the way we live. Other developments have made small incremental changes in our societies in an evolutionary way. Increasingly a formal, organized approach to the creation of new technical means and products has evolved. This technical knowledge and means has become more and more the province of people throughout the world instead of those nations who were the early creators of it. Typical of this change is Malaysia. John Hughes (1985) reported the following conversation with an American businessman who has Malaysians making all the electronic innards for his company's American labeled product:

> I doubt that we will ever manufacture these parts in the United States again. But anyway, Malyasian technology in this era has now overtaken our own. If we were to start producing these parts in the United States again, we would have to bring American workers to Malaysia to be trained by Malaysians (Hughes, p. 13).

The United States and other western nations are losing world markets. George McAlmon reported the trend in 1979. His study concluded that business and industry in the United States seemed to have lost its initiative and innovative potential. He noted:

> Management in the successful foreign industries has invested heavily in research and new technology, quality control, engineering, imaginative product design, and a willingness to go for higher long-term profits rather than lower short- term profits (McAlmon, p. 8).

In contrast, McAlmon noted that top American industrial management has cut back on research and development. The focus has been on management and profit rather than on innovation, invention, and product design. He found that U. S. research and development expenditures had declined thirty percent over the last fifteen years and most successful companies were technologically and research oriented such as International Business Machines, Xerox and Polaroid.

United States technological leadership is in the "high-tech" industries such as semiconductors, computers and lasers. Technical research created the base for these industries and a significant portion of this research came from Bell Laboratories, the research and development arm of American Telephone and Telegraph. From these laboratories, which focus on non-product oriented research, came the transistor, voice recording, radio astronomy, the solar cell and lasers.

The creation of new technical means, whether a new product or a new means of producing products, is critical to the economic health of a country. New product innovation is often conceived as being the most important, Christopher D. Stone suggests that new product innovation may not be as significant as innovation relating to the factors of production (Stone, 1979). He notes that the intoduction of commercially viable solar voltaic cells, which are highly efficient in producing electricity, would be an enormous contribution to society. The means for reducing the cost per unit of electricity would be the major breakthrough. Solar cells, as a product, have been in existence for a number of years.

Technical research involves not only the creation of new products but also the creation of the means of producing new products. This is one of the secrets of the success of the Japanese. Semiconductors were created and developed in the United States. First came the transistor, then the integrated circuit and then the microprocessor. Even though the United States still has the competitive edge in microprocessors, Japan is on the leading edge in integrated circuit production systems at the ultra-precise level of 1/1000th of a millimeter. The creation and development of carbon fibers, fifth-generation computers and optic fibers are examples of Japan's research capabilities in both product design and production.

Technical research has always been important to business, industry and society. Today the continued success of a business or an industry in meeting the challenge of national and international competition is related directly to a variety of technical research activities ranging from new products to more efficient means of production. For example, half of Hewlett-Packard's orders in 1982 came from products introduced during the previous three years. John Doyle, Hewlett-Packard vice-president for Research and Development, stated that "Hewlett-Packard would be less than a $300 million company today instead of a $4.3 billion company if we hadn't introduced any new products in the past decade" (1983, p. 3).

TECHNICAL CREATIVITY

The creation of technical means has been essential to the evolution and development of civilization as we know it. As critical as the process of creativity in the technologies has been, it is a little understood process. The creation, development and adoption of new technical means by society is a complex maze of human intellectual activity ranging from the lone inventor to highly organized corporate research and development efforts.

The nature of the creative act may be the same today, but the context and the knowledge components have changed significantly.

Knowledge and Technical Means

A technological society must, by its nature, be a knowledge society. Knowledge is necessary to create tools, machines, techniques and technical systems. It is also necessary to determine the nature and characteristics of the systems required to support a given social system.

The technical means created in the twentieth century are of a different order than those created during the period of industrialization. The tools of industrialism extended the physical capacity of human beings. The tools of today are of a broader and more encompassing order. They are *systemic* and require an entirely new order of thinking. An example is using electronic devices for sensing and controlling machine operations formerly performed by human operators. Cybernetics came into being with the advent of the computer with its capability of providing analog control of individual machines, digital control for coordination and control with feedback and self-correcting capabilities for the entire factory system.

The creation of new technical means requires new forms of knowledge, often different from knowledge organized in traditional disciplines which focus on unitary fields of inquiry. The future requires the integration of these traditional disciplines and the creation of new disciplines and modes of inquiry which focus on the design and development of new technical and social systems. The new disciplines and modes of inquiry will emphasize using information about all aspects of life and living for the creation of knowledge needed to solve human and societal problems.

Much of this new knowledge will be technical knowledge. Information about technical systems can be organized and integrated into conceptual, systematic and transmittable forms. This knowledge provides the user with the means to predict the behavior of these systems. This form of knowledge requires high level integration.

The belief that technical knowledge could be organized and integrated led to the institutionalization of the process of creating and developing technical means. The process allowed problems to be attacked systematically utilizing specialized equipment, laboratories and people. This was a major change in the evolution of technical means. At this point, rather than knowledge being the province of universities and scholars, knowledge became the concern of business and industry. This institutionalization of invention took the form of research expenditures by business and industry, the creation of independent research organizations and the establishment of special agencies of the government. Many cooperative ventures evolved, with colleges and universities focusing on basic research in the technologies and business and industry focusing on innovation, product design and development.

Creativity in the technologies is a complex interwoven maze. Traditionally, information about technological development has been focused on specific discoveries and individual inventors. However, technical research, which occurs mostly in industrial settings and is generally classified as product development or technological development, is not as well understood. According to Ralph E. Gomory, Vice President and Director of Research, IBM Corporation (p. 576), the day-to-day intellectual efforts of thousands of individuals conducting technical research related to product design and development provide the core for the evolutionary steps that eventually lead to significant advances.

A number of different terms are used to describe the technical research process. Among them are invention, discovery, innovation and development. Each has a distinct meaning.

Invention: a creative mental process through which knowledge and experience are combined over time to produce something which did not exist before and which is represented by some *physical* form (gyro-compass, long-playing record, shell molding), *social* form (banking, corporation, health insurance), or *mental* concept (hypothesis, theory, taxonomy).

Discovery: the process of observation and recognition of the phenomena which were inherent in the nature of things but unknown before. Example: oxygen, gravity.

Innovation: the process of refining and improving that which is already created and/or established. Example: all steel automobile body, monocoque aircraft construction.

Development: the process of using known methods and procedures of creating new methods and procedures for the purpose of evolving an invention or innovation from *initial concept to commercial application*. Examples: commercial production of nylon, the development and commercialization of the computer.

There is a continuum of creativity in the technologies ranging from inventions such as the transistor to technological developments such as the computer.

Technical research comes in many forms. There are certain characteristics of technical research that separate it from what is commonly called scientific research. Technical research is:

1. Usually conducted in an industrial setting.
2. Focused on problems associated with specific goals, applications or products.
3. A highly complex human endeavor involving questions ranging from the behavior of materials, to the design of criteria based components, to the reliability of components and systems over time in commercial use, to the problems of efficient production of the product.
4. Involved with the creation and development of products that are affected by and affect the society in which they are created and introduced.

THE TECHNICAL PROCESS

Why some people create while others do not is not known. The attributes of creativity and inventiveness are not the province of any one race, nation or culture. Some peoples have retained their inherited ways for long periods of time while others have created better and more efficient solutions to the problems of life and living.

There has been much speculation about using genetics to explain the differences between Western and so-called primitive people. Evidence indicates that inventiveness is not an ability specific to any one race of people. There is no objective evidence that the mental acuity of people of modern society is superior to that of primitive societies. In fact, the inventions of primitive people, including fire, the bow and arrow, preparation of animal skins for clothing, the spinning of fibers, taming of animals and the domestication of plants, provided the technical base for further advancement.

The inventive abilities of the Eskimo and the Indian are often overlooked. The Eskimos survive in an extremely limited environment. They use a high level of ingenuity in utilizing bones and hides of animals for clothing and tools, and ice and snow for shelter. In the extreme cold, the Eskimos freeze walrus hides into sleds which exploits the environment to advantage.

The Indians brought forth a number of inventions, innovations and discoveries before the discovery of America. Some of the more significant contributions were the tools and techniques for growing and harvesting maize. They also introduced irrigation systems in Peru and the southwestern portion of North America. Beans, potatoes in several varieties, artichokes, tapioca, sunflowers and tomatoes were contributions of the Indian. The Indians also discovered rubber and developed ways to mold, shape and cure it. These and other inventions and innovations illustrate that primitive people do invent.

Some insight into why some peoples continued to advance technically while others have reached a stable state can be obtained through an understanding of the process of how technical adaptive systems came into being.

The factors which seem to be critical to the technical process are cultural. They have to do with human perceptions and attitudes about creativity and change. Societies that provide for freedom of expression and have positive attitudes toward invention and change have made significant contribution to technological advancement.

Societies which are positive about creativity in the technologies support activities that enhance the creative process. There is within these societies a recognition that creativity can be enhanced. Many of the human traits associated with technological creativity are learned traits which can be examined, altered and improved through thought and intelligent action.

The ability of some societies to evolve complex technical systems relates not only to the cultural factor, but also to the cumulative nature of technical means. Tools, machines, techniques and technical systems of increasing complexity result from a series of separate but related inventions and innovations over a period of time. This has been particularly true of the complex machines of today, such as the computer, which evolved from the mechanical difference machine of Babbage in the 1820's to today's electronic computer. Today's computers are dependent on inventions and innovations ranging from the binary code to the transistor and printed circuit board. This coming together of essential elements at just the right time has been evident in the evolution of complex technical means. Examples include the long evolution of printing and the creation of the essential elements of the modern turbine aircraft engine which required advances in metallurgy, lubrication and precision fabrication.

THE CONTEXT OF TECHNICAL RESEARCH

The source of technical means is the human mind. Human thought processes are determined largely by the nature of the social and natural environment in which a person exists. A change in the technical content of society, in the tools or technical systems, alters the intellectual perspective. Any alteration in intellectual perspective changes the potential for the creation of new tools, machines or technical systems. Throughout history significant shifts in intellectual perspective have occurred. Such a shift began in the 1500's, giving rise to the industrial era. This shift was from a passive, contemplative mode to an activist, interventionist role. The new intellectual perspective was more analytical than in the past, establishing the base for a heightened ability to analyze the behavior of tools, machines and technical systems. The new mentality placed a more positive value on the use and function of technical means. The new mentality belonged to the realm of action and was characterized by:

1. *Ability to do* with a concern for how to do and how things work as a way to improve the means available for doing.
2. *Efficiency of doing* with a concern for the improvement of the performance of tools, machines and technical systems.
3. Extension of the *analysis of doing and application to practice* to all tools, machines, techniques and technical systems, with the goal of doing all things better.

The focus was also on thinking, but with a difference. Thinking was transferred to practice. The new intellect was an analytical one which asked, "Why?".

The new intellectual base focused on how things worked rather than on the essence of things. The mode of inquiry became knowledge based, with process as the primary focus. The knowledge base was concerned with facts, data, information, concepts and generalizations. The mode of inquiry was concerned with the application of knowledge to solving problems. In solving the problems and creating the new technology, a new mentality evolved. It utilized the intellectual processes of problem identification and definition, observing, analyzing, visualizing, computing, measuring, predicting, experimenting, testing and designing. This new mentality focused on learning-by-doing and direct observation of the physical world, the basis of today's technical research.

Human Factors

It is often assumed that a genius level of intellect is a necessary element for successful creativity in the technologies. Research indicates otherwise. A reasonably high level of intellect is necessary but IQ's much higher than 120 are not critical (Briggs, p. 75).

In addition to intelligence, most studies of the creative process conclude that those who have been highly creative in the technologies evidence:

1. A high level of motivation.
2. A dedication to the task.
3. Total immersion in the problem.
4. Ability to clearly identify the problem.
5. A mind prepared with broad, up-to-date technological information and knowledge base.
6. Perserverance and the ability to stick with the problem.
7. Intellectual delight in solving problems.

8. Dissatisfaction with the way things are.

9. A non-conformist perspective.

10. A wide range of diverse interests.

The Creative Environment

The nature of the environment in which the inventor or innovator works has a significant bearing on the creativity potential. Some of the more essential characteristics of a creative environment include: stability, communication, availability of new knowledge and information, a stimulating intellectual atmosphere, a perceived intellectual challenge and belief in the value of the research.

Context of Invention and Innovation

How do invention and innovation occur? Four theories of invention and innovation have been proposed, none of which has been accepted as a general theory. These are:

1. *Evolutionary Social Process*. Those who hold this view believe that inventions and innovations result naturally from the civilization process, that there is a cumulative synthesis and when the time is ripe someone, perhaps more than one person, will bring about the new invention or innovation. This theory is one of mechanistic determinism which says that when all the elements are available, someone will put them together.

2. *Transcendental Revelation*. This theory holds that invention and innovation are individual acts of inspiration brought forth by genius or people of unusual ability. The inventor achieves the new invention through a process of revelation or intuition. This theory rests on what is called mystical determinism, with no true analysis possible.

3. *Configurational Synthesis*. This theory is sometimes called the "Gestalt" theory of invention. The focus is on individuals who are capable of establishing relationships that did not exist before. Implied is a searching behavior with the goal of solving an existing problem. The invention or innovation occurs when a new pattern or configuration is created or synthesized, consisting of new combinations or groupings of known elements.

4. *Social-Economic Motivation*. This theory proposes that the technical act is induced by the complex relations existing between those who consume and those who invent. It assumes that

invention and innovation can be influenced if accumulated knowledge about a given technology and information about social needs and priorities are made available to inventors and innovators who are supported by appropriate resources.

Many factors are associated with invention and innovation. The primary factors are intellectual and those mental processes required for analyzing and synthesizing, among others. The question remains, "How do inventions and innovations come about?"

The Process

There are two common views concerning the nature of the invention and innovation process. One view suggests that it consists of non-linear, unstructured investigations into the behavior of technical phenomenon. The second suggests that invention and innovation are rational, orderly and linear procedures that can be planned and managed. Proponents of this view cite Thomas A. Edison's research laboratory at Menlo Park, New Jersey and the Bell Telephone laboratories or the General Electric Research laboratories. These research organizations were established to create and convert knowledge into new technical means. This process is perceived as an orderly process; it starts with the discovery of new knowledge, moving through various stages of development and eventually concluding with a new product, service or form. This view assumes that the inventive process can be analyzed, the various elements can be identified, assignments can be made and the entire process can be controlled. Those who hold the rational view of invention believe that the process is goal oriented, is orderly in procedure, utilizes selected knowledge from specific disciplines to solve problems and is, in reality, only a matter of applying intelligence to the solution of identified problems (Schon, 1967; p. 5).

This procedure has the greatest support among large corporations and government bureaus. It is best illustrated by large- scale projects such as the space program and the Polaris submarine. This procedure, as outlined in Figure 1-1, involves considerable planning using such methods as PERT (*P*lanning, *E*valuation and *R*eview *T*echnique).

The linear-sequential models have been questioned by those who have researched the process. These studies have concluded that uniqueness cannot be programmed. (Langrish, 1972). Langrish, Gibbons, Jevons and Evans concluded in their landmark study that the sources of innovation are multiple and that a new product or process is the historical outcome of the convergence of many strands of events (p. 7).

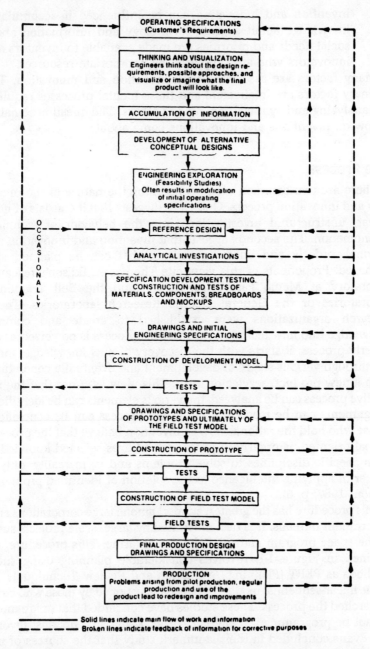

Figure 1-1: Diagram of Linear Perception of Creative Process and Product Design System. From *Technology and Change* by Donald Schon, 1967.

There is also considerable overlapping and interaction between the nature of the two views of invention and innovation. It is best to recognize that technical creativity and research are not one act or one kind of act, but a series of acts ranging from the least orderly to the most rational.

The two views of creativity in the technologies seem to be part of the same continuum and mutually supporting. In Table 1-1 the characteristics of the two views have been listed. The diagram visually depicts this continuum of creativity, ranging from invention and discovery through several types of innovation to development. It should be realized that these characteristics are not discrete and that linear melts into nonlinear at certain points on the continuum as do other elements.

The more each component of the process is studied, whether invention, innovation or development, the more it becomes obvious there are distinct differences between them. Each component is a part of the continuum but is also a separate and discrete process requiring certain intellectual and environmental prerequisites. Development involves large numbers of people in the complex task of perfecting and introducing a product into some social structure. Invention and discovery, on the other hand, involve individuals and small groups with the goal of adding to the knowledge reservoir and creating new or novel physical, social or mental forms. Both processes are part of the creative technical act and define its two distinct stages: 1) the act of *creating* new knowledge and forms through invention and innovation and 2) the act of *applying* new knowledge and forms through innovation and development.

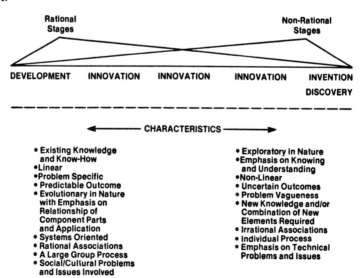

Table 1-1: The Technical Creativity Continuum Adapted From *Technology: An Introduction*, by Paul W. DeVore, 1980.

Both stages have goals. Those involved in the application of new knowledge and forms operate within specified boundaries with defined agreed-upon goals. Those involved in the creation of new knowledge and forms through invention-innovation operate within less structured and more flexible environments.

Invention-Innovation

Inventions and innovations do not occur in a vacuum. They begin at a given time and place and are products of the intellectual process. For this reason, all inventions and innovations have antecedents. Prior knowledge and information at some level are prerequisites, whether created by the inventor or by others. For invention to occur, the act must be carried out in an environment that is favorable to the process and by a mind prepared for the act of insight. The latter creates a new reality and the potential for further invention and innovation. The greater the size of the existing knowledge and component reservoir and the better prepared the potential inventor is intellectually, the greater the probability a new act of insight will occur.

It is also important to recognize the cumulative nature of technical means. Some inventions and innovations are the result of a series of discoveries, inventions and innovations over a period of time. An example of this cumulative nature of technology is the video tape recorder. It is a composite resulting from the efforts of many individuals over a number of years. At each stage in the evolution of the recorder, the antecedents necessary for an invention or innovation to occur were present. The lineage of the recorder includes developments in frequency modulation, electronics, magnetic theory, magnetic recording materials and control theory.

The social and intellectual environment in which the technical act takes place determines to a large extent the perspective of potential inventors and the focus of their intellectual endeavors. There are a number of theories about the process of creativity in the technologies. The primary element stressed in most descriptions of the process is being able to see things differently. Technical research progresses when that which is perceived by others as irrelevant or unrelated is perceived as relevant by the inventor or researcher. This process is termed "differentiation of wholes." A product of invention or research is a new configuration and results from the recombining of existing knowledge or elements.

The usual way of thinking is to think about objects and things rather than about the ideas or mental configurations of objects and things.

Configuration means a mental construct, a way of perceiving one's world and what makes up that world. Thinking in terms of things focuses one's thoughts on totalities rather than on the discrete elements that make up a configuration. By thinking in terms of the *idea of things*, or the *configuration of things* and the relationship of the elements within the configuration, it becomes possible to perceive new relationships. This is the source of new inventions, innovations and productive technical research.

Invention and innovation are the result of a reordering of thinking. Nontraditional, irrational and lateral thinking are essential for new configurations or the recombination of configurations to occur. Novelty occurs when new linkages are perceived between two or more elements which had not been joined before. The result is a product with properties entirely different from the properties of the individual antecedents.

Technological Development

The fact that a new device, process or technique is invented or a new physical or social phenomenon discovered does not mean that the invention or discovery will become a part of the adaptive system of society. What it does mean is that a new potential or choice exists. Inventions and discoveries go through a series of innovations and a process called development before adoption and commercial acceptance. This process is called *technological development*.

Technological development is a highly complex, little understood process that involves the transfer of new ideas into a social environment. It blends invention, innovation and technical research with adoption in a human and social context.

Whereas, invention and innovation generally deal with a single event or element, technological development is the integration of a series of events which brings an invention or innovation into commercial/social reality. Without development the process of invention would serve no social purpose.

The process of development includes the refinement and commercialization of a new product or process. Development is a process of integration and coordination which involves high risk and uncertainty. It also depends on the creation of new capital and the education and retraining of people to produce a product, provide a service, and market or inform people about the product or service. It is a change process involving diverse and complex human and social factors in a specific environment, at a specific time, with a specified goal.

The process of technological development has specific components, events and procedures, each related to the other in a functional way. The technological development process shown in Figure 1-2 is typical of systems associated with marketable products.

The process of technological development is more evolutionary and less revolutionary than generally perceived. It is dependent upon incremental development using technical research applied to numerous problems, each critical to the successful operation of the whole. Figure 1-3 illustrates a procedure used by Hewlett-Packard in product development which details the decision points step-by-step. At each step, various types of technical research are carried out.

Incorporating technical innovations into society often calls for social change and innovation. Conversely, the social environment directly affects the climate of technical research and innovation. There is a mutual and direct relationship. For instance, technological developments in housing, water supply systems, air quality monitoring, nuclear energy, turbine engines and satellite communications are categories where technical innovation brought about social changes.

Structuring and Managing the Research Process

To remain competitive today, businesses and industries have adopted two major types of research and development activities:

1. Structuring and managing the creative process in-house.
2. Collaborating efforts with other companies and/or associations.

In-house research and development involves an industry establishing its own research and development program to enhance the technical creative process, develop new materials and products and develop more efficient production procedures. Research endeavors range from support of day-to-day production operations or minor product design changes to those that are on the forefront of technological development such as computer aided tomography or the video recorder.

When General Electric, du Pont, Kodak and American Telephone and Telegraph established their pioneer research laboratories, the approach was novel and not fully accepted by other industries. Today research in the support of industry is taken for granted. Markets are highly competitive and the nature of technical means, whether in the field of electronics or construction, rests more and more on intellectual, conceptual and theoretical structures. For most product lines there is now world-wide competition, not only in the manufacturing of the product, but in product innovation and development as well.

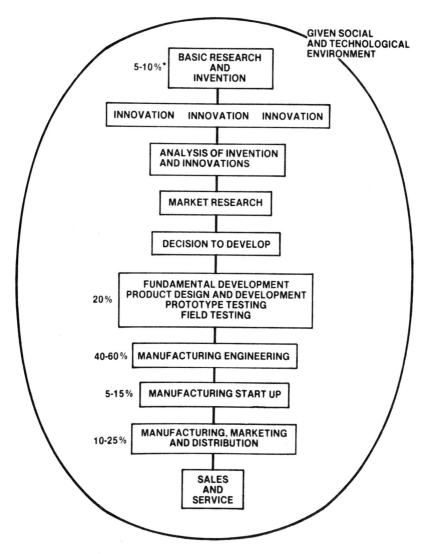

Figure 1-2: Typical Technological Development Processes for Marketable Technical Products with Percentage of Costs Per Stage of Development (From *Technological Innovation.* U.S. Department of Commerce, p. 7)

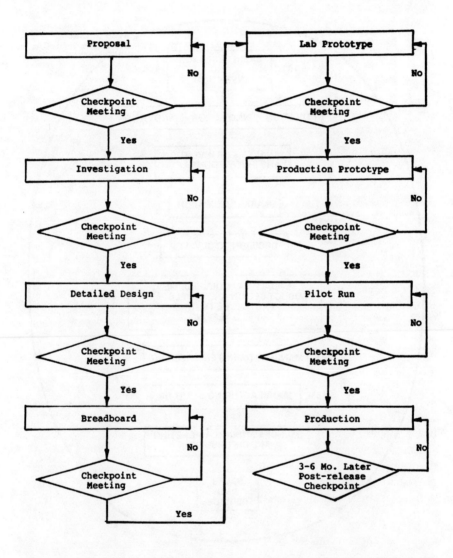

Figure 1-3: HP's Product Development Cycle. *Electronic Engineering Manager.*
April 1985, p. 28.

At the product design and development level, there is a consensus emerging that certain orderly steps are involved. Paul G. Waitkus, Engineering Operations Manager of Microsystems Development, Digital Equipment Corporation, has outlined the steps as they relate to today's advanced products such as computer systems. These are similar to other descriptions of the linear process. The four steps are:

1. *Strategy and requirements*: This step involves the determination of market requirements and review costs, delivery, functionality, quality, ease of use, performance, compatibility and serviceability.

2. *Planning*: Functional specifications of the product including product requirements—how it will look, how it will operate, and how its function will be distributed among various components.

3. *Implementation*: In this step the product is designed and prototypes built and tested to verify the design.

4. *Qualification*: Production units are built in a pilot run and qualified by specialists within and outside the company. This is the transition step from design to manufacturing. (Waitkus, pp. 92-95).

At each step there is a product design transition review and at the termination of the development effort the entire process is reviewed and a formal "lessons learned" report is prepared and distributed throughout the company to help refine the process (Waitkus, 1985). The latter is a critical process and is an on- going one in most companies searching for the means to remain competitive.

In 1981, Mark Shepherd, Jr., Chairman, Texas Instruments Incorporated (a business that started in 1930 to commercialize the reflection seismograph for petroleum exploration) presented a paper on "Ensuring Creativity in a Post-Industrial Society." In this paper he outlined Texas Instruments OST System (*O*bjectives, *S*trategies, *T*actics). OST is a management system that operates at all levels within the Texas Instrument Corporation and thus relates directly to the operation and management of the research function.* *Objectives* establish long-range goals, usually ten years or more for each business entity within the company. *Strategies* focus on an intermediate set of goals and define the course or direction to be pursued to attain these goals. *Tactics* are the

---

*The Texas Instruments OST system is one of a number of company management systems. It is cited here because of the long-term success of Texas Instruments in high technology endeavors.

action programs, usually funded on an annual basis. Tactics form the resource allocation part of the system. The OST system establishes a hierarchy of quantitative goals against which performance is measured.

Collaborative research involves a number of similar industries establishing consortiums to identify and complete research and development projects. Traditionally, businesses and industries in the United States have been highly secretive about their research efforts. However, the greatly increased competition from foreign firms has altered their stance. In addition, the increased complexity and costs of technical research have forced the issue and brought about the development of Research and Development (R & D) consortia. One of the earliest and most prominent R & D consortia is the Microelectronics and Computer Technology Corporation (MCC) initiated by William C. Norris, Chairman and CEO of Control Data.

Since the establishment of MCC a number of other R & D consortia have been established. Some of the more representative are:

1. Semiconductor Research Corporation
   Research Triangle Park, NC

2. Plastic Recycling Foundation
   New York, NY

3. Chemical Industry Institute of Toxicology
   Research Triangle Park, NC

4. Oncogen (cancer research)
   Seattle, WA

5. Bell Communications Research
   Composed of the group of telephone companies created with with the breakup of AT&T

6. Center for Advanced Television Studies
   Composed of major television networks—ABC, NBC, CBS, Ampex, PBS, RCA, HBO, Harris, 3M and Tektronix (Dwight B. Davis, 1985)

In 1972, the National Science Foundation established an Industry/University Cooperative Research Centers program. With the increased competition from industries in other countries the program has established and is supporting twenty centers with a faculty of 250, 30 postdoctoral fellows and 300 graduate students. The centers are sensitive to the needs of industry and are supported fully by business and industry after the initial five-year funding by the National Science Foundation (Maugh II, p. 48).

In 1984, additional centers were established:

1. Center for Robotics Systems in Microelectronics
   University of California at Santa Barbara

2. Engineering Research Center for Telecommunication
   Columbia University

3. Center for Composites Manufacturing Science and Engineering
   University of Delaware at Newark

4. Center on Systems Research
   University of Maryland and Harvard University

5. Center on Biotechnology Process Engineering
   Massachusetts Institute of Technology

6. Center for Intelligent Manufacturing Systems
   Purdue University (Maugh, p. 50).

Several critical factors account for the success of the centers. One, the cooperating industries make commitments to be involved by assigning researchers or engineers as liaison agents with the center. Second, the centers must produce. Third, there is the recognition that there are basic differences between basic science research and technological research.

In an interview conducted by Thomas Maugh for *High Technology* with Erich Block, Director of the National Science Foundation, Block stated: "Too many research scientists believe that *discoveries* flowing from their work drive engineering and technology. This is not only far too simple to describe the complex interactions. It is simply incorrect." "There have been many cases in which useful invention went forward without the benefit of scientific work and in fact led to the development of principles or theories—indeed, sometimes whole new areas of science" (Maugh, p. 50-51).

Some states, such as Ohio, have established technology application centers where the focus is on the application of new technology for the improvement of existing industries or the creation of new industries.

Industries such as Deere and Company have established their own Technical Centers. Advanced research is conducted on products and processes that may be eventually incorporated into new or improved products. Industries work cooperatively with various U. S. government research programs. Deere and Company have agreed to work with the National Aeronautics and Space Administration in several technical research areas. Categories include (1) investigating the shape of graphite steel at zero gravity, (2) determining the efficiency of the Sterling external combustion engine, (3) the use of ultrasonics to measure the properties of materials for nondestructive testing, (4) plasma coating for anti-corrosion protection of turbine engine parts and (5) using electronic sensors to determine the depth of an implement in the soil. Regardless of the approach used, the R & D activities must be structured and managed.

The goal of business and industry is to make a profit. To be competitive in today's technological environment it is necessary to create a dynamic environment from which new and improved products and services can emanate. The structuring of this environment varies from industry to industry, depending on the nature of the product line and the perception those who structured the process have of the creative process. All of the structured approaches are based on the belief that technical research and creativity in the technologies can be enhanced through appropriate organization and management.

SUMMARY

Technical research through invention, innovation and development provides us with new ways to meet human needs and social purposes. Basic to this process are inventors and/or researchers who address problems from a criteria-based approach in an industrial setting. These individuals must have the intellectual capacity to differentiate the whole and configure things.

Technical research involves creating new knowledge and forms through invention and innovation and applying the new knowledge and forms to meet human needs through innovation and development. These activities must always be in concert with societal and cultural factors, the cumulative knowledge base and the abilities of the researchers.

The focus of this book is on the linear or sequential procedures used to discover technical knowledge and the use of this knowledge to develop new products or services. This view suggests that the invention-development process is a managed process in which research and development assignments can be made, procedures can be organized and operations can be controlled.

Industrial research and development is a highly complex, little understood process that involves the creation, production and marketing of sophisticated technical means. The control and/or enhancement of the process, with the goal of improving creative productivity, requires an understanding of the behavior of the process. To be competitive, it is necessary to create a dynamic environment from which new and improved products and services will emanate. The structuring of this environment will vary from industry to industry depending upon the (1) nature of the product line and (2) perception of creativity by those who structure the process. The structured approaches are based on the belief that technical research and creativity can be enhanced through appropriate organization and management of the research environment.

BIBLIOGRAPHY

Barnett, H. G. *Innovation: The Basis of Cultural Change*. New York: McGraw-Hill Book Company, 1953.

Bell, C. Gordon; Mudge, J. Craig and McNamara, John E. *Computer Engineering*. A DEC View of Hardware Systems Design. Bedford, MA. Digital Press, 1978.

Bowser, Hal. "Technology and the Human Dimension." An Interview with Elting E. Morison. *American Heritage of Invention and Technology*, Summer 1985, pp. 35-41.

Briggs, John. "The Genius Mind." *Science Digest*, December 1984, pp. 75-77, 102-103.

Davis, Dwight B. 'R & D Consortia." *High Technology*, October 1985, pp. 42-47.

Devore, Paul W. *Technology: An Introduction*. Worcester: Davis Publications, Inc., 1980.

Gilfillan, S. C. *The Sociology of Invention*. Cambridge: M.I.T. Press, 1935.

Gomory, Ralph H. "Technology Development." *Science*, Vol. 220, May 6, 1983, pp. 576-580.

Haeffner, Erik A. "The Innovation Process." *Technology Review*, March-April 1973, pp. 18-25.

Haggerty, Patrick E. *Three Lectures at the Salzburg Seminar on Multinational Enterprise*. Dallas: Texas, Inc., 1977. ("Innovation and Development of the Multinational Corporation," "The Role of Institutional Culture in an Industrial Corporation" and "Forces for Technology Generation and Transfer in the Multinational Corporation.")

Hall, A. Rupert. "The Changing Technical Act." *Technology and Culture*, Fall 1962, pp. 501-515.

Harriman, Richard. "Creativity: Moving Beyond Linear Logic." *Futurist*, Vol. XVIII, No. 4., August 1984, pp. 17-20.

Helms, E. W. "Texas Instruments Objectives, Strategies and Tactics System." Remarks to the Institute Panamericano de Alta Direccion de Empresa, Mexico, May 1980, Texas Instruments, Inc. 1980, 16 pp.

Hewlett-Packard. "Doing R&D on R&D." *Measure*, July-August 1983, pp.3-6.

House, Charles H. "Product Development by the Numbers." *Engineering Manager*, April 1985, pp. 27-30.

Hughes, John. "The Future of Asia." *Christian Science Monitor*, Wednesday, March 20, 1985, p. 13.

Jewkes, John, Sawers, David and Stillerman, Richard. *The Sources of Invention*, 2nd ed., New York: W. W. Norton and Company, 1969.

Kidder, Tracy. *The Soul of a New Machine*. New York: Avon Books, 1981.

Langrish, J., Gibbons, M., Jevons, F. R. and Evans, W. G. *Wealth from Knowledge*. London: Halsted Press; New York: John Wiley and Sons, 1972.

Lips, Julius E. *The Origin of Things*. New York: A.A. Wyn, 1947.

Lowen, Walter. *Dichotomies of the Mind*. New York: John Wiley and Sons, 1982.

McAlmon, George. "American Manufacturers are Losing World Markets." *The Center Magazine*, Vol. XII, No. 6. November/December 1979, pp. 8-12.

Maclaurin, W. Rupert. *Invention and Innovation in the Radio Industry*. New York: The Macmillan Company, 1949.

Mason, Otis T. *The Origins of Invention: A Study of Industry Among Primitive Peoples*. Cambridge: M.I.T. Press, 1966.

Maugh, II, Thomas H. "Technology Centers Unite Industry and Academia." *High Technology*, October 1985, pp. 48-52.

Morison, Elting E. *Men, Machines and Modern Times*. Cambridge: M.I.T. Press, 1966.

Morton, J. A. *Organizing for Innovation—A Systems Approach to Technical Management*. New York: McGraw-Hill Book Company.

NASA. "Partners in Technology." *Spinoff, 1984*, NASA, 1984, pp. 52-55.

National Academy of Engineering. *The Process of Technological Innovation*. Washington, D.C.: National Academy of Sciences, 1969.

National Science Foundation. *Industrial Science and Technological Innovation—Program Report*. Washington, D.C.: National Science Foundation, 1984, p. 48.

Peters, Thomas J. and Waterman, Robert H., Jr. *In Search of Excellence*. New York: Harper and Row, 1981.

Scherer, F.M. "Invention and Innovation in the Watt-Boulton Steam-Engine." *Technology and Culture*, Spring 1965, pp.165-187.

Schmitt, Roland W. "Successful Corporate R&D." *Harvard Business Review*, May-June 1985, pp. 124-128.

Schmookler, Jacob. *Invention and Economic Growth*. Cambridge: Harvard University Press, 1966.

Schon, Donald. *Technology and Change*. New York: Delacorte Press, 1967.

Shepherd, Mark. "Ensuring Creativity in a Post-Industrial Society." Address to the European Management Forum. Texas Instruments, Inc., Davos, Switzerland, January 30, 1981, 8 pp.

Stone, Christopher D. 'A Variety of Innovations; But One Seems to be Most Important." *The Center Magazine*, Vol. XII, No. 6., November/December 1979, pp. 13-17.

Technological Innovation: Its Environment and Management. U.S. Department of Commerce. Washington, D.C.: U.S. Government Printing Office, 1967.

Tornatzky, Louis G., et al. *The Process of Technological Innovation: Reviewing the Literature*. Washington, D.C.: National Science Foundation, 1983.

Usher, Abbott Payson. *A History of Mechanical Inventions*. Boston: Beacon Press, 1929.

Waitkus, Paul G. "Managing High-Tech Product Development." *Machine Design*, June 20, 1985, pp. 91-96.

Zwicky, Fritz. *Discovery, Invention, Research: Through the Morphological Approach*. New York: The Macmillan Company, 1969.

CHAPTER 2

Technology and Science

by Paul W. DeVore

Sub-Topics:

- Exploring the Differences Between Technology and Science
- Alternative Views of Technology
- Intellectual Factors of Technology
- Knowledge and Technology
- The Relationship Between Scientific
  and Technological Development
- Technology and Science
- Summary

It is not possible to address the topic of technical research without being confronted with the long-standing debate on the relationship between technology and science. Much has been written on the topic ranging from attempts to obtain political and economic gain for "pure" science in the public arena to interest in metaphysical issues.

The issue is critical for those confronted with decisions concerning the allocation of resources for research whether for business, industry or government. Proponents of research in pure science perpetuate the myth that all technical advances follow scientific discoveries, even though a number of well designed studies conducted in the United States and England have documented the fallacy of this belief.

Confusion also exists in numerous standard reference publications and general use textbooks. In a typical publication it is generally stated that science began thousands of years before man learned to write. This "science" is described as the discovery of fire, the invention of the wheel, the wheel and axle and the bow and arrow. Further evidence in support of science is presented by noting that Europe could not have exploited vast continents without railroads, canals, steamships and weapons. In most histories of technology the developments cited would be listed as technological developments, not scientific. There was little

NOTE: Portions of this chapter are from DeVore, Paul W., *Technology: An Introduction*, Davis Publications, Inc., 1980.

or no connection between the science and the technical developments of the eras cited.

The confusion is enhanced by the gross personification of the terms science and technology with statements like: Science does *thus and so,* or Technology does *this or that.* This personification of large complex fields of human endeavor obscures the true nature of the actual behavior in these fields.

What has been taking place over the last several centuries is an evolution in ways of thinking and relating to the world. This change began in the sixteenth century with discoveries about the natural world including Nicholaus Copernicus' heliocentric theory that the Earth revolved around the Sun, Galileo's proof of the theory, Newton's contribution to gravitational theory and the calculus, Priestley's isolation of oxygen, Mendel's contributions to the field of genetics, Pasteur's germ theory of disease and Darwin's theory of evolution.

Concurrent with these contributions were major changes in the technical means of production, communication and transportation. Among the developments were: the three field system of agriculture, farming machinery, the lathe, spinning wheel, mechanical clock, surveying instruments, navigation instruments, atmospheric sensing devices, optical devices and precision instrument development. Other developments were the dividing engine by Jesse Ramsden, and the surface plate, bench micrometer, screw gauge, end measurement and plug and ring gauge by Joseph Whitworth.

The contributions of John Kays, Lewis Paul, John Wyatt, James Hargraves, Richard Arkwright, Samuel Crompton and Edward Cartwright in the design and development of the means for the mechanization of the textile industry were significant in the early part of the eighteenth century.

People like Charles Plumier, Jacques Besson, Jacques de Vaucanson, Henry Maudslay, David Wilkinson, John Wilkinson, James Nasmyth, Richard Roberts, Joseph Clement and James Fox created the machine tool base for the industrialization of the Western world. Equally significant were the contributions of Vannoccio Biringuccio, George Bauer and Rene Antoine de Reaumur to knowledge of the physical properties of iron.

The technical means to greatly increase the amount and quality of iron and steel rested on the contributions of Abraham Darby I (use of coke to smelt iron), Henry Cort (the puddling furnace and grooved rolling mill), Christopher Polhern (improved rolling mill), Henry Bessemer (iron to steel process), Percy Gilchrist and S.G. Thomas (improved the

Bessemer process) and the Siemens and Martin brothers (open hearth process).

Chemical industries were developed through the work of Joshua Ward, Karl Scheele, Charles Tennant, Charles Macintosh, Nicolas LeBlanc, James Muspratt, Ernest Solvay, Henry Perkins, Charles Martin Hall and Paul Louis Toussaint.

The means of energy conversion were improved during this era by people such as Olaus Magnus (overshot waterwheel), Lester Pelton (water turbine), Thomas Newcomen (atmospheric steam engine), James Watt (separate condenser and double acting steam engine), Gustav de Laval and Charles Parsons (steam turbine), Otto von Guericke (static electricity), Alessandro Volta (battery), Hans Christian Oersted (electricity and magnetism relation), Andre Marie Ampere (quantification of electricity-magnetism relation), Michael Faraday (production of electricity from magnetic effect), Z. T. Gramme (ring armature), Joseph Henry (D.C. electric motor), Nikola Tesla (A.C. electric motor), Nicolaus Otto (four-stroke cycle internal combustion engine) and Rudolf Diesel (compression ignition engine). Even though all the individuals listed above have contributed to the development of the technical means of energy conversion, the pure scientists would be readily identified in any name recognition game.

What has been occurring is the evolution of a new discipline, technology, which is not dependent upon nor subservient to science, as commonly known and perceived. *Technology is one of the new sciences.* The intellectual endeavors involved in the creation of the technical means of today are of a different order from those of the craft era of the past. The modes of thinking have established the base for the new disciplines and the new science, technology. Those involved in this new science are concerned with the behavior of tools, machines and technical systems. They base their work on information about the behavior of multiple variables and dynamic environments. Common outcomes or traits of the new science (technology) are predictability, replication, reliability, optimization and efficiency of system operations based on theoretical models. Rules and systematic predetermined procedures are based on objective knowledge. Emphasis is on logical, instrumental, orderly and disciplined approaches. This view is supported by most recent investigations that conclude that technology and science, as commonly perceived, are distinctly different forms of human behavior. The concept of technology and science being at different ends of the same continuum is probably false. What is probably true is (1) that technology is one of the sciences, as are biology, psychology, sociology and other disciplines concerned with human behavior, and

(2) that the source of the problem is the term science as it is commonly used. Even if the problem is explored using the commonly accepted definitions of science and technology, we find two distinctly different forms of activity with different goals, questions and means. Each field is mutually exclusive and not mutually dependent, although as with all sciences, each has been enhanced by the other.

EXPLORING THE DIFFERENCES BETWEEN TECHNOLOGY AND SCIENCE

Even if the the differences and relationships between technology and science are explored from commonly held perceptions, it is evident that adjustments in these perceptions are in order.

Most writers conclude that there are differences between technology and science, and attempt to show relationships with few definitive conclusions. This stems from at least two factors: (1) the background, experience and value context of the writer and (2) the changing nature of both technology and science. Many writers discuss differences or relationships based on seventeenth or eighteenth-century technology and science, and then project their findings to the twentieth century. These writers seem to exhibit a decided pro science perspective by suggesting that technological advance came only from the practical application of scientific discovery.

However, as other investigators have shown, the linkages between events in technology and science have not been proved. According to Lynn White, "until the middle of the nineteenth century there were remarkably few connections between science and technology" (p. 161). White maintains that, technology has had a greater influence on science than science on technology.

Technology and science have different antecedents. Technology has always been situated directly in the social milieu and conditioned by values, attitudes and economic factors. The latter is evident in the research by Schmookler, who investigated whether (1) important inventions are typically induced by scientific discoveries, and whether (2) inventions are typically induced by intellectual stimuli provided by earlier inventions (pp. 57-58).

Schmookler and his colleagues compiled chronologies of important inventions in four industries: petroleum refining, papermaking, railroading and farming. He noted that although none of these industries owed their origin to scientific discoveries, the petroleum and papermaking industries have had relationships with science similar to the electrical, plastics, nuclear and electronic industries. He concluded the hypothesis that scientific discoveries direct the course of invention, if true, would have a fair chance of surviving the test.

Two types of inventions that were included in the study: (1) inventions that were *economically* important in their effect on the industry and (2) inventions that were *technologically* important in providing a base for subsequent innovations which were economically significant. Nine hundred and thirty-four inventions were identified using these criteria for the period 1800 to 1957 with 235 of the inventions in agriculture, 284 in petroleum refining, 185 in papermaking and 230 in railroading.

It was found that few of the inventions were directly stimulated by specific scientific discoveries, although each field had inventions which did depend on other fields of science. Decisions on whether to invent or to develop an invention for commercial use were not automatic outgrowths of scientific discovery, rather, they depended on value judgments made in the "context of the times."

The investigators also established that scientific discovery is seldom a *sufficient* condition for invention, either in the short or the long run, and that particular scientific discoveries are seldom even *necessary* conditions for later inventions (Schmookler, pp. 70-71). It seems as though technological progress cannot be predicted from the progress of science even though science opens up a variety of alternative paths for invention and technological development. Choice of the path of development depends largely on extrascientific factors. In general, Schmookler's study supports Schrier's contention that "not all technology is scientifically based, nor is all scientific research directly applicable to technology" (p. 345).

The attempt to build a case by looking backward and placing a higher value on contemplation than on action has delayed the probability of gaining true insight into the nature of the differences. If a true perception of technology or science is to be attained at a given time in history, it is necessary to structure the perspective from that era, not the present. Why? Because there has been a continual evolution in the meaning of the words technology and science.

Differentiating between technology and science today is best accomplished, according to Otto Mayr, by focusing discussions on several categories. They include (1) the nature of the knowledge structure, (2) the type of work and activities engaged in by the people who do the work, (3) the motivation (ideologies) of the people who engage in technology or science and (4) the aims and goals toward which the activities are directed (Mayr, pp. 667-669).

31

None of the criteria will differentiate if used singly. The problems of differentiation between technology and science are too complex to rely on single variables. It may be that a clear, concise differentiation will never be attained unless current evidence is entertained and alternative approaches to the problem are entertained.

ALTERNATIVE VIEWS OF TECHNOLOGY

In most writings on technology, the nature of technology is discussed and also is the issue of knowledge and technology. There are numerous views expressed, all of which are based on a philosophical orientation. The philosophical orientation may be derived from two perspectives according to Skolimowski: a *philosophy of technology* or a *technological philosophy*. Those involved in the philosophy of technology are concerned with the questions of knowledge and technology, whereas those concerned about technological philosophy are involved in value questions relating to the social use and the future of human beings and society (1966).

The issue of whether technology is based on *knowledge* or *knowing* or *know-how* and *doing* is a relatively new question. Layton believes the separation of knowledge and technology is both recent, artificial and contradictory:

> Technique means detailed procedures and skill and their application. But complex procedures can only come into being through knowledge. Skill is the "ability to use one's knowledge effectively." A common synonym for technology is "know-how." But how can there be know-how without knowledge? (1974, p. 33).

The focus of Layton's view is on knowledge about the behavior of technical elements and systems.

In discussing knowledge and technology, many people equate the attainments in technology with prior work in science. This implies that science is the knowledge base for technology. Scholars such as Skolimowski and others state emphatically that technology is not science, nor is technology dependent on science. Skolimowski maintains that "the basic methodological factors that account for the growth of technology are quite different from the factors that account for the growth of science" (1966). He believes that technology is a form of human knowledge and that the idea of technology can be best understood by focusing on the idea of technological progress.

This suggestion is compatible with those who have studied the differences between past and present technology. Bell (p. 174) notes that there are major dissimilarities between the present and the past and cites "the nature of technology and the way it has transformed social relationships and our way of looking at the world" as the basic reason for these differences. It has been recognized that the modes of thinking, doing and acting associated with technological endeavors create new realities. As Skolimowski reminds us, "Science concerns itself with *what is*, technology with *what is to be*."

The creation of new realities and extending the boundaries of the possible requires a know-how based on knowledge. The question which bothers traditionalists is, What kind of knowledge is technological knowledge?

Jarvie believes technological knowledge is that knowledge which is part of humankind's "multiform attempts to adapt to the environment." Perceived in this fashion, technological knowledge is knowledge generated through thinking and action involved in creating adaptive systems as opposed to knowledge used to create ideological and/or social systems.

Jarvie's distinction between what he describes as two senses of the word "know" assists in clarifying types of knowledge. One form of knowing is "know-how." One can *know how* to create a design, build a machine, analyze traffic flow or develop a new communication system. One can *know that* designers exist or traffic flow is analyzed before a new system is proposed, or that the geographical limits of efficient government are a function of the speed and efficiency of communications. Whereas past technical means might have been created largely by "know-how," today is not only "know-how" at a more complex and sophisticated level, but also "know-that" and "know-why."

Jarvie proposes that the concept of tools must be expanded to include "knowing-that" side of knowledge. During early technological development, tools were largely extensions of the physical elements of human beings. Today, formulas and procedures are tools. A computer program is a tool as are procedures used to collect data for technological forecasting. Changes in tools have changed the character of our technical means and in the process, the structure of technological knowledge (Jarvie, 1967).

The character of the knowledge required to maintain life in a primitive preagricultural society is greatly different from today's highly complex technological societies. Primitive societies evolved slowly as did their technical means. Prior to the eighteenth century, technical work was purely pragmatic, inquiry was empirical and diffusion was slow. It was relatively easy for people to keep abreast of their technical means and control its use and influence.

According to Bunge, technology crossed an important threshold in the eighteenth century and became self-sustaining. This resulted from the establishment of rules for technology. Previously technology was controlled by *conventional rules* which were adopted with no particular reason. Conventional rules were culture-centered rather than technology-centered and consisted of rules such as tipping one's hat or striking the anvil twice before striking the metal (Bunge, p. 339).

The establishment of technology-centered *ground rules* based upon a set of formulas capable of measuring effectiveness, changed the nature of technology. Effectiveness could no longer be accepted from observation and consensus. It was now necessary to *know why*. The formulation of the rules that control the productive process was the beginning of the rationalization of technology. Perhaps it was also a return to the original meaning of *technologia*, the giving of rules to the arts (Buchanan, p. 157). Today, the primary characteristic that is evolving is the centrality of theory over empiricism.

The new theoretical knowledge is a source of invention and innovation and is the base for a new intellectual technology: a technology based more on intellectual and analytical processes than on mechanical, manipulative or physical processes. According to Daniel Bell, the new intellectual technology consists of "such varied techniques as linear programming, systems analysis, information theory, decision theory, games and simulation. When linked to the computer, they allow us to accumulate and manipulate large aggregates of data . . . . . . to have more complete knowledge of social and economic matters" (pp. 157-158).

In most discussions of knowledge and technology, a common descriptor is used: application. Drucker makes the case that knowledge is not at the cutting edge, technology is. Knowledge exists only insofar as it is applied to do something. Up to that point it is only information.

Technologists are concerned with the knowledge of application and the application of knowledge. One must know in order to do. This is true regardless of what stage of technological development is being analyzed. Knowledge of application is necessary to achieve any survival success. Survival potential increases as new information about the environment is obtained, tested, applied and refined to become the new knowledge base.

INTELLECTUAL FACTORS OF TECHNOLOGY

Another factor becomes evident in examining the nature of knowledge and technology. The character of thinking involved in creating a philosophical position, a new religion or an alternate form of government is different from the character of thinking involved in technological activities. Thinking in technology is problem and environmentally specific. It is concerned with efficiency and the relationship of elements in the *behavior of sub-systems and total systems*. The question of behavior engages the question of "why" one system is more effective than another as well as "how" the system works. The goal is predictability of outcome and performance.

Technological knowledge is more than knowing about such things as tools and machines. Jarvie points out that technological knowledge would have no place in the structure of knowledge if technology were only tools, what an inventor invents or what applied scientists do to show what a theory explains (1967, p. 9). To Jarvie and others, technological "knowing" must involve certain intellectual processes to be considered knowledge.

Layton analyzed the issue in some detail in his article, "Technology as Knowledge" (p. 39). He suggested that the common denominator is the "ability to design" which connotes "an adaptation of *means* to some preconceived end." Layton believes this is the central purpose of technology.

This point of view relates well with other characteristics such as being problem-oriented and problem- and environmentally- specific. It also emphasizes a characteristic that makes technological knowledge unique: the ability to combine many diverse factors and elements into a working whole in order to reach some preconceived end. It is necessary to "know" the way things function and to be able to analyze the relationships and synthesize new relationships, to create new inventions, innovations or designs. The nature of the thought processes in this hierarchy of thinking is unique and central to the generation of technological knowledge.

KNOWLEDGE AND TECHNOLOGY

Knowledge in technology is (1) *knowing that* something is true in a given context and (2) *knowing how* to accomplish a preconceived end.

Creativity in the technologies combines the *universe of knowing* with the *universe of doing*. It is a unique intellectual enterprise.

Layton views technology as a spectrum, with ideas at one end, techniques and things at the other. The design process is in the middle. Ordinarily, most analyses of knowledge and technology focus only on things and techniques. By doing so, they omit the entire intellectual component of technology. The origin of things and the process which brings things into being is with human intellect, not in the things.

It is also important to recognize that whereas science, as commonly perceived, is concerned primarily with *what is* and the nature and structure of the physical universe, technology is concerned with *what can be*. In determining "What can be?", values and the process of valuing become paramount. Therefore, rather than focusing on discrete elements, those involved in the creation of technical means must be concerned with totalities, with systems and the behavior of systems. It is here that the greatest difference exists between science and technology. Whereas those involved in other sciences are concerned with nature, technology is concerned with human beings, the physical world *and* society. It is one thing to determine the nature of physical phenomenon. It is quite a different thing to collect and analyze data related to a specific problem, create and test a design and implement the proposed solution in a human context. This is a new way of thinking. A new science which is the base for technical research.

THE RELATIONSHIP BETWEEN SCIENTIFIC AND TECHNOLOGICAL DEVELOPMENT

The literary scene has been dominated by those with a humanist tradition. Traditionally, humanists have shown a widespread disregard for technology's role in human affairs (Smith, p. 493). The same has been true of historians who have been more concerned with "great movements headed by kings, generals or businessmen." When they wrote about the events of technology and science, they emphasized that with which they were most familiar, traditional science and philosophical ideas. To the traditional humanist and historian, technology was merely the application of scientific laws and theories.

The importance of science and scientific ideas cannot be denied. They have had a great impact on our perception of ourselves and our universe. The problem has been the ignorance or indifference toward the importance of technology. As Smith reminds us: "Anyone who considers the nature of materials, advocates a new way of making pottery or advances a new theory of the hardening of steel meets with both intellectual and popular indifference" (p. 494). Importance has been assigned to contemplation rather than to action.

Yet in the world of reality, the world beyond traditional historical inquiry, there has been a uniting of "knowing" and "doing." Technology has become linked with social purpose. The goal has become the pursuit of knowledge and know-how for specific social ends. The range of technological activity today includes everything from problem identification to the design and implementation of solutions. This involves not only technical or physical elements but human elements as well.

Even so, many individuals exploring the relationship between technology and science restrict technology to invention or the application of a scientific theory or law to a specific technical device. By doing so, they restrict not only the true meaning of technology but that of science as well.

A more accurate relationship is presented by people like Rabi, who noted that in earlier civilizations technological progress was made without science; that there were developments in metals and metalworking before the advent of chemistry or metallurgy, as well as development in textiles, building and construction, transportation, mining, agriculture, forestry, food preservation, energy conversion and power development. The belief that science creates new knowledge which technologists then apply is stated so often that it has been accepted as true.

This belief was so prevalent that the U.S. Department of Defense funded Project Hindsight to determine what key events made possible the development of 20 weapons systems. Seven hundred key events were studied to determine whether they were technological or scientific. Over 99 percent of the events were found to be technological events. Only 0.3 percent of the events were found to result from basic science. The results were startling and contrary to commonly held views.

Another study, conducted by the Illinois Institute of Technology Research Institute in 1968, *Technology in Retrospect and Critical Events in Science* or TRACES* (1968), illustrated that a relationship between science and technology did exist, but not in a direct linear form. It was discovered that technology or mission-oriented research and development efforts brought about nonmission or basic science research which later influenced a given innovation (Layton, 1971).

---

*The TRACES project documented the events that were considered to be crucial in leading to five innovations: magnetic ferrites, videotape recorder, oral contraceptive pill, electron microscope and matrix isolation.

A follow-up study by Battelle Columbus Laboratories (Battelle, 1973) supported the findings of the TRACES research. The Battelle study, which focused on the identification of key influences on *decisive events* (an occurrence that provides a major and essential impetus to an innovation—without this event the innovation would not have occurred) in the innovation process, found that:

1. The recognition of technical opportunity ranged from moderately to highly important for 87 percent of the decisive events, indicating that the opportunity to create an improved product or process is a strong motivating force in the innovative process.

2. The recognition of consumer need or demand ranked second in importance and was judged important in 69 percent of the decisive events.

3. The technical entrepreneur (individual within the performing organization who champions a scientific or technical activity—a product champion) ranked as important in 56 percent of the events. (Battelle, p. 3-1).

The technical entrepreneur was identified as a "characteristic" that was important in nine of the ten innovations studied as a whole and was also a "factor" of significance with respect to individual decisive events. The fact that the technical entrepreneur is a significant driving force in the innovative process as identified in the Battelle study is important to note when the concern is with enhancing the technical research process.

Another factor which differentiates technological from "scientific" activities is the role "unplanned" confluences of technical events play in innovation. In the Battelle study this was a factor in six of the ten innovations. It was found that in all cases additional supporting innovations were required in order to refine and improve the original concept and to allow the ultimate product or process to reach the market place (Battelle, p. 3-2).

These and other studies support Layton's conclusion that the problem in discussing the technology-science relationship is the assumption that science and technology represent different functions performed by the same community. Science and technology represent different communities, each with different goals, sets of values, social controls and reward systems. The result is that science begets more science and technology more technology. Gibbons and Johnson found that science acts in a supporting rather than an initiating role (Langrish, p. 9).

Their study showed that there is a relationship, but the importance of science to the creation and development of technical means has been exaggerated. Kranzberg, attributes this exaggeration to "chronological fallacy," which is the belief that because one event preceded another chronologically the events were connected causally. The most common connections used to show the relationships between prior science and later technology are the development of the steam engine and the transistor. The 1500-year period from Heron's experiments with expanding steam to James Watts' improvement of Newcomen's atmospheric steam engine and the development of the transistor in the late 1940's are often cited to illustrate the decreasing period of time from scientific discovery to technological development. The problem with the comparisons is that the development of the steam engine did not begin with Heron, but with Newcomen and his predecessors, and that the steam engine was a technological development, not a scientific one. The development of the steam engine came about because of a problem with mine drainage. Historians such as Kranzberg conclude that "new technology grows mostly out of old technology, not out of science," and "scientists concern themselves chiefly with the problems posed by science, not by technology" (Kranzberg, p. 27).

J. M. Langrish and others also question the chronology methodology (p. 35). They offer four reasons:

1. Difficulty in defining the scientific discovery on which a technological application is based. Different time intervals are assigned by different authors for given innovations.

2. Possible biases in selection of innovations and events due to absence of standard selection procedures. "It is in fact not difficult to produce sets of example which show time-lags *increasing* substantially during the last hundred years or so."

3. Impossibility of observing anything other than a short time-lag for recent discoveries. "Discoveries made in the last few years may be exploited in the future, and such cases are of necessity excluded from consideration."

4. Many cases have negative time-lags. Many times technological advance comes *before* the scientific advances that help to make them understandable such as was the case with the first synthetic rubber and plastics which were produced prior to the development of polymer chemistry.

TECHNOLOGY AND SCIENCE

There are relationships between technology and science, but of a different order than commonly believed. According to Kranzberg, the relationship between technology and science can be best described as a disunity rather than a unity, and as *two distinct orders of activity* engaged in by human beings with an ongoing dialectic between them (1968, p. 30). Relationships are more dependent on the situation or problem than on doctrine. The relationships, according to Kranzberg, are pragmatic, free of formal protocol and exist in specific contexts which vary according to the situation (1968, pp. 32-33). Rather than one relationship there are many, with the initial entree and dialectic determined by the situation and the problem.

The difference between technology and science is distinct, particularly with reference to goals, nature of the problem and problem setting.

Technology	Science
Goal: to create the human capacity to do; to create new and useful products, devices, machines, or systems.	*Goal*: to obtain fundamental understanding of nature and the physical universe.
Problem: complex and interrelated problems involving design, materials, energy, information and control. Many variables, both technical and social. Involves total system design.	*Problem*: small, highly detailed, manageable problems designed to contribute to a body of information that may provide the base for generalizable theories.
Setting: situated directly in the social milieu.	*Setting*: isolated from requirements of meeting direct social needs.

One way to clarify the technology and science issue is to investigate the *goals* and *scope* of inquiry of each discipline and the critical variables for distinguishing between and among various human intellectual endeavors (Gruender, pp. 456-57).

Goals: The goals of the discipline concern the purposes of the activity while scope concerns the narrowness or breadth of the activity. If the goal of an activity is set by some specific human problem, the nature of the activity is technological. Whereas, if the goal of the activity is based on curiosity and interest in finding basic generalizable theories, the activity is scientific. Bunge (p. 68) believes that just as pure science focuses on objective patterns or laws, action-oriented research aims at establishing stable norms of successful human behavior: that is, rules. By rule, Bunge means a prescribed course of action to achieve a predetermined goal. However, caution should be exercised in making too simplistic a separation. Abstract theories can be used for the solution of practical problems and the solution of practical problems often leads to abstract theories.

Scope: Scope is generally established by the goal, aim or purpose of the problem, inquiry or activity. If the scope of the problem is clearly defined as solving a human or social problem within a specified environment, then the activity is technological. If the *goal* of the problem, inquiry or activity does not restrict the *scope* of the results sought or the direction of inquiry, then the activity is another form of scientific endeavor.

The creation of technical means is situated in a human and social context from which the *goals* that direct the activities of the discipline are derived and the *scope* of the field of inquiry is determined. In the process of development, the goals and scope of the discipline of technology are altered as new potential presents new choices. Today, rather than focusing on problems concerned with specific tools for a specific application in a given craft within a limited social environment, the goals and scope of technological problems include inquiry into total systems and their interrelateness, technically and socially.

In the traditional view, science would be different. In the pure sciences, it is essential that the human element be eliminated, and the variability of human responses be controlled (Ashby, p. 82). The *goal* of science is to seek explanation for the behavior of the natural world, not to solve problems related to creating adaptive means to aid humans to live in the natural world. However, Anna J. Harrison has proposed that science is the *process of investigation** of physical, biological, behavioral, social, economic and political phenomena. Harrison uses process in a collective sense, encompassing everything the investigator does from the selection of the phenomena to be investigated, to the assessment of the validity of the results. The outcome is scientific knowledge. Technology is perceived to be the *process of production** and the delivery of goods and services. Technological innovation is the *process of investigating** how to more effectively produce and deliver goods or services, modify significantly their characteristics or create and deliver new goods or services. The outcome is technological

---

*Italics added by author.

knowledge consisting of a data base with an array of concepts (p. 1242). Ziman notes a corpus of generally accepted principles has developed in every technical field. Modern technology is definitely scientific because there is continuous formal study and empirical investigation of the aspects of technique (Michalos, p. 24).

SUMMARY

Individual perceptions of various topics or phenomena are largely dependent on a person's background, the amount of study and reflection given to the topic and personal experiences with the phenomena. This is certainly true of the technology-science issue. With respect to technology, viewpoints about its nature range all the way from technology as a tool, to technology as a major component of the adaptive systems of civilization. It is thought of as skill, craftsmanship, artifacts, technique, work or a system of work, engineering, a body of knowledge, a discipline, a system of means, an effect and other similar constructs. Similar viewpoints exist with respect to science. Each viewpoint differs depending on the perception of the individual espousing that viewpoint.

The many diverse viewpoints are of little help to those concerned with establishing public or corporate policy with respect to industrial or technological research. If there are no common agreements about perceptions or meaning, it is not possible to develop an appropriate and successful research agenda with the *goal* of maintaining technological prominence and contributing to the improvement of human existence. Nor is it possible to establish programs of assessment to determine future directions for the allocation of resources for research for given goals. This is a primary and continuous problem facing leaders in business and industry.

There is a growing recognition that the character and nature of today's technology is more theoretically, intellectually and systematically derived. Those involved in the various fields of endeavor in the technologies are systematically pursuing the search for knowledge and understanding of the behavior of various technical systems concerned with the transformation of materials to useful products. This involves the transmission, reception, storage and retrieval of information and the efficient movement of goods and services. These human activities are associated with other branches of knowledge and know-how that have also been systematically derived.

The discipline of technology is the *systematic study* of the creation, utilization and behavior of adaptive systems. It includes the tools, machines, materials, techniques and technical means along with the behavior of these elements and systems in relation to human beings, society and the environment.

The question *is not one* of differentiating between technology and other sciences. The question *is* to determine the most appropriate direction for improving the creation and application of new technological knowledge through well designed technical research and development programs.

BIBLIOGRAPHY

Agassi, Joseph. "The Confusion Between Science and Technology in the Standard Philosophies of Science." *Technology and Culture*, Vol. VII, No. 3., Summer 1966.

Ashby, Eric. *Technology and the Academics*. New York: St. Martin's Press, Inc., 1963

Atkinson, Richard C. "Education for an Age of Science." *Science*, March 30, 1984.

Battelle Columbus Laboratories. "Interactions of Science and Technology in the Innovative Process: Some Case Studies." Springfield, Virginia: National Technical Information Service, U.S. Department of Commerce, 1973, p. 218.

Bell, Daniel. *The Coming of Post-Industrial Society*. New York: Basic Books Publishers, Inc., 1973.

Buchanan, Scott. "Technology as a System of Exploitation." *The Technological Order*, Detroit: Wayne State University Press, 1963.

Bunge, Mario. "Towards a Philosophy of Technology." ed. Alex C. Michalos. *Philosophical Problems of Science and Technology*, Boston: Allyn and Bacon, 1974, pp. 28-47.

Bush, Vannevar. *Science—The Endless Frontier*. Report to President Harry Truman, 1945. Reprinted May 1980, Washington, D.C.: National Science Foundation.

Cardwell, D.S.L. *Turning Points in Western Technology*. New York: Neale Watson Academic Publications, Inc., 1972.

Cassidy, Harold G. *Knowledge, Experience and Action*. New York: Teachers College Press, 1969.

Compton, W. Dale. *The Interaction of Science and Technology*. Urbana, Illinois: University of Illinois Press, 1969.

DeVore, Paul W. *Technology: An Introduction*. Worcester: Davis Publications, Inc., 1980.

Drucker, Peter. "Knowledge and Technology." *Dimensions for Exploration* Series. Oswego: Division of Industrial Arts and Technology, State University of New York—Oswego, 1964.

Durbin, Paul T. (ed.). "A Guide to the Culture of Science." *Technology and Medicine*, New York: The Free Press, 1980.

Friedman, Edward A. "Technology as an Academic Discipline." *Engineering Education*, December 1980, pp. 211-216.

Gruender, C. David. "On Distinguishing Science and Technology." *Technology and Culture*, Vol. 12, No. 3, July 1971, pp. 456-463.

Halfin, Harold H. *Technology—A Process Approach*. Morgantown: West Virginia University, Technology Education Program Doctoral Dissertation, 1973.

Harrison, Anna J. "Science, Engineering and Technology" (editorial). *Science*, February 10, 1984.

Hood, Webster F. *A Heideggerian Approach to the Problem of Technology*. University Park: The Pennsylvania State University, Doctoral Dissertation, 1968.

Illinois Institute of Technology Research Institute. *Technology in Retrospect And Critical Events in Science*. Chicago: Illinois Institute of Technology, 1968.

Jarvie, Ian Charles. "Technology and the Structure of Knowledge." *Dimensions for Exploration*, Series. Oswego: Division of Industrial Arts and Technology, State University of New York—Oswego, 1967.

Kranzberg, Melvin. "The Disunity of Science-Technology." *American Scientist*, Vol. 56, No. 1, 1968, pp. 21-44.

Kranzberg, Melvin and Pursell, Carroll W. *Technology in Western Civilization*. Vol. I, New York: Oxford University Press, 1967.

Langrish, J., Gibbons, M., Evans, W.G. and Jevons, R. *Wealth From Knowledge*. New York: John Wiley and Sons, 1972.

Layton, Edwin. "Mirror-Image Twins: The Communities of Science and Technology in the 19th Century America." *Technology and Culture*, Vol. 12, No. 4, October 1971, pp. 562-580.

——————. "Technology as Knowledge." *Technology and Culture*, Vol 15, No. 1, January 1974, pp. 31-41.

Mayr, Otto. "The Science-Technology Relationship as a Historiographic Problem." *Technology and Culture*, Vol. 17, No. 4, October 1976, pp. 663-673.

Michalos, Alex C. *Philosophical Problems of Science and Technology*. (John Ziman, "The Nature of Science and Technology"), Boston: Allyn and Bacon, Inc., 1974.

Mitcham, Carl and Mackey, Robert. *Philosophy and Technology* (Mario Bunge, "Toward a Philosophy of Technology"), Free Press, 1972.

National Science Board Commission on Precollege Education in Mathematics, Science and Technology. *Educating Americans for the 21st Century*, Washington, D.C., 1984.

Ortegay Gasset, Jose. *History as a System*. New York: W.W. Norton and Company, 1961.

Pacey, Arnold. *The Maze of Ingenuity—Ideas and Idealism in the Development of Technology*. Cambridge: MIT Press, 1976.

Rabi, I.I. "The Interaction of Science and Technology." *The Impact of Science on Technology*, Aaron W. Warner, Dean Morese and Alfred S. Eichner, eds. New York: Columbia University Press, 1965, pp. 9-36.

Roy, Rustum. "STS: Core of Technological Literacy." (editorial). *Bulletin Science, Technology Society*, No. 2, 1982, pp. 289-290.

Sahal, Devendra. *Patterns of Technological Innovation*. Reading, MA: Addison-Wesley Publishing Company, Inc., 1981.

Saxon, David S. *The Place of Science and Technology in the Liberal Arts Curriculum*. Washington, D.C.: Association of American Colleges, A Report of the Wingspread Conference, June 1982, p. 37.

Schmookler, Jacob. *Invention and Economic Growth*. Cambridge: Harvard University Press, 1966.

Schofield, Robert E. "Comment: On the Equilibrium of a Heterogeneous Social System." *Technology and Culture*, Vol. 6, No. 4, Fall 1965, p. 591.

Shamos, Morris H. "Scientific Literacy: Reality or Illusion." ERIC, Paper presented at the Annual Meeting of the American Educational Research Association, New Orleans, April 24, 1984, p. 17.

Skolimowski, Henryk. "The Structure of Thinking in Technology." *Technology and Culture*, Vol. 3, No. 3, Summer 1966, pp. 371-390.

Smith, Cyril Stanley. "Art, Technology and Science: Notes on Their Historical Interaction." Vol. 3, No.3, Summer 1966, pp. 371-390.

Van Melsen, Andrew G. *Science and Technology*. Duquesne Studies. Philosophical Series 13. Pittsburgh: Duquesne Univeristy Press, 1961.

White, Leslie A. *The Science of Culture: A Study of Man and Civilization*. New York: Farrar Straus and Company, 1949.

White, Lynn, Jr. *Machine Ex Deo: Essays in the Dynamism of Western Culture*. Cambridge: M.I.T. Press, 1968.

Whitehead, Alfred North. *Science and the Modern World*. New York: Macmillan Company, 1925, pp. 137-292.

Zvorikine, A. "Technology and the Laws of Its Development." *Technology and Culture*, Vol. 3, No. 4, Fall 1962, pp. 443-458.

CHAPTER 3

A Model of the Technical Research Project

by Richard D. Seymour

Sub-Topics:

- Technical Research in Perspective
- The Technical Research Process
- Conceptualization of the Research Project
- Selecting the Technical Research Procedure
- Finalizing the Technical Research Design
- Development of a Proposal
- Conducting the Research
- Analyzing the Project Results
- Reporting the Project Results
- Evaluation of the Project
- Summary

Webster defines research as the "careful, systematic, patient study and investigation in some field of knowledge" (1968). Research provides the means for humans to discover new insights and solutions to problems which hinder civilization. It helps us expand our understanding of how and why this complex world functions or how to apply knowledge to solve problems in a given social/cultural setting. Research is a structured mental process by which we investigate our universe in order to increase our knowledge base.

Research is conducted in all disciplines and contributes to human understanding in different ways. For example, market research serves as a vital competitive tool as manufacturing firms try to predict the behavior of consumers in the marketplace. Scientists explore the oceans and continents to more fully comprehend the nature of biological lifeforms. Agricultural researchers attempt to produce new hybrids that will yield more productive field crops. Laboratory researchers in the medical field continually strive to discover new cures for diseases such as cancer or heart disorders. Research in other areas has yielded more convenient and comfortable housing, better ways of predicting the weather, stronger materials for household appliances or tools and improved methods of educating our young. The purpose of this chapter is to present a simplified structure for technical research. This background is necessary for understanding more complex technological research activities which are characterized by many interconnected tasks and feedback loops.

DeVore suggests that technical research "involves creating new knowledge and forms . . . to meet human needs through innovation and development." The complex mental process involved in researching technical topics will be explained using a linear model that illustrates the major steps in developing technical knowledge. Technological investigations traditionally follow a sequence of interrelated events which ultimately produce some tangible rewards. The model introduced in this chapter, although not applicable to every technical problem, may best serve to introduce the procedures generally associated with technical methods of investigation.

TECHNICAL RESEARCH IN PERSPECTIVE

All research activities can be described as either applied or basic. Applied research involves developing knowledge for specific purposes. In industrial settings the primary goal is to solve technical problems or develop new products for the marketplace. New knowledge is sought that will aid in the development of new processes or products that will be of benefit to humans or products that will be of benefit to humans or sytems. In contrast, basic research offers the means for expanding human understanding. Basic research results in gains in knowledge without regard to specific applications.

Improved technical understanding has resulted from both applied and pure research. Most technical research projects have an emphasis on specific goals. Industrial firms conducting technical research usually have practical applications for their work. The strong competitive climate in today's business and industrial sectors has kept a constant pressure on research and development laboratories worldwide. New technologies have continually been developed and brought into the marketplace (McHenry, 1983).

It is not easy to differentiate the methodology used in technical research from other forms of inquiry. In the preceding chapters, DeVore provided a context for the technical research conducted in an industrial setting. His discussion of "what is science?" and "what is technology?"

helps to narrow our focus in the study of technical investigation. As Poe (1983) suggests, [technical] research ". . . involves the practical application of scientific knowledge to definite problems or needs" (p. 308). Technical researchers attempt to apply knowledge to particular problems using their intellect, imagination, observation, and deductive powers. The following example may better describe the differences between scientific and technical means of inquiry.

Few individuals would question the critical problem of environmental (air, land and water) pollution in today's society. Scientific researchers spend their time observing and quantifying the extent of damage to the environment due to various sources of pollution. Their task is to observe nature, survey existing natural conditions and report dangers to plant and animal life. A technical researcher will use human "know how" to develop methods that reduce or eliminate the pollution. The scientific data provides valuable information in proposing a solution to the problem. The technical researcher is the individual who develops the technical means to solve a specific problem, such as the way in which pollution is harming the environment.

When atmospheric pollution exists, a variety of technical systems or sources may be involved in contaminating the air. Researchers may propose numerous technical solutions. It may involve altering the fuel consumed at a local power station or changing an entire transportation structure of the city to reduce particulate matter in the atmosphere. Another remedy may require local manufacturing firms to install filtering systems for their exhaust stacks. Other researchers might suggest that area manufacturers use more efficient production methods to reduce the hazardous output of airborne particulates. As illustrated by these proposed solutions, the technical researcher often uses basic investigative techniques or practices with a focused mission, to develop the efficient technical means to reduce a specific problem.

THE TECHNICAL RESEARCH PROCESS

Technical research is one of the most difficult activities to plan and structure. Jewkes (1969) states that beyond a certain stage, [technical] research is impossible to organize and administer. The basic nature of investigating "unexplored territory" suggests that an individual may wish to impose as few restrictive procedures as possible because the scope of a research assignment may quickly change in unforeseen ways. Random skipping or recycling of outlined procedures may occur (Emory,

1980). Revisions in funding, staffing, schedules or other factors may change the research project.

Efficient investigators often seem to skip or alter the process. Normally it is their foresight, experience or judgment that allows them to reduce the time or effort required for the inquiry and deal with the interrelationships among the research activities.

The beginning researcher can best understand technical research by viewing it as a linear process involving eight formal steps (See Figure 3-1). These include: (1) conceptualizing the project, (2) selecting the research procedure, (3) finalizing the project, (4) developing a proposal, (5) conducting the research project, (6) analyzing the results, (7) reporting the results and (8) evaluating the research project. This chapter will describe the model while subsequent chapters will discuss each step in greater detail. In addition, Chapter 7 on research management and other chapters addressing technical innovation support the themes of the book.

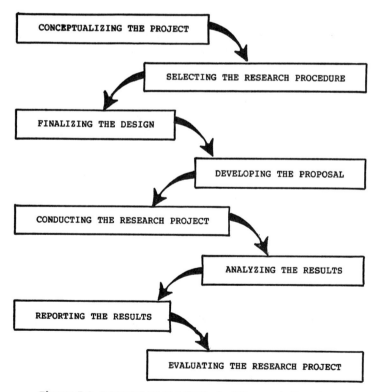

Figure 3-1: A Model of the Technical Research Process

CONCEPTUALIZATION OF THE RESEARCH PROJECT

Technical research starts with the identification of a problem. A verbal or written concept statement serves as the beginning of the research activity. This allows the researcher(s) to focus on a common theme for the investigation. All possible facts that have a bearing on the problem are accumulated. The state-of-the-art in technical advancement related to the problem is considered. All formal planning will be based upon the conceptualized statement as the process of technical research officially begins.

Conceptualization of a technical project provides more than a starting point for a research problem. It allows various parties (researcher, management, customers, clients, etc.) to view the "big picture" and place the project in perspective. This includes examining the anticipated goals, costs and benefits of the project. A timetable may be introduced at this point. The conceptualization stage also provides an opportunity for the researchers to estimate investigative capabilities and resource requirements. The proposed methodology is considered along with ways to manipulate extraneous and intervening variables. Any limitations which may hinder the success of the research project should be identified at this early stage.

The act of developing a concept statement is a mental procedure for describing a potential avenue of technical exploration. It consists of countless trial associations to explain the dynamics of the problem. Ideas for identifying the nature of the project may be derived from many sources. Researchers often seek suggestions from their peers, production and marketing personnel and management. Brainstorming sessions produce many creative possibilities for the project. Researchers also utilize mathematical and computer models to help shape the final concept statement.

The result should be a clearly defined and formulated research problem. This statement is frequently in the form of a hypothetical question. The entire research focus will then involve attempts to prove or disprove the statement.

SELECTING THE TECHNICAL RESEARCH PROCEDURE

The selection of an appropriate research procedure is a demanding task. The term "appropriate" rather than "best" is used because time and resources often limit the types of inquiry which can be performed. The capabilities of the laboratory may restrict the options available for the research activity. The important requirement is to identify the technical research procedure. The design must allow the investigator(s) to gain the needed information or results.

A selection of research procedures involves examining three elements of the project. First, the problem statement must be reexamined to determine the nature of the research. Second, various research designs must be considered and an appropriate model selected. Third, a large body of insufficient knowledge may require preliminary inquiry to solve a primary need or problem before beginning the formal investigation (Fernelius & Waldo, 1983). The chances for a successful investigation are greatly improved with careful analysis and planning at this early stage.

Formal planning results in the clarification of a technical problem. The planning phase will result in a "road map" for the technical inquiry. Research goals, testing procedures, budgets and resources are assessed at this time. A timetable is established to determine if the project will be short- or long-term in nature.

The size of the activity is another key factor to be considered. Certain research projects will necessitate hiring staff numbering into the hundreds and involve budgets totaling millions of dollars. Under these circumstances, a highly detailed picture of the proposed research is essential. However, these estimates are often educated guesses and may lack accuracy.

Selecting a promising research design is the next step. Common technical research designs can be classified as experimentational or descriptive. Laboratory or on-site experimentation is the most common form of technical investigation. Experimental designs allow the research to show that one element influences or causes another factor to occur. This research design typically makes use of scale models, test specimens, specially designed chambers, simulations or a variety of other equipment and facilities. Descriptive designs involve observation of systems or trends. They have many applications in the studying of integrated systems in almost every area of modern technology.

FINALIZING THE TECHNICAL RESEARCH DESIGN

The completed proposal for a technical research project includes the statement of the research problem and the selected research design. Competent researchers will have explored all practical avenues before concluding this preliminary phase. A review of related research is completed to gain a fundamental understanding of the problem. By this stage, projected benefits, procedures, and resources are fairly well established. Technical literature and data banks have been thoroughly examined for information associated with the research problem. The researcher is now ready to seek approval of the research activity.

DEVELOPMENT OF A PROPOSAL

Most technical research projects must be approved at a higher level of authority. Each company will have its own criteria and procedures for evaluating proposed research activity. In some industrial settings, the ultimate decision may be made by top management using a systematic method (formulas, equations, etc.) of evaluation. Other organizations have individuals or committees *judge* the proposed research activity and make recommendations. Review boards are often used to determine if the inquiry adds value to a product, service or system. Researchers may be called before the board to explain or defend their proposal at a planning session. While difficult to generalize for every case, two distinct means of obtaining approval are available, formal and informal.

A formal proposal must be prepared if approval is being sought from a client, the government or another outside party. Decisions will be based on analysis of the planned research activity outlined in the proposal. A document is assembled for review and consideration. The development of a research proposal involves a variety of formats but the information contained in the document generally includes: (1) a statement of a problem or purpose, (2) specific procedures, (3) methods of data collection, (4) data analysis techniques, (5) personnel, (6) budget, (7) resources and (8) a timetable. The documented proposal may include charts, graphs and other graphic materials that will play a significant role in obtaining project approval.

Many research organizations and funding agencies require only printed documentation for consideration of a project. Other firms invite the researcher(s) to make an oral presentation. Feedback during oral presentations is helpful in developing an acceptable proposal.

Informal methods of approving research proposals vary considerably. Verbal acceptance is given for small- to medium- sized projects in many organizations. Small research teams often receive their approval by informal consent of management. A letter is generally the formal approval for the technical investigation.

Final approval marks the last step prior to actually conducting the research. Upon receiving approval, the project is organized and the investigation(s) begins. Effective planning minimizes the chance of interruptions which might be encountered during the research project.

During the formulation stage, it is important for the researcher to realize that problems are very likely to surface at any time. Learning to cope with set-backs and failures is critical in becoming a successful researcher. Unexpected problems are a normal part of conducting research and should be readily accepted during the activity.

CONDUCTING THE RESEARCH

The organization of a research project and collection of data varies considerably with the research design. Several common steps precede the actual conduct of any research. For example, staff members must be identified and trained. Test equipment must be acquired or built before the research begins. Instrumentation (data gathering devices) should be tested for accuracy. Management and recording-keeping systems should be developed to control the project. Test samples, models and related items must be selected and prepared.

Technical research involves obtaining measurements or data by a variety of means. Specific properties or systems are analyzed using a variety of measurement standards and procedures. If a test hypothesis is being used, variables are manipulated and controlled to compare behaviors or interactions. The data are interpreted, findings are reported and recommendations are made.

The time required for completing research activities varies considerably by the number and complexity of the tasks involved. The interval for conducting technical research may last from a few months to several decades (Fernelius & Walls, 1983).

The technical research project may yield unexpected results which create needs for new research. Some thoroughly planned research activities have undergone major changes after the accumulation of relatively small amounts of data. This indicates the important need for the willingness and ability to take corrective actions. Occasionally research may produce results that indicate the project has reached a "dead end" and should be abandoned.

An important part of conducting a technical research project, which involves directing, controlling and evaluating research activities, is the management function. To manage any project, the researcher(s) must keep the project's objective or goal in mind. Researchers utilize many management "tools" to track their work including schedules, Gantt charts, computer-reporting techniques and even "guesswork" (Roberts). Cost-accounting tools are frequently used to monitor research activities.

ANALYZING THE PROJECT RESULTS

The next step in the technical research process involves analyzing and summarizing the data collected. The researcher has two basic data analysis techniques available. These are visual inspection and statistical analysis.

The data can be reviewed and analyzed using photographs, charts and graphs. These visual techniques are used to summarize and illustrate the data for written and oral reports.

Statistical analysis allows the researcher to use various mathematical procedures to interpret the data collected. These procedures can be classified as descriptive and inferential. Descriptive techniques present the data using measures of central tendency, variability and data patterns. Inferential statistics are based on the probability of an event occurring by chance rather than a result of specific actions.

The statistical analysis of the data allows researchers to draw defensible conclusions. The credibility of the results is based on the selection of data analysis methods which are compatible with the research design and data collection techniques.

From these conclusions, recommendations for various courses of action are made. These may include process change, product development or improvements and equipment modifications.

REPORTING THE PROJECT RESULTS

Communication of project results is vital to the successful conclusion of any technical investigation. This may include formal documentation through written reports and/or oral presentations. In a proprietary situation, results may only be explained to top officials pending direction from management on future use of the research. If an outside agency is involved, a major presentation is often scheduled to explain details of the project. The agency personnel will review the data collected quite extensively to determine the effectiveness or usefulness of the investigation. In addition, the researcher is expected to place a detailed account of all activities in the departmental files for future reference by the organization.

The dissemination of technical research may include supplying the information to a variety of other sources. Research findings that are funded by a company and provide a competitive edge will not be disseminated widely within or outside the company. Important non-proprietary findings from research projects may be published in technical bulletins which range from small, in-house correspondence, to literature sponsored by major associations. The information might also be released to the profession through journal articles or trade publications. Presentations of papers or workshops at technical meetings are other means of reporting valuable research findings. Frequently, an entire professional conference is devoted to the dissemination of technical research results.

EVALUATION OF THE PROJECT

The process of technical research concludes with an evaluation of the project. This includes the results of the technical data and the procedures used while collecting data using the specified research design. Various evaluation techniques are used to review the project. The value of the project is then determined by careful analysis of all factors related to the investigation.

Technical research is designed to gain new knowledge or solve some impending problem. Therefore, the project may be evaluated to determine if the stated goals were realized. A close examination of the research findings and recommendations will indicate what action should be taken. Occasionally the data suggests that further research is required.

The review of a technical research project should include an examination of the selected design and analysis of test procedures. The resulting knowledge may be rendered useless if a flaw is found in the research methodology. Investigations may yield little technical advance if improper testing procedures were used or uncorrected problems were encountered during the data collection process.

The findings and recommendations of the technical investigation are now ready for application. They may provide valuable knowledge for a new process, service or product. This marks the successful completion of a technical research project.

SUMMARY

Technical research is an orderly mental procedure involving a detailed analysis of technological concepts, behaviors and systems. Effective organization is critical to performing any investigation of technical topics. Prior planning is important in initiating the proposed technical research.

The model for learning the technical research process outlined in this chapter includes eight steps. The steps are not mutually exclusive in either content or sequence. An overlap should be anticipated. Several phases are often in progress at any one time. While each phase is not readily evident in every technical investigation, researchers generally follow these guidelines to maintain the integrity of the activity.

All technical research projects are designed to achieve results over a period of time. The resulting data or new knowledge should have direct application to the identified problem. Following the investigation, information and results must be communicated in appropriate form to other people. Actions or recommendations may be taken based on the results of the project.

Rarely is a technical research project conducted exactly as envisioned at the inception of the activity. This illustrates the critical importance of human organization and management. Decisions concerning continuation, modification or termination of the project must be based on the best information available.

BIBLIOGRAPHY

Budworth, D. "Innovation, Accounts, & Engineers." *Engineering*, 5, 314-315, 1985.

DeVore, P. W. *Technology: An Introduction*. Worcester, Massachusetts: Davis Publications, 1980.

Drew, C. J. *Introduction to Designing and Conducting Research*. 2nd ed. St. Louis: C. V. Mosby, 1980.

Emory, C. W. *Business Research Methods*. Homewood, Illinois: Richard D. Irwin, Inc., 1980.

Fernilius, W. C. & Waldo, W. H. "Innovation's Debt to Basic Research." *Chemtech*, 5, 148-151, 1983.

Hertz, D. B. *The Theory and Practice of Industrial Research*. New York: McGraw-Hill Book Co., 1950.

Heyel, C. (Ed.) *Handbook of Industrial Research Management*. 2nd ed. New York: Reinhold Book Co., 1968.

Jewkes, J., Sawers, D., & Stilman, R. *The Sources of Invention*. 2nd ed. New York: W. W. Norton & Co., 1969.

Killeffer, D. H. *The Genius of Industrial Research*. New York: Reinhold Publishing, 1948.

Li, Y. T., Jansson, D. G. & Cravalho, E. G. *Technological Innovation in Education and Industry*. New York: Van Nostrand Reinhold Co., 1980.

Mansfield, E., et al. *The Production and Application of New Industrial Technology*. New York: W. W. Norton & Co., 1977.

McHenry, K. "Who Does What in R & D?" *Chemtech*, 5, 156-161, 1983.

Morris, J. M. "Real-World Savvy and Adaptability." *Chemtech*, 5, 280-282, 1985.

Niebel, B. W. & Draper, A. B. *Product Design and Process Engineering*. New York: McGraw-Hill Book Co., 1974.

Poe, J. B. *An Introduction to the American Business Enterprise*. 5th ed. Homewood, Illinois: Richard D. Irwin, Inc., 1983.

Roberts, E. B. *The Dynamics of R & D*. New York: Harper & Row Publ., 1964.

Shurter, R. L., Willamson, J. P., & Broehl, W. G., Jr. *Business Research and Report Writing*. New York: McGraw-Hill Book Co., 1985.

Vagtborg, H. *Research and American Industrial Development*. New York: Pergamon Press, 1976.

Webster's New World Dictionary. (College Ed.) Cleveland, Ohio: The New World Publishing Co., 1968.

CHAPTER 4

Conceptualizing the Research Topic

by Gary D. Weede

Sub-Topics:

- Identification of a Technical Research Problem
- Identifying and Defining Variables
- Tools for Planning and Conducting the Technical Research
- Assessing Project Feasibility
- Planning and Scheduling the Research Project
- Review of a Research Idea by Others
- Approving the Research Idea

All major projects begin somewhere. Technical research starts with the recognition that a problem exists. Project ideas typically center around a need to more fully understand a complex problem. To undertake this task, pertinent information must be gathered and factors that have a bearing on the problem must be explored. The technological "state-of-the-art" related to the problem should also be considered. Using these perspectives, a verbal or written concept statement which serves as the beginning of the research activity is prepared. The development of this statement allows the researchers to interact and focus on the common theme for the anticipated investigation. Formal planning for the research project is based on this conceptual statement. The process of technical research officially begins at this point.

The conceptualization of the technical project idea allows various parties (researchers, managers, customers and clients) to view the "big picture," and to place the project in perspective. This results in all parties being able to identify the goals of, establish the feasibility and cost of, and establish a tentative timetable for the project. This stage also provides an opportunity for the researcher and other people involved to determine their capabilities and the resources available. Individual and/or company limitations can hinder the success of a project. It is best to recognize these factors at this early stage.

Developing a concept statement is essentially a mental activity that identifies potential avenues to be explored. The development of this statement involves numerous attempts to explain the dynamics of the problem. The ideas for identifying the nature of the project may be derived from many sources. Research staff members can use past experiences to provide suggestions and valuable input. Researchers may utilize mathematical and computer models to draft the concept statement.

The result of these activities is a clear definition of the research problem or task. The entire research focus will then be directed to finding an appropriate solution to the identified problem.

IDENTIFICATION OF A TECHNICAL RESEARCH PROBLEM

One of the frequently asked questions concerning technical research is: "Where do the ideas for technical research come from?" There are several sources of good ideas. The first source is from the *employees* of the company. Employees are hired by a company because of their expertise in a technology. They have gained this expertise through formal training and/or past experience. They draw on these attributes to formulate questions about their field of interest. They also have personal contacts which may stimulate ideas for further research. In addition, researchers read current technical literature (such as government, industry and professional association reports) and attend conferences that keep them current about technological advancements. This prompts their thinking about the "step beyond" in their field of technology. Some larger industries hire people to follow new technologies that relate to their company and formulate new ideas for research.

Appropriate past experiences in a technical field along with up-to-date knowledge of the state-of-the-art provide the basis for conducting quality technical research. If the experiences are truly meaningful, the inquiring mind will generate a number of avenues for investigating identified research problems.

New thoughts can be quickly developed and analyzed through a second source called brainstorming. This is a process whereby two or more people meet to freely exchange creative ideas on a topic or problem. Brainstorming allows researchers to compare their ideas and share past experiences which should result in a list of possible approaches to finding a solution to the research problem. As one experienced research and development (R&D) person stated, "This will often result in a change in thinking and definitely requires an open mind."

Another source for ideas is the consumers of the company's products or services. Sales or marketing personnel, when they contact customers, can determine current or anticipated needs. This information can be shared with R&D personnel who can provide insight into possible research projects. More ideas may be stimulated by the customer through returned goods, complaints and requests for products.

A fourth source is the company's competition. The success and/or limitations of a competitor's product or service may suggest research priorities. There are obvious challenges: avoiding patent infringements and developing a product or service that can be differentiated in the market place. It is not too uncommon, but often considered unethical, for one or more of the competition's key personnel familiar with the project idea or service to be hired.

Identification of Criteria for Evaluating Ideas

The selection of a technical research project should be based on identified needs of the company or the customer. The results of the project must have a potential use within the company or generate income through sales of products or services to the customer. If the need criteria cannot be met, the project idea cannot be economically justified.

Freedom to think creatively is valuable to the research process, but an attitude of realism must also prevail. In a company, criteria for project selection must be established to avoid expending excessive resources in an unsuccessful project. A researcher should realize that a prime consideration for evaluating proposed research activities is project idea feasibility, which indicates whether the project can be completed within the company's economic and technical capabilities. If the initial response is, "It can be done.", then the question should be asked, "Can it be done efficiently?" Stated another way, "Will the maximum results be obtained from the effort expended?"

Another criteria is, "How valuable will the results be?" Some things may be interesting to research but would be of little or no benefit to the company or the consumer. Some technical research may be valuable to the company but cost factors would make it prohibitively expensive. The bottom line is "What is the probability of success?" and "How much will it cost?"

Evaluating Research Problems

After the research tasks have been clearly defined, they need to be subjected to a more rigorous examination. This is usually done with established criteria that reflect the philosophy and direction of the company. The result of this evaluation will be a better understanding of the problems and a priority listing of those that are acceptable. In the more sophisticated research-oriented industries, this evaluation is often done by assigning a weight to each criterion which reduces the subjectivity of project selection. Costello (1983) identifies several techniques for project selection.

The technical project selection process should be formalized to insure that decisions will be consistent with the established company goals. Each project idea presented for review should include several major objectives. These help clarify what should be accomplished and the limits for each project idea.

Another aspect of evaluating research problems relates to other research efforts within the company. This would include research that has been or is being conducted as part of other projects. A search of literature should be conducted for the necessary foundation and perspective of the project idea. This can also yield information about how the research may be designed which will be of major concern later.

Evaluating the research problem is a very important step and should not be taken lightly. The information gathered and evaluated against stated criteria can later be measured in the company's profit column.

Assessing Human Resources

The training and experience of people conducting and managing the research is a major determinant of the project's success. The abilities of the company's research personnel must be evaluated with the same care as the research proposal. If a major new area of concentration is being developed, the corporation may decide to hire qualified personnel who have the necessary training and experience. If the need is for special expertise for a shorter term project, one or more consultants may be employed to conduct the research on site. For some types of research, a consulting firm may be used to provide the desired information. It must be recognized that each employee has his/her limitations in formal training, experience and expertise. For some research, formal instruction will be required.

Although an employee may not have the desired education and experience, his/her motivation should not be overlooked. Motivation has been a major factor in the success of a project when numerous positive incentives such as pride in the company, recognition for team efforts and acceptance as a worthy contributor to the project are evident.

Establishing a Research Team

A commitment to study the feasibility of a research project idea is done after the need for the project idea has been verified and the project idea has been identified as a goal for the company. A technical research team is organized to undertake the project idea. A successful team is made up of creative and analytical thinkers, preferably with a variety of experiences that will contribute to the success of the project. The best single selection criteria for team members is success on past projects.

IDENTIFYING AND DEFINING VARIABLES

As the research project idea is developed, there are a number of topics to be considered. As in any field of study, carefully defined terms allow co-workers to communicate thoughts and ideas without misunderstandings.

A major concept in all research is variables. Variables are factors that are subject to change and research projects are designed to investigate the relationship among them. There are several different types of variables which researchers must identify, classify and then define.

Variables may be arranged into three classifications. The first classification is *explanatory variables* which are the factors of major interest to the researcher. The relationship among explanatory variables is the focus of research projects. There are three types of explanatory variables: dependent, independent and moderating. The dependent variable is the factor or phenomenon that is being studied or investigated. Independent variables are the factors or conditions that are controlled or changed to determine what effect they have on the dependent variable. Moderating variables are those factors, conditions, settings or circumstances that can influence or change the results of the research but are secondary to the independent variables. These variables are more fully explained in Chapter 5.

The second classification is *extraneous variables*. They include a number of factors that could influence the relationships between the independent and dependent explanatory variables. These variables can be either controlled or uncontrolled. If these variables could affect the relationship between selected explanatory variables, they should be controlled and not allowed to change during the study. If these variables will have little effect on the study, they are allowed to be uncontrolled. It should be noted that there is always the possibility that one or more of these uncontrolled extraneous variables could affect the relationship between the explanatory variables in a systematic way. This action is referred to as a "confounding" effect.

The third classification of variables is the *intervening variables*. These variables are described as observed phenomena or conceptual mechanisms that cannot be measured or controlled but could affect the relationship between the explanatory variables. (Emory, 1980).

TECHNICAL RESEARCH DESIGN

A research design is formulated after the research problem has been stated and the various variables have been identified and defined. This research design is an organized plan or structure which will systematically advance the research project to completion. A simple analogy for a research design could be planning an extended vacation. This would include the routes to be traveled, the sights to be observed and the experiences to be encountered. This plan would be formulated within a given time period depending on the money available. These factors would be stated in the research problem.

The research design must include:

1. A plan for collection of the information relevant to the problem.
2. A strategy for the conditions under which the information will be collected.
3. A method with which it will be analyzed with regard to the costs involved. (Emory, 1980, p. 82-83).

A continued discussion of the role of the research design is presented in Chapter 5.

TOOLS FOR PLANNING AND CONDUCTING THE TECHNICAL RESEARCH

After the research design has been selected, consideration is given to tools or specialized equipment which are needed to collect, control and process the data. It is important that the accuracy of acquired data is not contaminated by poor practices, improper tools and equipment or tools and equipment that lack the required precision.

Technical research implies that more instrumentation would be used than in market, business or historical research. There is an almost inexhaustible list of these "specialized tools." Technical research may require a tool that does not exist and must be fabricated. Chapter 8 will provide more detail on these tools. The researcher should have some concept early in the research planning of the types of tools to complete a project.

Tools for conducting technical research may be grouped in the categories of data gathering, data controlling and date processing. A partial list of specialized tools for data gathering would include:

A. The electrical and mechanical items such as counters, timers, tachometers, frequency analyzers, pressure sensors, velocity meters, balances, scales, linear measuring devices, light meters, gloss meters, colorimeters, calorimeters, dosimeters, moisture meters, flow meters, spectrophotometers, chemical analyzers, sequencers, strip chart recorders, comparators, simulators and computers.

B. Other non-electrical and mechanical tools such as data collection tables; charts and graphs for raw data; computer tapes and disks; heat, light, and chemical sensitive papers and other materials; computer programs; survey instruments; and instructional packages for preparing research assistants.

The specialized tools for controlling data may include some of the sensing tools used in data collection. They would be set up to feed back information to keep the experiment within predetermined limits. Equipment for environmental control of heat, humidity, light, mechanical vibration and radio frequency would be some of the tools in this category. The control of electrical and other forms of power would require data-controlling tools. Data processing tools are used to analyze data or put them in more understandable and/or usable forms. Calculators, statistical analysis procedures and the computer itself are tools in this category. The tools for presenting the data in final form, such as tables, charts, graphs, diagrams, drawings and photos, would also be included. More information on data processing and reporting the results is given in Chapters 9 and 10.

ASSESSING PROJECT FEASIBILITY

Probably the most important item in conceptualizing a research project idea is the feasibility consideration. There are many factors which must be considered. If ignored, they could make the research very difficult, if not disastrous. These factors can be classified as either internal or external, although the same considerations will be found in each classification. Internal factors are those that are within the discretion and control of the researcher while external factors are imposed on the research project from outside sources.

In industry, the prime internal factor for consideration of any technical research project is *cost*. Since research costs can exceed available financing of the company, an itemized budget for the research project must be developed. The budget should consider both direct and indirect costs anticipated for the project. If the budget exceeds the company's financial resources, outside funding sources such as economic development agencies may be approached.

A second consideration is *human resources*. Consideration must be given to the abilities of the company's research and support personnel. In some cases, external human resources must be sought.

Space is a third research consideration. Many research projects require specialized space and equipment. If these are not available, plans for their acquisition must be developed.

The state-of-the-art or *level of technology* is a fourth consideration. It is much easier and more economical to pursue research that is in line with the company's resources and knowledge. Better results are obtained if the technology gap is not too large.

The fifth consideration is *environmental*. Many research projects require special environmental considerations. For example, the exposure of humans to excessive noise, fumes, radiation and particulate matter must be controlled. Some projects require special environments, such as controlled humidity or atmospheric pressure, extreme temperatures or shielding from external radiation. Externally, the Environmental Protection Agency has established standards to minimize external environmental damage, and companies have a moral and legal obligation to meet these standards.

The sixth consideration is *legal, contractual or policy constraints*. The company may have internal policies dealing with using human subjects in research or accepting defense contracts. External constraints of research are imposed by factors such as liability considerations, patent laws and anti-trust regulations.

Ergonomic considerations are a seventh type. These are human factors in engineering and are necessary to protect researchers and subjects from undue stress and strain.

The eighth consideration is realistic *scheduling* of research events and human, capital and material resources. The timing and coordination of all factors is mandatory for smooth progression of the research project.

Societal impact is the last major consideration. Care should be taken to ensure that the research does not adversely impact people or the community. The entire project idea should be reviewed to identify any actions or results that could discredit the company or be of disservice to society.

PLANNING AND SCHEDULING THE RESEARCH PROJECT

After the feasibility check has determined that the research project is viable, major steps in the project should be planned and scheduled. Various management programs and tools exist that can be used to schedule and monitor the progress of the project. These tools, which include Gantt charts, milestone charts, network systems (PERT and CPM) and progress organization charts, are presented in Chapter 7.

REVIEW OF A RESEARCH IDEA BY OTHERS

Review of a research project idea by other people is usually required and nearly always beneficial. Formal and informal discussions solidify thoughts and justify decisions.

A formal presentation is usually necessary to obtain support and approval of the project idea. The presentation itself should be well-planned and organized, properly timed, and smoothly, confidently and enthusiastically presented. The information presented should include a clear statement of the research problem including the expected results, variables, the research design, the results of the feasibility assessment, procedures for planning and scheduling the research, cost estimates and special research tools needed. More specific coverage of preparing a complete proposal is presented in Chapter 6.

Formal presentations normally are followed by discussion. The presenter should welcome this opportunity to clarify any information or correct misconceptions. The presenter should listen to the concerns and perceptions of the audience and be objective in his/her responses.

APPROVING THE RESEARCH IDEA

Following the presentation, the research idea will be considered for approval by management. They will most likely review the information to confirm that:

1. The objectives, variables and desired outcomes are clear, complete, and sound.
2. The project idea is feasible and likely to succeed.
3. The schedule of events is reasonable and within the time available.
4. The projected cost of the research is within reasonable limits.

The research idea may be approved, returned for further development or rejected. If it is approved, the researcher or team should finalize the technical research design which is the subject of the next chapter.

BIBLIOGRAPHY

Costello, D., "A Practical Approach to R&D Project Selection." *Technological Forecasting and Social Change*, Vol. 23, No. 4, 1983.

Emory, C. W. *Business Research Methods*. Homewood, Illinois: Richard D. Irwin, Inc., 1980.

Leiner, Kevin, Senior Project Engineer III, Cobe Laboratories, Inc., Lakewood, CO, Personal Interview, August 9, 1985.

Tellin, Earl, Manager of Qualtiy Assurance and Ballistics (Retired), Remington Arms Company, Personal Interview, July 15, 1985.

CHAPTER 5

Selecting a Technical Research Design

by Michael R. White

Sub-Topics:

- Determining Research Direction
- Problem Definition
- Methods of Collecting Data from Various Sources
- Selecting the Appropriate Research Design
- Summary

Any research must be carried out in a systematic, methodical and appropriate manner to assure that the results, conclusions and recommendations are warranted. Once the problem is identified, the research design establishes the soundness of all that follows. Any research-based decision is only as good as the process utilized to arrive at that decision.

Bennis and Nanus (1985), in discussing the difference between leaders and managers, note that: "Managers are people who do things right and leaders are people who do the right things" (p. 21). This summarizes two crucial roles for the researcher in the technological environment. It is extremely important to do things right (methods, statistics, processes, and other technologies of doing research). However, all of this "doing things right" is wasted if the research is also not doing the right thing.

Before selecting the research methodology, it is crucial that the researcher and the researcher's constituents are in agreement and are equally committed to the research problem. The crucial decision is "what to study" and this decision will, by its very nature, affect the methodology employed.

DETERMINING RESEARCH DIRECTION

First the overall purpose of industrial research must be established. Consensus needs to evolve as to whether the research team is *looking for problems* or *looking to solve problems*. Much of what follows in methodology will relate to this basic dichotomy. The technique used to do exploratory surgery (looking) is not used to treat a specific ailment (solving). Many of the problems in industry may not respond to research results. Sometimes the best developed problem analysis and research design will lead to conclusive results only to have the manager indicate that the data is nice ". . .but that's not what I want to do." The researcher and the management team must decide very early in the research problem identification and design consideration stages which problems are researchable and worthwhile.

An example of this dilemma: a company employed an outside researcher/consultant to conduct research into the training needs of a group within the organizational hierarchy. The research identified significant training needs for the group and indicated that upper management practices needed to be modified *before* training would be effective. However, the decision makers were reluctant to implement significant self-change strategies that were discovered to be necessary. All they thought necessary was "the workers needed training" not "we as managers needed to behave differently."

Another pre-design consideration is, "Can the problem be located or solved using informal methods rather than formal methods?" The cost/benefit relationship of any research in terms of the return on investment must be considered. It would be unwise to spend three months and $50,000 locating the causes of and developing strategies for dealing with material scrap if the same results could be obtained by asking for and implementing suggestions from shop floor people. Peters and Waterman (1982, p. 119) call this "A Bias for Action" approach to decision making. It's trying it, adjusting, trying again, adjusting and keeping at it. It's getting the people who know involved in problem identification, resolution and implementation (White, 1978). While technically not research, much of what goes on in industrial settings would be of this informal research/problem resolution nature. When these methods yield positive results, they are often the most effective way to approach the resolution of the problem and have the additional organizational benefit of increased motivation due to participation in the process (Lehrer, 1983).

69

Another prerequisite to the research design process is to determine if the solution is best sought using inductive or deductive methods of reasoning. Inductive methods of research and problem solving involve the study of many individual instances or occurrences leading to the formulation of a generalized conclusion from those occurrences. Deductive methods of reasoning and research are on the opposite end of the logic continuum. In this method, a general principle is stated, assumed or postulated. Ideas, positions or data are offered to support the principle and the principle is accepted as "truth." Then the rule is used for applications which fit the same conditions.

Both inductive and deductive reasoning have benefits and hazards when associated with research design (Clover & Balsley, 1984). Since most industrial research uses inductive thinking, the rules of inductive reasoning must be applied to test the validity of any research design that uses data collected from a sample and extrapolated to the population. These rules can serve as check points for the research design to assure that the inductive principles are supported.

Four essential conditions must be present for satisfactory inductive reasoning:

1. Observations must be correctly performed and recorded; data studied must be accurate and must be collected from the universe in which the researcher is interested.
2. Observations must cover representative cases.
3. Observations must cover a sufficient number of cases.
4. Conclusions must be confined to statements that are fully substantiated by the findings and are not too general or too inclusive. (Clover & Balsley, 1984, p. 20).

A concerted effort must be made during the research design phase to assure that the study adheres to these four principles. The time to plan for those assurances is before the study is conducted, not after the data is collected and it is discovered that one or more of the basic principles was violated. The four rules are foundational to any inductive research design and a brief explanation is appropriate at this point.

Recording Observations

The information must be collected accurately and consistently over time and over all the observations. The researcher must have a plan that collects the same data from all the observations. The records used or the observations made must be accurate, clear and verifiable. The data must be collected from sources that have knowledge about the universes of concern. For example, if the researcher is concerned about the incidents of rework in a particular manufacturing process, data must be collected from all those manufacturing processes that could contribute to the rework incidents. Manufacturing processes that could not contribute to the rework problem would not make up the universe for this particular study. One error that is often made in conjunction with this rule is collecting a lot of information and then looking for potential causes or relationships. Research studies that commit this error tend to get out of hand by trying to go beyond the capability of the research design.

Choosing Representative Cases

The population must be defined in terms of observable variables in the population and the sample must represent the population. If the population is made up of all the production processes involved in the manufacturing of a particular component, then the sample must include data and information from that universe. Data must be collected across all shifts from representative operations, and over a representative time frame of the production. If there is variability from day to day or week to week in the manufacturing process under study, then the sample from which data is collected must contain representation with the same variability.

Selecting Sample Size

The question of sample size is important in all research. Although no set formula can be proposed for sample size, the sample must be large enough to insure that all possible variability associated with the population is included. Sample size also must be large enough to reduce the probability of error, from the characteristics of the universe, to a predetermined level. This concern will be addressed in detail in the section on sampling techniques.

Drawing Conclusions

The researcher can draw conclusions only from the data and the population investigated. The researcher will often discover tangential data or "best guesses" and will feel compelled to include this in the report. This must be avoided. An example of this error would be a researcher who was investigating a particular management group in an organization, then drew conclusions about all management in the organization. The researcher must avoid going beyond the data, the defined problem, the design limitations or the universe of the study.

PROBLEM DEFINITION

With these four essential conditions in mind, the process of defining the research problem may begin. The type of research problem and how it is defined and stated impact on every aspect of the research design. Research failures can more often be attributed to poor problem definition than poor methods or poor research design (Buckley, Buckley, & Chiang, 1976).

An appropriate research problem is characterized by these attributes:

1. The problem is defined properly, is labeled and described accurately.
2. The problem is posed in solvable terms.
3. The problem is connected logically to the environment from which it is drawn—and the solution is applied within the environment.
4. The problem has been screened against the existing body of knowledge to assure its uniqueness, i.e., it has not been solved previously.
5. The solution to the problem must be viewed as making a potential contribution to the body of knowledge, i.e., the problem must be significant. (Buckley, *et al*, 1976, p. 19).

Two research problems might serve to illustrate these concerns: (1) *"Is* Statistical Process Control (SPC) used extensively in the manufacture of plastic molding?" or (2) *"Should* SPC be used extensively in the manufacture of plastic moldings?" The distinction between descriptive research (what is) in *(1)* and normative research (what should be) in *(2)* must be recognized because the research design and methodology are different. Empirical data must be collected in the case of *(1)* while opinion research would be appropriate in *(2)*. The population of respondents in *(1)* might be plant managers while the population of respondents in *(2)* might be quality assurance personnel, industrial technologists or engineers, supervisors or machine operators. Case studies or interview methodology may be appropriate in *(1)* while in *(2)* survey questionnaire techniques may be appropriate (Buckley, *et al*, 1976).

Setting Objectives

Once the research problem has been clearly defined, objectives for the research will be established. The objectives of the study are those things that are going to be accomplished or discerned as the result of the research effort. These objectives can be stated as research questions or hypotheses.

In some cases, there is enough information from the literature or current practice to suggest, or hypothesize, what will be found as the result of the study under the parameters of the investigation. A study is then designed to test the hypothesis. The purpose of testing hypotheses is to *explain* a relationship.

In other cases, research questions guide the *search* for what is or could happen. The question may be simply stated as "How much 'x' is going on in our organization?" "What material is best studied for this new year?" or "What changes will have to be made in this process to achieve a specific performance criteria?" Most technical research is formulated around research questions, and not hypotheses.

Regardless of the nature of the study, it is important to remember that there is a direct relationship between the research questions or hypotheses and the research problem. The former must contribute to and solve the latter. To accomplish this, the research problem should be written with the research objectives listed under the problem. Next the researcher should be assured that each of the research questions or hypotheses will contribute to the resolution of the research problem. Graduate programs in industrial technology have long sought the linking of research efforts to practical problem resolution (White, 1984). Some of the research objectives may be "non-researchable" due to the unavailability of the data, cost of collecting the data or the proprietary nature of the data. These research questions, if critical to the overall success of the project, may require additional managerial support, additional research activities or be eliminated from the study.

The research objectives must be analyzed to determine the variables that they contain. The variables should be classified as explanatory, intervening and extraneous variables. Data on the variables will be collected and used to answer the research questions or confirm or reject the research hypotheses. There are three types of explanatory variables. A variable capable of effecting change in another variable is an *independent* variable. The variable that is affected by the independent variable is the *dependent* variable and a variable that could alter the affect of an independent variable on a dependent variable is called a *moderating* variable. For example, a technical project exploring the reasons for scrap in a particular manufacturing process, might use the following design development sequence:

1. What processes are contributing to more than 5% scrap in *xyz* process? (A research question).

2. List all the processes that could produce or contribute to the production of scrap in the *xyz* process (Potential independent variables).

3. List the ways in which scrap is measured or shows up in the *xyz* process (Potential dependent variables).

4. List the way in which the independent variable(s) can be measured.

5. List the ways that the independent variable's affect on the dependent variable could be altered by some other variable or action (Potential moderating variables).

6. List the ways in which the dependent variables can be measured.

7. Determine which independent variables have the greatest potential for affecting the dependent variables and how the moderating variables can be eliminated, controlled, or minimized. Determine (a) which independent variables have multivariate components; that is, which ones are connected to other variables in some way and (b) which independent variables combine to affect, in a multivariate way, the dependent variable(s).

8. Determine the costs (i.e. dollars, time, personnel) of collecting the data on the independent and dependent variables especially in respect to the importance of the information in solving the problem.

9. Design a study to (a) control the intervening and extraneous variables when necessary, (b) maximize control over the independent and moderating variable(s) and (c) clearly show the relationship between the independent variable and the dependent variable so the observed variability of the dependent variable can be associated with the known variability of the independent variable.

METHODS OF COLLECTING DATA FROM VARIOUS SOURCES

Once the research questions or the hypotheses have been defined and variables identified, a plan to collect the data to solve the research problem is needed. As discussed earlier, the research design can be either inductive or deductive. Inductive methods often used in technical research are:

1. *Opinion Strategy*: The collection of opinion from those who have knowledge about the independent variable.

2. *Archival Strategy*: Records and historical data are examined to determine how the variability in the dependent variable is associated with, or affected by, variability in one or more of the independent variables.

3. *Analytic Strategy*: Logical analysis of what is to determine the nature of the causes of what was observed or what could be.

4. *Empirical Strategy*: The creation of an experimental design where all the variables are controlled and one independent variable is manipulated to determine its effect on the dependent variable.

Buckley, *et* al, (1976) discussed each of these strategies from an accounting perspective. They showed how each of these strategies may have inductive and deductive methods of obtaining information to answer the research questions or test research hypotheses. Also each strategy often has a unique source for obtaining the data.

Opinion strategy gathers opinions from individuals or groups using formal techniques such as survey research (groups) or Delphi technique (individuals). Informal techniques such as individual interviews, individual or group role playing or brainstorming are often used to collect data during pilot studies.

The archival strategy is an inexpensive way to do research because existing information is used to answer the research problems. The archival strategy, however, has many pitfalls for the unwary. The accuracy of existing data is a primary concern. The researcher must address sometimes sensitive issues of (1) secondary versus primary sources of data and (2) the potential "error" of forming "research" conclusions based on non-systematic data collection. These two pitfalls can be easily avoided through careful problem identification, by examining primary data and by systemizing the data search. However, the researcher using the archival strategy is sometimes tempted to look for what is expected rather than what is actually there.

The analytic strategy operates in the domain of internal logic of an individual or a directed group. Formal techniques are mathematical modeling, some operations research and artificial intelligence systems. Informal techniques are philosophical arguments and discussions and group task forces designed to do creative problem solving. The strength of the analytic technique is dependent upon the ability of participants to engage in logical thinking and focus on a specific task.

The empirical strategy is most closely associated with the pure experimental design of controlled research, and while often appropriate in industrial settings, it frequently does not lend itself to the multivariate problems inherent in industrial research. Where the environment can be controlled and the independent variable(s) identified and controlled, empirical studies are the preferred, and in many cases the required, methodology to draw cause-and-effect conclusions. These types of studies are often conducted in industrial laboratories and testing centers where the environment and the input/output measures can be precisely controlled. Some field testing, case studies and computer modeling or simulation also lend themselves to empirical strategy.

SELECTING THE APPROPRIATE RESEARCH DESIGN

The crucial issue in research design selection is to make sure that the design used is appropriate for the research problem, research questions or hypotheses, variables and the environment. Decisions need to be made to design the best study that will tell the most about the problem without going beyond the limitations of the particular design. Some of the specific methodologies of descriptive, experimental, quasi-experimental, ex post facto and correlational will be described in this chapter. If and when needed, additional or indepth information should be explored about each methodology. This chapter provides a starting point for the first time technical research method designer.

Sampling Techniques

An understanding of sampling procedures or methods of selecting people or things to be investigated is fundamental. One of the crucial concerns in any research is the similarity of the sample to the population. Sampling methodology is, therefore, very important in research design. Samples are selected from the populations in numerous ways. The most common is the random sample method, with variations to accommodate different population and research needs. The truly random sample is drawing the item (name of a respondent) from a list (all possible respondents) with no order (random) to the drawing.

Another sampling technique is the systematic random sample where the population is determined or assumed to be equally disbursed. The researcher draws *1/nth* of the population as the sample where *(n)* equals the size of the sample to assure representativeness.

If the items or respondents may be very different on specific independent variables, a stratified random sampling technique could be used. A stratified random sample is obtained by first separating the population into groups that are similar internally to each other yet different externally from the other sub-groups on the specific independent variable(s). The groups must be mutually exclusive from each other and totally representative of all individuals who make up membership in the group (Bailey, 1982). A foundry scrap problem could use the following stratified random sample descriptive design:*

X_1 (parts from furnace A and shakeout 1; n=100) O_1

X_2 (parts from furnace B and shakeout 1; n=100) O_2

X_3 (parts from furnace A and shakeout 2; n=100) O_3

X_4 (parts from furnace B and shakeout 2; n=100) O_4

The parts are separated into the four groups shown above (O_1 - O_4) and then random or systematic random samples are then drawn from each of the lots.

Proportional random sampling is often employed where it is known that the population is unevenly dispersed on some important independent variable and the researcher wants the sample to represent the population on that variable. The population is separated into groups according to differences in the identified variable. Then proportional random samples are drawn from each group. In the above example, if $(X_1)=100$, $(X_2)=200$, $(X_3)=300$ and $(X_4)=400$ (a total population of 1000), then a proportional random sample of (X_1) could be 1/10 of the total population, $(X_2)=2/10$, $(X_3)=3/10$ and $(X_4)=4/10$.

Samples that are not drawn at random are called nonprobability samples. In rare cases there may be a reason or reasons why a researcher cannot conduct a truly random sample of the population. When

---

*In all diagrams that follow, an "X" represents a treatment (introduction of a stimulus, manipulation of a variable, change in a condition, etc.) and "O" is a measurement of observation.

nonprobability sampling is used, the findings *cannot be generalized.* Second, the statistics used would have less power to detect a difference that existed.

In many cases, convenience or quota nonprobability sampling are used when it would have been just as easy for the researcher to use random sampling. For example, a researcher may have taken the first 20 items off an assembly line or recorded the opinions of the first five workers willing to talk about a specific technical problem rather than define the population and take a random sample. This occurs frequently in descriptive, historical and action research. In these situations, the findings cannot be generalized to a situation the researcher thinks he or she is sampling or to a given population.

Sample Size

For all research methodologies used, researchers determine the number of subjects that must be examined (sampled) to make inferences about the population. The subject of sample size is presented in most research methodology books and these should be consulted in establishing samples for a particular technical research project (Bailey, 1982; Emory, 1980; Kidder, 1981). All sources indicate the researcher should make the sample as large as possible. However, the question of how much is enough is not a simple question. Some sources will give formulas and charts for sample size, but the researcher must know certain critical characteristics of the population before these precise methods can be employed.

Four general questions must be answered before the sample size can be established:

1. How precise must the sample be in respect to the population? Do the research findings have to be "right" 99 times out of 100 (the .01 level) or is 95 times out of 100 "close enough" (.05 level)?

2. How much variability is expected in the population? For populations with a great deal of variability, the samples must be larger; for homogeneous populations, the samples can be smaller.

3. How are the samples going to be grouped for analysis? A sample that could fall into one of six categories on a variable will need to be larger than one that could potentially fall into only two categories.

4. What is the magnitude of the effect expected to be exhibited as the result of the independent variable? If the differences expected

are small, then larger samples are required to insure that one does not lose those differences due to a small sample.

Different types and designs of studies require different sample sizes. There are some general rules (Gay, 1976) that can be considered for determining sample size:

1. Sample sizes of less than 30 are generally to be avoided.
2. A sample of 10% is considered the minimum for descriptive research. A 20% sample may be required with small populations (less than 1000).
3. At least 30 subjects for each related component are required for most correlational studies.
4. Correlational and causal-comparative studies should have at least 15 in each sample.

Sample size is not easy to determine in the quantitative sense. Many of the qualitative components of the population must be known or estimated and built into any formula for determining the size of the sample to be drawn from the population.

Descriptive Research Designs

Descriptive research is designed to discover *what is* rather than to determine *why it is*. Descriptive research could be used to determine the distribution of defects among finished components or how the opinions of the employees about their supervisor relate to the performance appraisal of that supervisor by the plant manager. In the first example, the descriptive research is attempting to determine the "facts." In the second example the "facts" (employee's opinions about the supervisor) are compared with the plant manager's performance evaluation to determine if a correlation between the employee's and the plant manager's ratings exist. Both examples are descriptive research that can be conducted *without controlling any variables*. Descriptive research studies naturally occurring phenomena as opposed to manipulated variables in experimental or quasi-experimental designed research (Kidder, 1981).

The most frequently used method of collecting descriptive information is surveys. There are various forms of surveys such as questionnaires, interviews and non-intrusive measurements (item count as products pass an electric eye on a conveyor belt). The survey method collects information on the incidence and distribution of characteristics of the sample and then infers the results back to the population. In some cases, relationships are drawn *among* measured characteristics in the sample. Common examples of this technique are the opinion polls of Lou Harris and the Gallup Organization. The crucial concern of this methodology is to assure that the sample is representative of the population. In large populations, randomization sampling techniques are used to assure that the sample represents the population on *every* independent variable that could impact the dependent variable.

A pre-experimental design, Campbell and Stanley's (1963) static-group comparison can be used to determine what dependent variable characteristics are related to and/or vary with the independent variable. Using the common shorthand for explaining research design, "0" is the observation or measurement of "X" the variable being measured. Different subscript numbers represent different samples from the population. The dash line indicates that the groups have not been selected by randomization. If, for example, to determine the fatigue rate "0" of several different metal parts processed by different operators/machines X_n, the following design could be used:

$$\frac{X_1 \qquad O_1}{X_2 \qquad O_2}$$

It may be found that O_2 varies from O_1. However, it cannot be determined that the variability in O_2 was *caused* by the variability in X_2. The fact that two things are associated or correlated together does not mean that there is a causal relationship between the two. Other empirical research designs would have to be employed to test this relationship. Descriptive studies are very useful in describing phenomenon and identifying relationships which can be further isolated using more powerful techniques (DeGroot, 1969).

Survey data in the static-group comparison type design may be very time sensitive, especially for opinion type data. Therefore, it is important that the data be collected in the *same* time frame. Descriptive studies are often seen as less than real research because of the lack of control and the inability to draw conclusive, causal results.

This is an unfair criticism of the methodology and may lead to both poor descriptive and experimental studies. Without good descriptive methodologies to "strain the sea of information," more rigorous experimental studies may be "...untimely, and based on immature hypothesis construction, insufficiently anchored in the world of common experience, or premature fixation on a theoretical model." (De Groot, 1969, p. 305). Descriptive survey techniques, including the structured interview, are extremely appropriate for locating and clarifying problems and for studying variables that may later be structured into a more controlled environment to determine the nature of the relationships among variables.

Experimental and Quasi-Experimental Designs

Technical research that seeks to show that X causes Y must use a design (1) that controls and manipulates the independent variables, (2) isolates, measures and eliminates the moderating variables and (3) provides a way of observing the effect of the independent variable, in a controlled environment, on the dependent variable. This kind of study is called an experimental study. When variable or intervention management control varies slightly from the rigid requirements of an experimental design, the design is said to be almost experimental or quasi-experimental. In industrial settings, these types of studies are conducted in laboratories or production settings where the variables can be controlled and the effect of any moderating variables is controlled or eliminated. In some cases, models and computer simulations are used to provide control where the actual environment cannot do so.

For over two decades Campbell and Stanley's *Experimental and Quasi-Experimental Designs for Research* (1963) has been the foundation upon which most researchers have built their empirical designs. Their discussion of each design, methods of controlling for internal validity, factors jeopardizing external validity and the recommended statistics to be used should be a familiar source for the technical researcher.

Campbell and Stanley (1963) classify the research designs into four types:

1. Pre-experimental designs
2. True experimental designs
3. Quasi-experimental designs
4. Ex post facto and correlational designs

Pre-experimental Designs: The simplest and crudest forms of experimentation are pre-experimental designs. "They are the weakest designs in terms of scientific value and measurement power" (Emory, 1980, p. 337). However, their value lies in their ability to inexpensively gather information which can be used to provide direction and focus in planning more sophisticated research projects. The three pre-experimental designs are:

1. *One-shot case study*: All the population receives the treatment and the results are compared to "common knowledge." The procedure fails to control extraneous variables. The one-shot case study may be diagrammed as follows:

2. *One-group pretest-posttest design*: All the population receives a pretest, then a treatment followed by a posttest. The design has no control group to provide a benchmark for comparison and therefore is subject to uncontrolled extraneous variables. The one-group pretest-posttest is diagrammed as follows:

$$O_1 \text{ ----- } X \text{ ----- } O_2$$
Pretest   Treatment   Posttest

3. *Static-group Comparison*: Uses two existing populations, one of which receives a treatment and the other serves as a control. The groups are not chosen at random and therefore may not be comparable. The static group comparison design is diagrammed as follows:

$$\text{Group} \quad \text{I} \; X_1 \text{ ------- } O_1$$
$$\text{Group} \quad \text{II} \; X_2 \text{ ------- } O_2$$

These research designs are not experimental designs, but are widely employed in descriptive and action research settings. They should be used with extreme caution because they do not possess enough control in the design to warrant cause and effect conclusions.

True Experimental Designs: These are used to measure the effect of an independent variable on the dependent variable to determine how the independent variable *causes* a change in the dependent variable. Several guidelines must be followed to develop a valid experimental design:

1. Control over the independent variable and the effects that any moderating variables have on the dependent variable must be established.

2. The hypothesis, expectations of how things will come out, must be clearly defined and stated.

3. A control group, a sample from the population, must be used to compare the effects of the independent variable (treatment) on the experimental group.

4. The research design must concentrate on controlling all variables except the independent variable.

5. Random selection of subjects, subject assignment to groups (treatment and control), and assignment of treatments to groups must be assured.
6. Internal validity must be assured. Hence, the question: "Did the manipulation of the independent variable cause an effect on the dependent variable?" must be answered.
7. The sample must represent the population on every variable under study (external validity).

Three types of true experimental designs are pretest-posttest, Solomon four-group design and posttest-only control group. The *pretest-posttest control group design* (Leedy, 1980; Clover & Balsley, 1984; Miller & Barnett, 1986) is commonly displayed as:

$$R \quad O_1 \quad X \quad O_2$$
$$R \quad O_3 \quad \quad O_4$$

The "R" indicates that subjects are randomly assigned to either the experimental or treatment group (top) or the control group (bottom). The single variable, X, is manipulated for the treatment group. The observations for the experimental and control groups, $O_1 - O_4$, are conducted to measure the before and after effect of X. For example, a technical research project may test the effect of excess heat on the wear of engine parts. The selected parts are measured, then randomly installed and operated under two conditions: (1) engines running within the normal operating temperature (control group) and (2) engines operating above normal temperature (experimental group). After the engines have run for a predetermined running time, the parts would be removed and measured for wear.

The *Solomon four-group design* is commonly used to control for the effects of testing and the interaction of testing and X. (Campbell & Stanley, 1963). The design is diagrammed as:

$$R \quad O_1 \quad X \quad O_2$$
$$R \quad O_3 \quad \quad O_4$$
$$R \quad \quad X \quad O_5$$
$$R \quad \quad \quad O_6$$

This design uses two experimental and two control groups. One of each of these does not receive a pretest. By incorporating the characteristics of the pretest-posttest design with another randomly assigned set of treatments and observations, this design can control for, and determine the potential effects of, the pretest. For example, a pretest may require

X ray measurements. If the researcher was concerned about the effect of the X ray on the posttest results, the Solomon four-group design could be used. Randomization of assignments to groups and to treatments allows the researcher to confidently answer the question, Did X make a difference?

When randomization is correctly done with large populations, a pretest is not needed to assure that the groups are the same prior to the treatment "X." The *posttest-only control group design* builds on this premise (Campbell & Stanley, 1963). The diagram of this design is:

$$R \quad X \quad 0_1$$
$$R \qquad 0_2$$

This design can be very useful in industrial research where it is known that the population can be assigned to groups at random (parts into job batches) and then one of the groups is randomly selected for the treatment (a new heat treating process). The effect of X (the heat treating process) can then be measured by comparing the treatment observation, 0_1, to the control observation, 0_2.

True experimental designs are used widely in industry, where the researcher is attempting to determine how X affects, or causes, 0. These designs do, however, require control through randomization. The researcher cannot take groups (parts or people) as they naturally occur in the industrial setting and collect data from them.

Quasi-Experimental Research: These designs often fill the need for doing experimental research where randomization is not possible. There are many various designs that are appropriately called quasi-experimental (Campbell & Stanley, 1963; Leedy, 1980).

Two examples of the numerous types of quasi-experimental designs are:

1. Time series experiments.

$$0_1 \; 0_2 \; 0_3 \; 0_4 \quad X \quad 0_5 \; 0_6 \; 0_7 \; 0_8$$

2. Equivalent time samples design

$$X_1 \; 0 \; X_0 \; 0 \; X_1 \; 0 \; X_0 \; 0$$

whereby X_0 means no treatment.

Quasi-experimental designs test moderating or extraneous variables by taking *repeated* measures, over time, to assure that X caused 0.

Ex Post Facto Design: These designs attempt to determine what has happened "after the fact" or after the treatment has occurred. Industrial accident investigation and machine breakdown analyses are examples of ex post facto research. This research design is sometimes called

causal-comparative (Miller & Barnett, 1986) because the research is conducted to determine casualty by comparing what has happened (results)
to what has caused the results (treatment). Since data are not collected
in controlled conditions, the researcher can miss the real cause of the
effect.

Most ex post facto designs are a variation on the static-group comparison design, where observations 0_1 and 0_2 are made to determine
the effect of X. Ex post facto designs are commonly diagrammed as:

$$\_X\_\_\underline{0_1}\_$$
$$0_2$$

With no control over the independent variable X, the researcher
employing ex post facto projects should explore *all* possibilities of the
observed event. Since this is never fully possible, the validity of the
research rests on the ability of the design and the researcher to come
as close as possible to examining and eliminating all possible explana-
tions but one, the cause. Ex post facto designs, although used extensively in industrial and medical research, must be used with great caution and with the recognition of their limitations. One of the best uses
of ex post facto design may be the isolation of a *field* of potentially important independent variables for further experimental study.

Correlational Design: These designs attempt to determine if the
variance in the independent variable is *related to* the variance in the
dependent variable through the use of correlational coefficients. These
types of designs are appropriate where the variables are very complex
or they do not lend themselves to controlled manipulation.

The advantage of correlational research designs is that several
variables are measured simultaneously in a naturally occurring environment. Like ex post facto designs, correlational studies do not *imply
causality*. An example of this type of research design could be the job
performance of welders (0) correlated with the type (X) of welding training that they received.

$$\_X\_\_\underline{0_1}\_$$
$$0_2$$

If a difference is observed in performance 0_1 compared to 0_2, the researcher may assume that X caused 0_1. Because of the number of internal
validity (self-selection, interaction between subjects, or lack of control
of moderating or independent variables) and external validity questions
not answered, the researcher cannot assume that changes in "0" were
caused by "X." The major disadvantage of correlational design is that,

85

even though the variable(s) may be correlated with the dependent variable, the reseacher does not know, nor should it be implied, that "X" caused changes in "0."

SUMMARY

It is imperative that the theory (-logy) of the research process is supported by the action (techno-). The technologist must take into account the defining of the problem and designing and carrying through of the systematic treatment of the art of research. The research design, because it is a roadmap to be used for a specific destination, is a crucial step in the process. The world of the technologist is a multivariate one with complex interrelationships among variables. It is, in the best of situations, very difficult to control all the variables that might be involved in a particular situation. The essence of research design is to strive for the maximum control of the research situation. The technologist, in the practice of research, will more often find a complex, multifaceted, holistic environment rather than the one-dimensional setting of the controlled laboratory (Kilmann, 1984). Systematic research designs must be utilized to assist in these settings. The overriding principle of controlling for effects and measuring for results is most likely with a thorough understanding and practice of good research design.

BIBLIOGRAPHY

Bailey, K. D. *Methods of Social Research.* 2nd ed. New York: The Free Press, 1982.

Bennis, W. & Nanus, B. *Leaders: The Strategies for Taking Charge.* New York: Harper and Row, 1985.

Buckley, J. W., Buckley, M. H. & Chiang, H. *Research Methodology and Business Decisions.* New York and Hamilton, Ontario: National Association of Accountants and The Society of Industrial Accountants of Canada, 1976.

Campbell, D. T. & Stanley, J. C. *Experimental and Quasi-Experimental Designs for Research.* Chicago, Rand McNally, 1963.

Clover, V. T. & Balsley, H. L. *Business Research Methods.* 3rd. ed. Columbus, Ohio: Grid Publishing, Inc., 1984.

De Groot, A. D. *Methodology: Foundations of Inference and Research in the Behavioral Sciences.* The Hague, Belgium: Mouton and Co., 1969.

Emory, C. W. *Business Research Methods.* Homewood, Illinois: Richard D. Irwin, Inc., 1980.

Kidder, L. H. *Research Methods in Social Relations.* 4th ed. New York: Holt, Rinehart and Winston, 1981.

Kilmann, R. H. *Beyond the Quick Fix: Managing Five Tracks to Organizational Success*. San Francisco: Jossey-Bass, 1984.

Leedy, P. D. *Practical Research: Planning and Design*. New York: Holt, Rinehart and Winston, 1981.

Lehrer, R. N. (ed.). *White Collar Productivity*. New York: McGraw- Hill, 1980.

Miller, D. W. & Barnett, S. T. *The How-To Handbook on Doing Research in Human Resource Development*. Alexandria, Virginia: American Society for Training and Development, 1986.

Peters, T. J. & Waterman, R. H. *In Search of Excellence: Lessons from America's Best-Run Companies*. New York: Harper and Row, 1982.

White, M. R. Administration of Industrial Education programs. *Journal of Industrial Teacher Education, 15*(3), 75-84, 1978.

White, M. R. Graduate Education and the Doctor of Industrial Technology Degree. *The Technology Teacher, 44*(3), 9-12, 1984.

CHAPTER 6

Preparing and Presenting the Technical Research Proposal

by Harold H. Halfin
and Orville W. Nelson

Sub-Topics:
- Components of a Formal Technical Proposal
- A Sample Technical Research Proposal

The conceptualization of a technical research project has involved:
1. Identifying and evaluating research ideas that fulfilled specified needs.
2. Evaluating potential research problems.
3. Specifying research questions or hypotheses.
4. Determining and classifying research variables.
5. Selecting a research design based upon the problem to be solved.
6. Outlining sampling techniques.
7. Identifying the major steps for conducting the study which includes implementing the research design, managing the project, instrumentation, measurement and collecting data.
8. Identifying how the data will be analyzed.
9. Specifying how the results, conclusions and recommendations may be derived.

It is understood that these conceptualization tasks must have generated a research idea that has been deemed feasible, reviewed by peers and supervisors and approved by company managers.

The next step in conducting technical research is to prepare a proposal. This chapter will identify the components of informal and formal proposals, identify major topics that need to be addressed in each component and give an example of a formal proposal.

COMPONENTS OF A FORMAL TECHNICAL PROPOSAL

There are two types of proposals, informal and formal. Each type should include a problem statement and a section on what will be done during the project. Other detailed sections, such as (1) specific instrumentation that will be used, (2) a population/sampling plan, (3) data analysis procedures and (4) decision strategies, may be included.

The informal research proposal is usually a short presentation including a problem statement and a statement on what, how and when it will be done. The informal proposal is usually used when there is not a clear idea of the problem to be studied or the problem is new and vague. The proposal provides an opportunity to explore ideas and concepts so that a more clearly stated approach may be developed. Exploration, typically done with informal proposals, may save time and money by identifying problems that are not as important as first thought. The informal research proposal should be used for doing much of the exploration type of research prior to developing a formal proposal.

Formalized research proposals are well structured and have clearly stated objectives and research questions or hypotheses. The formal proposal will usually include the following:

1. Purpose of the research, statement of the problem, and research questions or hypotheses.
2. Need and related research, limitations and assumptions.
3. Research methodology.
4. Budget.

Purpose of the Research, Statement of the Problem and Research Questions or Hypotheses

The research proposal should start with a clear statement of purpose. This statement presents the research topic being addressed, provides a brief overview of the project and identifies the value of the results.

The statement of the problem states exactly what the research expects to accomplish. This statement focuses on a clearly stated objective(s) which gives direction to the research process. It must detail the performance criteria expected of the outcomes. The statement of problem must limit the scope so that definite conclusions can be drawn and recommendations can be made.

The statement of the problem is followed by a series of research questions or hypotheses. Technical research usually uses research questions which give direction and focus to the investigation, identify the explanatory, intervening, and extraneous variables, and provide direction for selecting a research design. The research questions or hypotheses should be:

1. Stated as concisely as possible.
2. Capable of being answered or tested.
3. Reasonable.
4. Consistent with known facts.

Need and Related Research, Limitations and Assumptions

The need statement discusses how the answer to the research problem(s) will influence the plant operations or the design of the products, the processes used to produce products or the people who are responsible for or are involved in designing or producing the product. The need, in most cases, will center on personnel, materials, machines and/or existing technology. Need statements may come from:

1. Management reports which include production, warehousing, inventory problems, future trends or personnel problems.
2. Special reports which include information about products, new equipment or machinery, technological advancements or changes in policies.
3. Past research.
4. Customer complaints or service reports.

Failure to include this step in the proposal may result in a research program which will not contribute to the overall goals of management and/or improve the design or production processes.

Related research should be reviewed in this section. Previous research on the topic should be included to show that the proposed research will give the company a competitive advantage. Similar research strategies should be reviewed as they relate to the proposed project.

Included in this section are assumptions and limitations which bring the project into focus and operational definitions of new or unfamiliar terms.

Research Methodology

The research methodology includes selecting the research design, outlining sampling techniques, identifying major steps for conducting the study, instrumentation and data collecting procedures, data analysis procedures and decision strategies. The plan includes:

1. The major research activities needed to test the research questions or hypotheses.
2. A timetable for the events that will take place.

The research design presented in Chapter 5 identified methods and procedures for collecting and analyzing data. The research design needs to be described in terms of type of study, population to be sampled and procedures to be followed to conduct the study. Below are major questions that should be addressed in the research design section of a research proposal.

1. *What type of research design will be used?* The proposal should communicate whether the research will be descriptive, experimental or correlational in nature. The experimental type design may be further described as pre-experimental, true-experimental or quasi-experimental.

Typical descriptive studies include case or field studies, surveys, causal comparative studies, activity analysis studies, time and motion studies, content or document analysis studies and follow-up and trend studies. Examples of experimental studies are:

1. One-shot case study.
2. One-group pretest-posttest.
3. Static group comparison.
4. Pretest-posttest control group.
5. Solomon four-group.
6. Posttest-only control group.
7. Single and multiple group time-series.
8. Equivalent time sample.
9. Expost facto.
10. Correlational.
11. Simulation.

Correlational studies are classified as bivariate, multiple, non-parametric, partial and regression.

Included in the discussion of the research design should be the rationale for choosing the particular approach that will be used. This decision is generally based upon such questions as:

a. Is the study exploratory or in-depth?
b. Will the research be conducted in the field or laboratory, or will it be a simulation?
c. Will it be a one-shot study or longitudinal?
d. Will observations or experiments answer the research questions?

   e. Will selected variables be affected or will relationships among variables be described?

The research design section should clearly communicate the type of research that has been chosen and the reasons for choosing it.

2. *What are the variables present in the research?* All research activities must consider the variables which are present. The proposal should describe those variables which will be controlled, studied or left to operate on their own. The main types of variables are:

   a. Explanatory: factors of major interest to the research which are believed to explain specific conditions.

   b. Intervening: observed phenomena or conceptual mechanisms that cannot be measured or controlled but could affect the relationships among the explanatory variables.

   c. Extraneous: factors that could influence the relationship among the independent and dependent explanatory variables.

Identification of the variables will result from answering such questions as:

   a. What factors are being measured? (Dependent variables)

   b. What factors are being controlled? (Control variables)

   c. What factors are being manipulated? (Independent variables)

   d. What factors have an influence on the dependent and independent variables? (Independent variables)

   e. What conditions can change the results of the research? (Moderating variables)

   f. What outside factors might influence the results of the research? (Extraneous variables)

In some cases the proposal will contain a diagram showing the relationships among the different variables identified for the research.

3. *How will the sample for the research be identified?* The proposal should clearly describe the population from which the sample will be taken and the procedure used to select the sample. Sampling involves selecting a representative subset of parts, people, agencies or businesses from the total group available.

A population comprises all of the parts, people or agencies that meet the criteria for the total group. For example, if a study is designed to inspect all parts produced by a plant, the population would consist of all parts produced within a defined time period.

A sample is a representative group of individuals or parts from the total population. In the above example a portion or sample of the total population of parts produced in a given time frame may be inspected. The sample must be representative of the population if generalizations or conclusions about the population are to be drawn.

Samples can be drawn from the population using one of several techniques including random sampling, stratified random sampling, systematic random sampling and proportional random sampling.

The sampling technique is chosen after some basic questions are answered. These questions include:

a. Is there a population to be sampled?

b. Can the study be conducted with the entire population?

c. What characteristics of the population are being studied in the research project?

d. Does the population vary greatly on the characteristics being studied?

e. How can a representative sample be selected?

f. What size sample is needed to adequately represent the population?

This section of the proposal should provide a rationale for the sampling technique chosen. It should provide confidence that the sample truly represents the population.

4. *What major steps will be followed in conducting the research?* A method for collecting data from the sample must be selected once the variables being measured and the sample to be used have been identified. Four basic strategies are available: (1) opinion, (2) archival, (3) analytic and (4) empirical. After the data collection strategy is selected, the major steps for conducting the research project should be identified. These steps are based on major decisions which include:

a. What parameter, characteristic, activity or feature will be measured?

b. How will these traits be measured?

c. What measurements should be taken?

d. How accurate must the measurements be?

e. What instrument can be used to provide the required measurements?

f. How can the data (measurements) be recorded?

g. How can the recorded data be put into a readable form?

h. What procedures must be followed to collect accurate, reliable and valid data?

    i. How much will it cost to complete each step?

The proposal should describe and give a rationale for the data collection strategy and procedures selected for the research project.

5. *How will the research project be managed?* Technical research projects are managed activities. The proposal should describe the tools and techniques that will be used to insure that the project meets time schedules. Gantt and/or PERT charts (See Figures 6-1 and 6-2) or other management techniques which are described in Chapter 7, are often used.

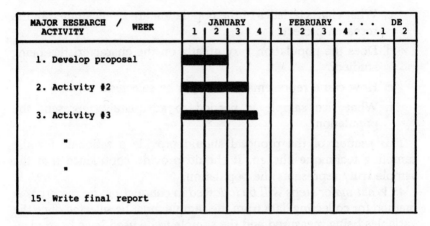

MAJOR RESEARCH / WEEK ACTIVITY	JANUARY				FEBRUARY . . . . DE					
	1	2	3	4	1	2	3	4 . . .1	2	
1. Develop proposal										
2. Activity #2										
3. Activity #3										
.										
.										
15. Write final report										

Figure 6-1: Sample Gantt Chart

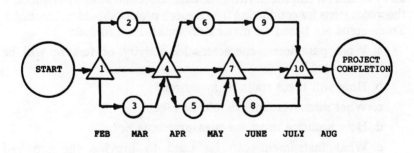

FEB   MAR   APR   MAY   JUNE   JULY   AUG

◯ = Activities which are not on the critical path but need completed to accomplish the next major step

△ = Major activity or critical path

Figure 6-2: Sample Pert Chart

Gantt charts plot the major activities in the research project against the weeks or months of the year. PERT provides visual display of the sequencing and timing of critical events for the research project.

6. *How will the data be analyzed and decisions made?* The final portion of the research proposal should present data analysis and decision-making procedures. The statistical procedures that will be used to analyze the data should be identified and described. The data may be described by:

a. Patterns of occurrence: frequency, percentage, graphs, line charts, etc.

b. Measures of central tendency: mean, mode, median.

c. Measures of variability: range, variance, standard deviation.

Often inferential and/or correlation statistics are used in the decision-making process. These statistics help in the interpretation of the data for drawing conclusions and making recommendations. The statistical procedures are selected based on answers to some basic questions including:

a. What type of measurement scale will be used? (nominal, ordinal, interval, ratio)

b. Will random sampling procedures be used? (nonparametric or parametric statistics)

c. Will the test of significance for the data be based on measures of central tendency or variability? (i.e., t test, F test, Chi square)

d. Are relationships among variables being tested? (Spearman r, multiple correlation, regression)

e. Will the validity and reliability of the data be measured?

The results of the statistical treatment of the data, findings from similar research projects and judgement of the research are used to draw conclusions about the research questions or hypotheses and make recommendations for action.

Budget

The final segment of the proposal should detail the cost elements for the research project. These elements are included in a budget which lists personnel, travel, supply and material, equipment, contractual service and overhead costs.

A SAMPLE TECHNICAL RESEARCH PROPOSAL

An example of a formal research proposal is presented. Background information on the company and how the problem and objectives for the proposal were identified are discussed first. The second portion of this section presents a research proposal based on this problem situation.

Background on the Problem

High Tech Plastics Corporation produces a variety of plastic parts that are sold to other manufacturers. With the exception of a small number of specialty parts, the High Tech Plastics Corporation does not sell directly to consumers. High Tech has a reputation for producing a quality product. Management and staff are very concerned about maintaining and improving the quality of the parts produced.

During the last three months, the High Tech Corporation has been experiencing some problems in producing the Series H Control Arms. Variations in the width of these plastic control arms has caused some of them to be too wide and thus bind in the sub assembly.

Staff members in the quality department have been collecting data on the variability in the width of these control arms. These data were collected over the last three months through systematically sampling the output from the molding machines which produced them. The averages calculated for these samples indicated that the process is running on target. However, the standard deviations for the samples indicated that the variability is too large to meet the specification.

While the quality control members were collecting the data, the High Tech Corporation Research Department was also reviewing reports of related research and technical articles relevant to the problem. No direct answers were found in the research and articles reviewed. However, several potential factors were identified.

After reviewing the data acquired by the quality staff members and the results of the review of related research, the researcher decided to bring together a team comprised of individuals who had experience with the process in the plant and a knowledge of the materials used. A five-member team comprised of a representative from the quality department, a molding machine operator, supervisor, inspector and the researcher met to discuss the problem and identify potential causes.

The researcher directed the meeting. During the first phase of the session, the members of the team discussed the possible causes of the

96

problem. These were listed on a flip chart as they were presented by the team members. The purpose of this portion of the meeting was to identify as many potential causes as possible.

After the team members had exhausted all of their ideas for potential causes, the team turned its attention to developing a cause-effect diagram. The final diagram developed is given in Figure 6-3. The problem (effect) was listed on the right and an arrow was drawn to it from the left. Potential causes of the problem were categorized in four major areas: materials, equipment, worker techniques and process technology. Specific problems or factors associated with each of these areas were then organized as twigs on these main branches. For instance, in the materials area, the composition of the material, moisture content and granule size were identified as potential factors. Potential causes associated with the equipment area included the mold design and maintenance.

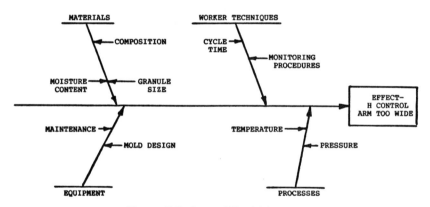

Figure 6-3: Cause-Effect Diagram

The next portion of the meeting was spent reviewing the cause-effect diagram. First participants scanned the diagram to determine if all of the potential causes of which they were aware were included. No additional causes were added during this time. The team members then identified high potential or priority causes. Based on their experience and knowledge of the factors involved with the problem, each person identified the three most critical causes. This was done individually. The researcher then tallied the priorities assigned to each cause on the cause-effect diagram. The two causes given the highest priority were the mold design and temperature of the mold.

The researcher left this meeting with the responsibility to develop a formal research proposal. The team members also understood that they would have an opportunity to review a draft copy of this proposal before it was presented to management for approval.

Developing the Formal Research Design

The discussion process and the cause-effect diagram developed by the quality team provided a good framework for the researcher to use in developing the proposal. Considerable information was available on the nature of the problem and potential causes. Although the researcher realized that a research study might determine that the high priority causes were not really the causes of the problem, the data available and the input from the quality team provided an appropriate starting point.

In order to obtain a more systematic view of the potential variables involved, the researcher conducted a systems analysis on the problem. This systems analysis is reproduced in Figure 6-4. The causes identified in the cause-effect diagram were used in developing this systems view of the process. In addition, the knowledge gained from the review of related research and technical articles on the process were used.

System
Manufacturing Environment
• Management system
• Climate control in the plant
• Employee skills
• Maintenance program
• Equipment - press and mold

	Processes		
	• Process steps		
	• Sequence of steps		width
Input	• Inspection	Output	specification
Plastic raw material	• Temperature of mold	Control Arms	.25±.02
	• Processing speed		

Figure 6-4: Systems Analysis Diagram

A SAMPLE OF A FORMAL RESEARCH PROPOSAL

The following is the proposal developed by the researcher at the High Tech Corporation. This proposal is consistent with High Tech's format and the level of detail preferred by management. Formats and the level of detail will vary somewhat from company to company. However, the contents of this proposal will provide an appropriate starting place.

ABSTRACT

Approximately five percent of the Series H Control arms are too large. A quality team has reviewed the problem and identified several potential factors or causes. The team members concluded that the mold design and temperature were the most likely causes. This study is designed to experimentally evaluate the impacts of these two variables on control arm width.

The problem in this study is to determine the amount of variability in the width of Series H Control arms caused by differences in mold cavities and temperature levels. Major research questions to be answered are:

Does the width of parts produced by different cavities in the mold vary significantly?

Does the temperature of the mold have an effect on the width of the Series H Control Arm?

Do some temperature levels and cavity locations produce significantly wider control arms?

The design of the study has been carefully developed to minimize the effects of extraneous variables and permit an efficient evaluation of the impacts of the independent variables, temperature and mold cavity, on the dependent variable, control arm width. A competent molding machine operator will run all of the parts. All parts will be run from the same lot of raw material.

Width of the control arms will be measured by the Quality Department. This measurement will be entered directly from the measuring instrument into our quality analysis software.

Total cost of the project is estimated to be $3277. This cost will be recovered in six months if the results of the experiment help reduce the proportion of rejects from 5.1% to .5%.

INTRODUCTION

Since production of the Series H Control arms started, 5.1% of the arms have been too wide. A quality team identified variations in mold cavities and temperature levels as the most likely causes of this problem. This study will use an experimental design to determine the amount of variation in control arm widths caused by these two factors.

PURPOSE

The purpose of this research is twofold:
1. Identify factors that can be controlled to reduce the variability in the present process.
2. Expand knowledge of the molding process so that future processes can be more efficiently designed.

PROBLEM

The problem of this research study is to determine the amount of variability in the Series H Control arms caused by differences in mold cavities and mold temperature levels.

RESEARCH QUESTIONS

The research questions to be answered are:
1. Does the width of parts produced by different cavities in the mold vary significantly?
2. Does the temperature of the mold have an effect on the width of the plastic control arms?
3. Is there any interaction between the cavity locations and temperature levels?

NEED AND RELATED RESEARCH

Since production of the Series H Control Arm was initiated, we have had problems with excess variability in the control arms produced. For one or more reasons, the process being used is too variable. Data collected on samples of the control arms during the first three months of production are summarized in Table 6-1.

| Week | Sample | |
	Mean	Std. Deviation
1	.251	.011
2	.248	.009
3	.251	.012
4	.252	.011
5	.249	.009
6	.253	.011
7	.251	.012
8	.248	.010
9	.250	.009
10	.251	.012
11	.249	.013
12	.250	.011
	$\bar{\bar{X}} = .250$	$\bar{s} = .011$

Table 6-1: Series H Control Arm: Width Data

It is apparent from reviewing the data in Table 1 that the process is running on target. The average control arm widths for the samples do not vary significantly from what would be expected when sampling from a process that is running at .25 inches.

The standard deviations for the samples, however, indicate that there is too much variability in the process. In other words, the variation in the widths of the individual parts produced by the process is too great. We need more consistency in the output from the process. At the present time, 5.1 percent of the parts produced are too wide. If the variability in the process could be reduced by 20 percent, only one-tenth of one percent of the parts would be too wide.

A quality review team was formed to more clearly define this problem and gain further information about the factors related to it. The team was comprised of Mary Jones from the quality department; Ned Anderson, molding machine operator, Joan Smith, supervisor; Tom Block, inspector; and the researcher. Team members identified 23 possible causes of this problem. These causes were organized in a cause-effect diagram which is given in Figure 1. The team identified variations in mold cavities and differences in temperature levels as the two most likely causes of excess control arm width. These two factors are a logical starting place for research on this process. They are consistent with the technical and research information available on this process.

LIMITATIONS

The following limitations will apply to this study.

1. Measuring equipment used in this study has ±.001 accuracy.
2. The study will be limited to eight cavity molds.

ASSUMPTIONS

The following assumptions underlie this study. It is assumed that:

1. The specification for the control arm width is valid.
2. The molding machine operator will be able to function at the same performance level during the two-hour period required to conduct the experiment.

DEFINITIONS

Series H Control Arm — the activating lever used in the 981 Electronic Metering Control to activate the by-pass system. Specifications for this control arm are given in S.F.5018-B.

Lot — refers to the raw materials produced in one production run. These may be shipped to High Tech in one or more containers.

RELATED RESEARCH AND INFORMATION

A review of related studies conducted in our plant indicated that each mold cavity is typically within specifications. However, these studies have not investigated the variability in the final parts that is assignable to differences in the output characteristics of individual mold cavities.

Our research department has also studied the effects of differences in raw materials and their impacts on the parts produced. We have found that different lots of the same raw material have different processing and output characteristics. In other words, even though each lot of material meets our specifications, each lot will have somewhat unique processing and output characteristics. Some variations have been found within lots; however, these variations are significantly smaller than the lot-to-lot variations.

Our studies also reveal some operator impact on the quality and characteristics of the parts produced. More experienced operators produce parts that have less variability. They also tend to detect problems more quickly. Parts produced by the evening and night shifts usually have less variability.

An analysis of the research literature provided several useful pieces of information. A number of researchers (Forslim, 1983; Person, 1985; and Roseberg, 1986) have found that mold temperatures can vary enough during normal processing cycles to influence dimensional characteristics of parts. Through the use of a sophisticated sensing device, Wicklund (1985) found that there is a significant temperature variation from cavity to cavity within the same mold as parts are processed.

These are the most relevant studies. They identify the potential impact of mold cavities and temperature on size of parts produced. In addition, they indicate the potential confounding effects of operators, shifts and lots of materials. These factors will need to be controlled in the research design for this study.

RESEARCH DESIGN AND METHODOLOGY

Design. A factorial design will be used for this experiment. The two independent variables will be temperature level and cavity location. Control arm width will be the dependent variable.

Four temperature levels will be studied. These levels will be the standard processing temperature presently used, one temperature level 15 degrees below the standard, and temperature levels that are 15 and 30 degrees above the standard. The eight cavities in the mold will form the eight levels for the cavity within the same mold as parts are processed.

The systems analysis completed for this process and the related research identified the following potential independent variables.

Operator skills.

Maintenance level and quality.

Press used to produce the parts.

Lot of raw materials.

Humidity in the processing area.

Work shift.

Since the goal of this study is to determine the effects of cavity and temperature (independent variables) on control arm width (dependent variable), the research design will be developed to assure that these potential variables do not have a systematic impact on the dependent variable. One operator will operate the molding machine. An experienced operator will be selected. The same press will be used throughout the experiment. Raw material from one lot will be used. The experiment will be conducted during a three-hour period. This will minimize changes in humidity and other environmental conditions.

Sample size for the experiment will be 9. Nine shots will be made at each temperature setting. Each shot will be inspected to determine if eight useable control arms are produced. If less than eight control arms are available, another shot will be used.

Procedure. Raw material for the study will be selected from one lot. The mold and molding machine will be set up using standard procedures. They will be tested and adjusted as needed to assure that they are operating normally. The low temperature sample will be run first. Then the die temperature will be increased to the next higher temperature and the second sample run. This process will be followed for the next two higher temperature levels. The mold will be inspected between each sample and cleaned as necessary. Output for each temperature level will be labeled and kept separate. Each of the cavities has a signature that will allow identification of the output from each.

After the parts have cooled to room temperature, they will be measured. Our standard measurement equipment will be used. This equipment is accurate within ±.001 and the data are fed directly into the computer system.

Statistical Analysis. The data will be analyzed with a two-way analysis of variance program that is a part of our statistical analysis package (SAP). This program provides an F test for the two main effects (cavity and temperature) and the interaction between these two variables.

The .05 level of significance will be used for the statistical tests. Descriptive statistics will also be run for each variable and levels within the variables. Average width and the standard deviation will be reported for each level.

Research Activity Schedule. The proposed research activity schedule is given below.

Research Activity	Schedule
1. Project proposal reviewed and approved by management.	June 2-5, 1986
2. Experimental schedule checked with production schedule.	June 9-10
3. Molding machine and operator scheduled for experiment.	June 11
4. Lot of raw material selected.	June 11-12
5. Experimental procedures discussed with molding machine operator, quality staff, and other persons involved in the experiment.	June 16
6. Press and mold setup checked and adjusted for experiment.	June 17
7. Experiment conducted.	June 17
a. Run at low heat	
b. Run at standard heat	
c. Run at standard +15 degrees	
d. Run at standard +30 degrees	
8. Measure width of control arms.	June 18
9. Analyze data.	June 19-20
10. Prepare report of results.	June 23-25
11. Present results to management.	June 30

Project Budget. The estimated cost of this research project is $3277. If the knowledge generated by this study can be used to reduce the percentage of nonconforming control arms from 5.1% to .5%, the cost of this project will be recovered in six months. All budget costs are based on our standard cost factors.

A. Personnel
  1. Researcher (64 hours @ $20.15/hr) $1290.00
  2. Molding machine operator (4 hours @ $9.81/hr)   39.00
  3. Support staff for molding operation
     (8 hours @ $10.00/hr)   69.00
  4. Quality technician (6.5 hours @ $10.11/hr)   66.00
  5. Computer Operator (2 hours @ $12.31/hr)   25.00
  6. Secretary (8 hours @ $7.13/hr)   57.00
  7.   TOTAL SALARIES + WAGES $1546.00
  8. Fringe Benefits (35% of wages + salaries)   541.00
B. Supplies, Services and Materials
  9. Clerical supplies and photocopying   90.00
  10. Raw materials for control arms   28.00
  11. Press time (4 hours @ $2.75/hr)   11.00
  12. Computer time   125.00
  13. Total Supplies, Services & Materials   254.00
  14. Total Direct Costs   2341.00
  15. Overhead Costs (40% of direct costs)   936.00
  16. Total Project Costs $3277.00

BIBLIOGRAPHY

Emory, C. William. *Business Research Methods*. Homewood, Illinois: Richard D. Irwin, Inc., 1985.

SUMMARY

The preparation for and presentation of a technical proposal involves identifying and verifying a need, evaluating and stating a technical research problem, identifying and classifying research variables, selecting a research design, outlining sampling techniques and outlining the major steps for conducting the project. These steps include managing the project, instrumentation, measurement and collection, analyzing the data, interpreting the results, drawing conclusions and making recommendations. The written proposal must include an abstract and be well written. The proposal should be brief, to the point and concise. The authors of the proposal must be prepared to present the proposal verbally. They need to have visuals which explain major points in the proposal. The presentors must realize that their job is to present the proposal with objectivity so that management will be able to make the best decision possible.

BIBLIOGRAPHY

Forslim, A. (1983) "Variations in Die Temperatures During Production Runs." *Plastics Research Newsletter*, 15, March, pp. 15-31.

Person, B. (1985) "Fluctuations in Die Temperatures During Long Production Runs." *Plastics Manufacturing Memo*, 21, pp. 89-94.

Roseberg, G. (1968) "Die Operating Characteristics." *Plastics Research Newsletter*, 18, April, pp. 28-37.

Wicklund, M. (1985) "Cavity to Cavity Variations in Die Temperatures During Production Runs." *Plastics Manufacturing Memo*, 21, August, pp. 39-43.

CHAPTER 7

Managing the Technical Research Project

by Donald L. Clark

Sub-Topics:
- **Definition of a Project and Project Management**
- **Planning, Organizing and Controlling of the Project**
- **Management Systems**
- **Summary**

In the previous chapters of this yearbook, topics dealing with the nature of technical research, including problem identification, selection of the research technique, and documentation of these in the proposal have been discussed. In the chapters that follow, topics dealing with conducting the research, including collecting and analyzing the data and evaluating and reporting the results will be discussed. The management functions that are discussed in this chapter should evolve during the preliminary phases, be documented in the proposal and then implemented during the project execution and reporting phases. Thus, the material presented in this chapter could be considered to be a bridge between the previous chapters and those that follow.

In the model of the research process as presented by Seymour in Chapter 3 of this yearbook, the management plan would evolve during steps one through three of the model, be documented in step four, and be implemented in steps five through eight. In each of these phases, Seymour places considerable emphasis on the importance of the management function. The authors of most of the other chapters of this yearbook also make reference to the importance of the management function. For example, in Chapter 4, Weede calls attention to the need to consider factors related to the management function.

It is obvious that the management function must be considered in selecting the research procedure as discussed by Halfin and Nelson in Chapter 6. The activities discussed in the chapters that follow by Shackelford, Kovac, Andrews, and Kanagy, dealing with conducting, analyzing, evaluating, and reporting can only be as successful as the management plan that supports these activities.

The philosophy that undergirds the material presented in this chapter is based upon the belief that even though there are commonalities among projects, each project, by definition, is a unique entity. Thus, the management plan for each project must evolve during the ideation phase with specific details of the plan being designed to fit both the project and the host environment.

DEFINITION OF A PROJECT AND PROJECT MANAGEMENT

Projects by their very nature are finite in character. They have a beginning point and, once the objective is accomplished, the project is terminated (Karger & Murdick, 1980, p. 78; Cook, 1971, pp. 4-5; Schmenner, 1984, p. 379). "... the management of a project is quite different from that of an ongoing operation" (Schroeder, 1985, p. 353).

A simple definition of a project, yet one that includes many elements that relate to the need for effective and efficient management, would include the following:

1. Finite in character, with a given beginning and ending. The life cycle is limited from a few months to five or more years.
2. Set within established time, cost and performance specifications.
3. Consists of a series of tasks which relate only to that project.
4. Generally consists of a once-through, non-repetitive or one-of-a-kind activity. A particular project will be done only once. (Cook, 1971, pp. 4-5).

With the foregoing definition of a project, it follows that project management functions facilitate the effective and efficient completion of the project. Included in this successful completion would be:

1. Was the project completed on time?
2. Was the project completed within budget?
3. Was the project completed within the specified standards of quality?

A related series of questions would include:

1. When should project management start?
2. Who is responsible for the effective management of the project?
3. What elements need to be considered in effective project management?

4. When are the responsibilities of the project manager complete? (Clark, 1976, p. 80).

All too often, project management is not included in the ideation phase with the assumption that an effective plan will evolve during the implementation phase. However, in successful projects, the management function starts during the ideation phase.

The companion question of who is responsible for the effective management of a project must also be clarified in the management plan. The project director is ultimately responsible for the total operation of the project. In most research environments, there is a support staff that can be of great assistance in the effective completion of the project. The successful director also integrates members of the research team into appropriate management activities. This is especially important because the definition of project management includes the concept of getting things done through people (Cook, 1971, p. 4).

The management team must function within the host environment which is impacted by both internal and external constraints. Depending upon the setting of the research, internal constraints may be staffing, facilities and institutional policies, including purchasing and accounting procedures. External constraints include federal, state, and/or local regulations that are often based upon federal or state laws (Lefferts, 1983, pp. 49-68).

PLANNING, ORGANIZING, AND CONTROLLING OF THE PROJECT

Various management functions have been identified and developed which have proven to be of benefit to the project manager. Three to six functions tend to be identified by most authorities (An Introduction to Management in the Air Force, 1967; Karger & Murdick, 1980, p. 37). However, the umbrella functions tend to be planning, organizing and controlling.

The Planning Function

The planning function should begin with the ideation phase of the project so that the management plan can be clearly specified in the proposal. The planning function does not stop with documentation in the proposal. Weekly or daily planning should also be conducted throughout the life of the project (Karger & Murdick, 1980, pp. 41-42). The adage that no one plans to fail, they simply fail to plan, certainly relates to project management.

Four major elements in planning include:

1. Defining and establishing project goals and objectives.

2. Identifying processes or procedures to accomplish the established goals and objectives.

3. Identifying constraints to accomplish the established goals and objectives and providing alternative methods of overcoming these constraints.

4. Scheduling activities to achieve established goals and objectives.

Each of these elements should be considered within the internal and external constraints that impinge upon a project. The scheduling function, which is a sub-unit of planning, is impacted by numerous constraints. Depending upon the project, the timing of printing a document or using a unique piece of equipment may have to be adjusted to meet the needs of other research or production schedules.

The Organizing Function

In considering the term organizing, most people consider only the factors related to the structural organization within the project. This is an important consideration, but of equal importance, is the placement of the project within the structure of the company. Some companies have a very structured system through which all projects are administered. Other organizations allow sufficient flexibility to establish the organizational structure that would best facilitate each individual project. Examples of various structures include:

1. Separate organization approach.

2. Vertical or centralized approach.

3. Horizontal or decentralized approach.

4. The executive staff approach.

5. Project staff approach. (Cook, 1971, pp. 6-9).

In establishing the organizational structure within the project, consideration must be given to those elements that will allow for leadership to be developed at all levels and draw upon the strengths of each individual on the project team. In this organizational process, several factors, including responsibility and authority, need to be addressed. It must be determined who has the authority to take action. If there is a delegation of responsibility, then the individual receiving this responsibility must also receive the authority needed to accomplish the assigned tasks. This is in the context that the final authority always lies with the project director.

Congruent with responsibility and authority are the staffing elements of (1) unit of command, (2) span of control and (3) homogeneous assignments. The element of unity of command relates to the concept of to whom does one report. It should be clear to each individual that he or she has one "boss." The principle of span of control relates to how many individuals report to one supervisor. Management theory suggests that for the greatest productivity the span of control should be limited to no more than five to seven individuals. The concept of homogeneous assignment relates to grouping tasks of a similar nature together. Staff assignments can then be made to accomplish the greatest level of productivity with the highest level of quality for each job assignment (Cook, 1971).

Most successful project directors indicate that, without quality staff, all other planning and organizing functions are of little value. However, without a proper plan and organization, even a superior staff could not achieve the highest level of productivity. In order to staff the project with individuals who have the appropriate knowledge and skills, a set of job specifications must be developed for each position. It is only after the development of the job specifications that effective recruitment, selection, employment, and training can be facilitated (Schroeder, 1985, pp. 497-500).

The Controlling Function

The controlling function deals with the question: Is the work being done being directed toward the attainment of the established goals and objectives? There are situations where individuals have been completing numerous tasks of high quality but their activities have not been directed toward established goals and objectives of the project. Then the project cannot be brought to a successful completion. The controlling function includes setting performance standards and measuring the performance of each activity or staff member against these established standards. Taking corrective action to maintain proper time, cost, and performance levels to correct any incongruence with the established standards is the final step in the controlling function. Just as planning continues throughout the project, controlling is also a continuing cyclic endeavor in which the project manager must draw upon both internal and external information to maintain the project schedule (Gaither, 1980, pp. 359-379).

MANAGEMENT SYSTEMS

Various management systems have been developed to assist the project manager. The system to be used depends upon the preference of the researcher and the nature of the project. Most of the management systems include a visual presentation of the research activities in relationship to time. Some systems also portray staff assignments and cost factors. A management system that is presented in a visual form can be of assistance in both planning and conducting the research. This includes communicating the plan in the proposal as well as to fellow-workers during the actual conduct of the project. The visual plan can both facilitate and track the progress being made during the research process (Venit & Burns, 1985, pp. 37-52).

Computer utilization has enhanced the level of sophistication included in many of the project management systems. As was noted in the advertisement of a computer-aided management system, "It can't fasten, cut, hammer, drill, dig, bend, level, or lift, but it could be the most valuable construction tool you'll ever own."

Examples and a brief explanation of graphic systems that have been used in project management are presented in the following section of this chapter. Citations are provided to direct the reader to selected publications that would provide greater detail to the full development and utilization of each.

Gantt Charts

The Gantt Chart is named after Henry L. Gantt who developed this scientific management schema during World War I. Gantt was an early proponent of visual displays to indicate work schedules. The Gantt Chart allowed staff members to know where they fit in the organization and how their efforts contributed to the total project. The Chart uses a bar-chart system to depict when each activity is scheduled to be done. The open bars extend across time-period columns. As the work is completed, the bar is entered as a solid line. This allows the project manager, the research and development team, support staff and administrative personnel to readily track the progress of the project. It also allows for the assignment of resources to those activities that have not yet been completed or are behind schedule. The example presented in Figure 7-1 includes an activity and time schedule with a coding system that indicates who is responsible for each task (Barndt & Carvey, 1982, pp. 101-103; Gaither, 1980, pp. 309-354).

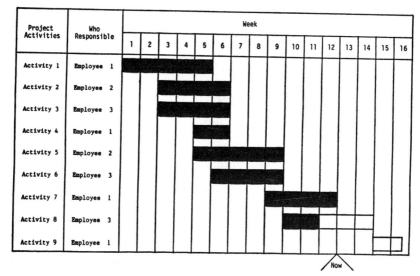

Figure 7-1: Gantt Progress Chart

The Gantt Chart can be developed and utilized without the aid of a computer. However, there are computer programs for creating and updating Gantt Charts. Some of these computer programs will also display budgeted funds and expenditures (Layman, 1985).

Milestone Chart

The Milestone Chart is an extension of the Gantt Chart with critical decision points or deadlines for major reports or products being highlighted. Since Milestone Charts do not indicate the relationship between various activities, they are not "stand alone" systems. However, cost factors can be associated with each milestone and, with staff involvement in the development of the Chart, it can serve as a motivational tool (Cook, 1971, p. 50).

One of the major advantages of the Milestone Chart is that critical points are clearly identified. This allows the project manager to direct staff efforts in accomplishing the tasks needed to meet each milestone.

The Milestone Chart depicted in Figure 7-2 includes not only the proposed schedule but also the actual completed schedule. Through a coding system, rescheduling of milestones created by either early or

113

late completion of previous activities can also be noted (Barndt & Carvey, 1982, p. 104).

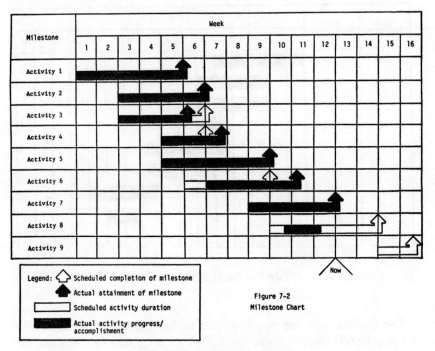

Figure 7-2
Milestone Chart

Figure 7-2: Milestone Chart

Network Systems

There are at least three major systems that utilize the network concept. The most familiar is the Program Evaluation and Review Technique, known as PERT. Critical Path Method (CMP) and Precedence Diagramming Method (PDM) are also recognized techniques.

PERT was introduced in 1958 by the consulting firm of Booz, Allen and Hamilton and the Special Projects Office of the U.S. Navy to be used on the Polaris Missile project. Through the use of PERT, the original time estimate for the completion of the engineering and development of the missile project was reduced by two years. The network system allowed the project managers to place in proper sequence or order each task that had to be completed. It also provided a schema through which tasks that could be done at the same time could be readily identified. By calculating the time associated with each task the project managers could than allocate resources and make staff assignments based upon those tasks that made the greatest impact on the total project time (Ivancevich, Donnelly & Gibson, 1983, p. 455).

CPM was introduced by du Pont and Sperry Rand in 1957, one year earlier than PERT. CPM was developed to assist in the start-up of new plants in the chemical industry. It has now gained wide acceptance in the total construction industry (Antill & Woodhead, 1970).

PERT and CPM, although developed by two different groups, have many commonalities. Each system uses nodes or circles to represent completed tasks. These completed tasks are referred to as EVENTS. Each system also uses arrows to connect the circles. Since these arrows represent activities or tasks in progress, they also represent time, effort and resources.

The major difference between CPM and PERT is in the time calculation function. CPM uses only one time estimate, while in PERT three estimates are used. One reason for this variance is that CPM was developed and has been used in projects in which there is a better experience base from which the time estimation can be made. This is known as deterministic time. In most of the early applications of PERT there was not an extensive experience base from which to make the time estimates. Three time estimates were then established with a formula for combining these estimates to yield the average time. Deterministic time estimates, or those that are based upon a previous base of experience, can also be used in PERT. However, when the experience base is not there, then the time estimates are based on a probalistic estimate. Estimates of the earliest (optimistic), the latest (pessimistic), and the most likely, are combined to yield the average or projected time needed to complete each activity (Buffa, 1983, p. 430; Federal Electric Corporation, 1963).

A second difference between PERT and CPM is that in the CPM system, after the time estimates have been completed, the combination of connecting arrows through the network that consumes the greatest amount of time are identified as double-lined arrows. This path throughout the network is then designated as the critical path.

Precedence Diagramming Method (PDM) is also a network system that uses arrows and nodes (See Figure 7-3). In PDM the activity or task in progress is identified by the nodes and the connecting arrows, which are referred to as dependency arrows. There is one time calculation or estimate that is often included in the node with a word description of the activity. Just as the nodes can be elongated into ovals, the ovals can also be developed into time bars on a chart and a schedule can readily be completed (Schroeder, 1985, p. 372).

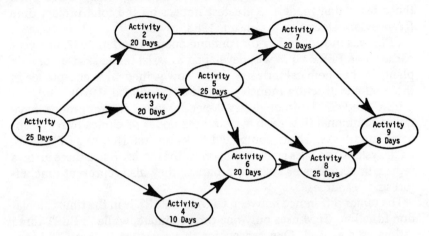

Figure 7-3: Precedence Diagram

As the systems have evolved, PERT and CPM have become the standards. These two are often combined into a PERT/CPM network (See Figure 7-4). The completed PERT/CPM network shows the relationship among all activities as well as the estimated time needed to complete each of the tasks. An important aspect of each network system is that activities that can be done in parallel are readily visible. Those that must be completed before the next one can start are also displayed.

Applications of the various network systems are not limited to multi-year or complex projects. As referenced in an early text devoted to the management system, "PERT [or other network systems] can be applied to any field of endeavor which requires planned, controlled, and integrated work efforts to accomplish established goals and complete a program on time" (Federal Electric Corporation, 1963, p. 2).

Most project management and research texts provide greater detail on the intricacies of the development of a network and the calculation of time estimates than can be covered in this brief chapter. (Beakley & Leach, 1972, pp. 317-385; Buffa, 1983, pp. 422-435; Cook, 1971; Federal Electric Corporation, 1963; Ivancevich, Donnelly & Gibson, 1983, pp. 455-458).

There are also various computer based programs for developing a network system. When the computer is used to generate the graphics, the circles are generally presented as squares or rectangles (Layman, 1985). In any of these systems, the basic steps would include:

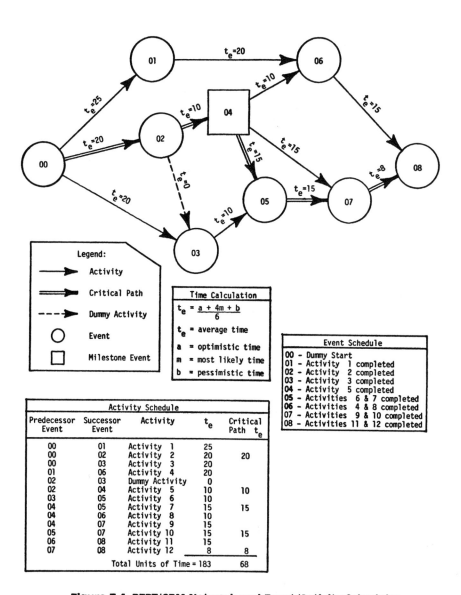

Figure 7-4: PERT/CPM Network and Event/Activity Schedules

Legend:
- ➤ Activity
- ⇒ Critical Path
- ⇢ Dummy Activity
- ○ Event
- ☐ Milestone Event

Time Calculation
$t_e = \dfrac{a + 4m + b}{6}$
t_e = average time
a = optimistic time
m = most likely time
b = pessimistic time

Event Schedule
00 – Dummy Start
01 – Activity 1 completed
02 – Activity 2 completed
03 – Activity 3 completed
04 – Activity 5 completed
05 – Activities 6 & 7 completed
06 – Activities 4 & 8 completed
07 – Activities 9 & 10 completed
08 – Activities 11 & 12 completed

Activity Schedule				
Predecessor Event	Successor Event	Activity	t_e	Critical Path t_e
00	01	Activity 1	25	
00	02	Activity 2	20	20
00	03	Activity 3	20	
01	06	Activity 4	20	
02	03	Dummy Activity	0	
02	04	Activity 5	10	10
03	05	Activity 6	10	
04	05	Activity 7	15	15
04	06	Activity 8	10	
04	07	Activity 9	15	
05	07	Activity 10	15	15
06	08	Activity 11	15	
07	08	Activity 12	8	8
		Total Units of Time = 183		68

117

1. Developing the list of activities.
2. Developing the network.
3. Estimating and calculating the time factors.
4. Identifying the critical path.

Project Organization Charts

Earlier in this chapter, reference was made to both the placement of the project in the host environment and the internal organization of the project staff. Through organizational charts, both internal and external staff relationships can be depicted. The formal relationships of a given project to other projects or program functions can also be highlighted.

An advantage of the project organization chart is that the formal line and staff relationships and the span of control for each supervisor are displayed. Since project management is getting things done through people, there is also the need to cultivate the informal lines of communication that cannot be depicted in an organizational chart (Cook, 1971, pp. 6-9; Fearon et al., 1979, pp. 96-101; Karger & Murdick, 1980).

An example of the placement of the project within the organization is shown in Figure 7-5. The organization of a given project is depicted in Figure 7-6.

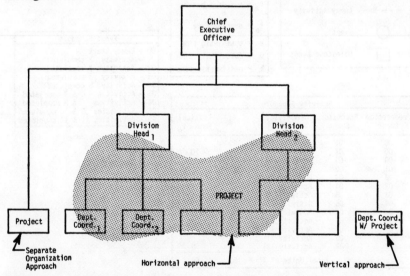

Figure 7-5: Organizational Chart for Host Institutions (Adapted from Cook, 1971, p. 7)

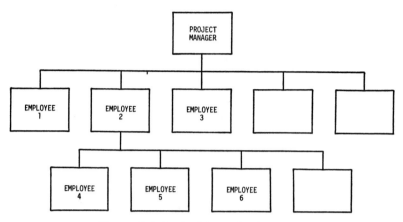

Figure 7-6: Project Organization Chart

Other Graphic Aids

The graphic aids that are available to the project manager are almost unlimited. The nature of the project and host organization may call for very specialized charts. Examples of such graphic aids could include:

Paradigm of the Research Design: This graphic aid can depict both the dependent and independent variables under consideration as well as their relationship to extraneous variables. All of these can be set within the context of the research or project being conducted. The paradigm can consist primarily of word descriptions arranged in a chart format or be arranged as a series of symbols connected by lines or arrows (Gage, 1963; Shulman, 1986).

Cost Analysis Schedule: With the advent of computers, financial records for research projects are more easily developed and maintained. Software programs are available that will assist in the preparation and maintenance of a wide variety of financial data. These records can be of great benefit in tracking the costs associated with the project as well as in the preparation of summary reports. These records may be developed and maintained in conjunction with the company's cost accounting department or as a separate research project control activity (Sladek & Stein, 1981).

SUMMARY

The importance of developing and implementing an effective management system that fits both the project and host institution cannot be over emphasized. Management systems are not ends in themselves, but only aids for managing the project.

The ultimate success of any project is dependent upon planning which evolves into an effective schedule that can be adjusted to meet the daily demands of the research project in a given working environment. An effective plan and work schedule can result in building staff morale, productivity and a quality research project.

BIBLIOGRAPHY

An Introduction to Management in the Air Force. *Military Management*, Vol. II. (pp. 2-12). Washington, D. C.: Air University, Air Force ROTC, 1967.

Antill, J. M. and Woodhead, R. W. *Critical Path Methods in Construction Practice*. (2nd ed.) New York: Wiley-Interscience, 1970.

Barndt, S. E. and Carvey, D. W. *Essentials of Operations Management*. Englewood Cliffs, New Jersey: Prentice-Hall, Inc., 1982.

Beakley, G. C. and Leach, H. W. *Engineering: An Introduction to a Creative Profession*. (2nd ed.), New York: The Macmillian Co., 1972.

Buffa, E. S. *Modern Production/Operations Management*. New York: John Wiley & Sons, 1983.

Clark, D. L. "Effective Management of Contract Activities." In *Addresses and Proceeding of the 38th National and 5th International Annual Conference of the American Industrial Arts Association*, pp. 79-82. Washington, D. C.: American Industrial Arts Association, 1976.

Cook, D. L. *Educational Project Management*. Columbus, Ohio: Charles E. Merril Publishing Co., 1971.

Fearon, H. E., Ruch, W. A., Decker, P. G., Reck, R.R., Reuter V.G., and Wieters, C.D. *Fundamentals of Production/Operations Management*. St. Paul: West Publishing Co., 1979.

Federal Electric Corporation. *A Programmed Introduction to PERT*. New York: John Wiley & Sons, Inc.

Gage, N. L. Paradigms for Research on Teaching. In N. L. Gage (Ed.), *Handbook of Research on Teaching*, (pp. 94-141). Chicago: Rand McNally & Co., 1963.

Gaither, N. *Production and Operations Management*. Hinsdale, Illinois: The Dryden Press, 1980.

Ivancevich, J. M., Donnelly, J.H. Jr., and Gibson, J. L. *Managing for Performance*. Plano, Texas: Business Publications, Inc., 1983.

Karger, D. W. and Murdick, R. G. *Managing Engineering and Research*. (3rd ed.), New York: Industrial Press Inc., 1980.

Layman, A. *Timeline Manual*. Novato, California: Breakthrough Software Corporation. 1985.

Lefferts, R. *The Basic Handbook of Grants Management*. New York: Basic Books, Inc., 1983.

Schmenner, R.W. *Production/Operations Management Concepts and Situations* (2nd ed.). Chicago: Science Research Associates, Inc., 1984.

Schroeder, R.G. *Operations Management: Decision Making in the Operations Function*. (2nd ed.), New York: McGraw-Hill Book Co., 1985.

Shulman, L. S. "Paradigms and Research Programs in the Study of Teaching: A Contemporary Perspective." In M.C. Wittrock (Ed.), *Handbook of Research on Teaching*, (3rd ed.), pp. 3-26. New York: Macmillan Publishing Co., 1986.

Sladek, F. E. and Stein, E. L. *Grant Budgeting and Finance: Getting the Most Out of Your Grant Dollar*. New York: Plenum Press, 1981.

Venit, S. and Burns, D. *MAC at Work*. New York: John Wiley & Sons, Inc., 1985.

CHAPTER 8

Conducting the Technical Research Project

by Ray Shackleford

Sub-Topics:

- Measurement
- Measurement System Design
- Human and Mechanism Measurement
- Instrumentation Signal Inputs and Outputs
- Summary

The act of conducting a technical research project is primarily a process of measurement. It involves monitoring, measuring and/or recording the characteristics and interaction among people, materials, processes, machines, energy, information, products and services. In the measurement process, data is collected about one or more of the variables in the activity under investigation. "Measurement is essentially a decision- making activity, and the usefulness of measurements must be evaluated in terms of their ability to provide information that will improve accuracy and validity of the decisions made." (Tarrants, p. 4.).

MEASUREMENT

Measurement is basic to all technical research and development activities. As a process, measurement can be defined as the result of a quantitative comparison between an identified standard and an unknown quantity. For the comparison to be meaningful the standard (1) must be accurately defined and commonly accepted and (2) the measuring procedure and device must be valid and reliable.

According to Beckwith and Buck, there are two basic forms or processes of measurement: "(a) direct comparison with either a primary or a secondary standard, and (b) indirect comparison with a standard through the use of a calibrated system" (pp. 10-11). The length of a 2 x 4 can be measured with a steel tape and its units of length can be compared to a known standard. During this direct comparison, the primary standard, determined by the National Bureau of Standards, was not used. A secondary standard, in English units, several generations removed from the primary standard was selected. When measurements need to be very accurate, direct comparison measurements are limited by humans inability to make direct comparisons consistently.

Accurate measurements generally depend upon the use of calibrated systems for indirect comparisons. A sensor/transducing device is used in conjunction with an indirect comparison measurement system. These transducing devices convert basic input forms of energy into analog data which is processed into a output which can be directly understood by humans or used by additional processing elements in the system. A simple example of this type of system is a fishing scale where the weight of a fish applies stress on a spring. The strain of the spring converts the weight of the fish to known units of measure.

The processing of analog data and signals can take many forms. It is often necessary to amplify, filter, transmit and record this data during the measurement process.

A basic measurement system, as seen in Figure 8-1, consists of five elements:

1. *Measurand*: the property, characteristic or phenomenon being measured.

2. *Detector/transducer*: a device that provides a usable comparison, response, or output about a specified property, characteristic or phenomenon being measured.

3. *Output*: unit equivalent or analog signal.

4. *Display/readout device*: displays data or units about the measurand.

5. *Data interpretation*: analysis and understanding of measured activity.

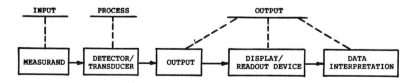

Figure 8-1: Basic Measurement System

Additional measurement elements may be added to the system as these systems become more sophisticated and utilize other forms of energy to transmit input and output signals. These elements include signal conditioners, power supplies, telemetry components, calibration signals, indicators, recorders and controllers.

When gathering and reporting data, the researcher must take into consideration applicable scales of measurement and the validity and reliability of all data collected. Some scales, which lack precision, are too primitive for use as scientific instruments. Scales are often divided into four types: nominal, ordinal, interval and ratio (listed in ascending order of power). See Table 8-1. Nominal scales measure entities placed in two or more categories. The only requirement is that the categories be different from one another. The identified categories have no relationship to each other nor do they imply that one is better than the other. Typical examples of measurements used in nominal scales would include the numbering of football players, assignment of code numbers to high school classes or part numbers to a product.

A Classification of Applicable Scales of Measurement

Scale	Basic Empirical Operations	Typical Examples
Nominal	Assessment of equality	"Numbering" of football players, assignment of H. S. class code numbers or product part numbers
Ordinal	Assessment of greater or less	Hardness of minerals; street numbers; grades of abrasives, diamonds, lumber, intelligence test raw scores
Interval	Assessment of the equality of intervals or of differences	Faherenheit or Celsius temperature scales, positions in line, calendar dates, measurements of energy, intelligence tests "standard scores"
Ratio	Assessment of the equality of ratios	Physical properties (length, density, mass), work, time intervals, Rankine or Kelvin temperatures, loudness, brightness

Table 8-1: Scales of Measurement (Tarrants, p. 13).

Ordinal scales are used when the researcher wants to identify whether the entities vary in degree. Ordinal scales rank people or objects in varying degrees (greater, equal or less than) on a characteristic with no implications of the distance between intervals on the scale. Typical examples of measurements used in ordinal scales would include the hardness of minerals, street numbers, grades of lumber and gravel and intelligence test raw scores. Ordinal scales place items in clearly defined rank order. The distances between the entries are unknown and not necessarily equal.

Interval scales perform two functions: (1) place entries in clearly defined order and (2) place entries into categories in which intervals of measurement among them are equal. Interval scales allow the researcher to state that the distance between entity "A" and "B" equals the distance between entity "B" and "C". However, it does not allow the researcher to state that "B" is twice as good as "C" or "A" three times as good as "C". Typical examples of measurement used in interval scales would include Fahrenheit and Celsius temperature scales, calendar dates, product-moment correlations and measures of energy.

A ratio scale has all the characteristics of an interval scale plus it contains an absolute zero. The addition of the zero scale offers a measurement constant or a base point of reference. With a ratio scale, the researcher can describe relative amounts and differences in amounts. Measurements on a ratio scale allow researchers to use the more powerful research procedures. Normal statistics such as geometric mean, harmonic mean, percent variation, coefficient of variation and other number manipulations can be performed using measurements from a ratio scale. Typical examples of measurements using a ratio scale include such physical properties as mass, density, dimensions, time intervals, loudness and brightness (Tarrants, pp. 7- 13) (Van Dalen, p. 341-342).

MEASUREMENT SYSTEM DESIGN

The characteristics of an effective measuring system must be considered when designing or selecting devices or procedures to measure or monitor an identified entity. These include:

1. Administrative feasibility.
2. Constant units of measure.
3. Quantifiable measurement criterion.
4. Sensitivity.

5. Reliability.
6. Stability.
7. Validity.
8. Error-free results.
9. Efficient and understandable.

Consideration of personnel, time, financial resources and the construction and use of the measuring system are all variables in *administrative feasibility*. It is during this stage that the researcher should try to anticipate needs and problems in the system's design.

In the design, selection and use of effective measuring devices, the researcher should consider their ability to provide *constant units of measure* throughout the usable range of the instrument. The researcher will need to determine that the output of the system is *quantifiable and capable of a statistical analysis* appropriate for the research problem. For the statistical analysis to be accurate and meaningful, the system must be (1) *sensitive* enough to detect appropriate changes in the measurand and (2) *capable* of collecting and recording the appropriate data. "The frequency of occurrence of a measure must be large enough to permit statistical analyses to be conducted" (Tarrants, pp. 17-18).

Sensitivity is a primary characteristic of an effective measuring system. The researcher must evaluate and make system selections based on the type and quality of the data required. Without anticipating these factors, the researcher could select a mercury thermometer to measure temperature to the nearest one hundredth of a degree.

Data must be reliable for it to be useful. *Reliability* is the capability of a measurement technique to provide consistent results in multiple measurements of the same condition. Any changes recorded by a reliable measurement technique should be the result of changes in the variable and not internal fluctuations in the measurement process or system.

Stability and reliability are similar in nature and function. Reliability insures consistency in the measurement result, whereas stability refers to the ability of a measurement device to give consistent readings of unchanged parameters over time. For example, a thermometer with stability, placed in a controlled environment of 50 degrees Fahrenheit, will indicate that temperature as long as it is in that environment. If this temperature changes by ten units, the measuring system should indicate this change in temperature and remain stable. The need for stability requires the researcher to select measuring devices capable of performing satisfactorily within the anticipated range and environmental conditions (Tarrants, pp. 16-20).

Once the reliability of the data has been established the need arises to determine its internal and external *validity*. Validity refers to the ability of a system to accurately measure the intended measurand. Internal validity insures the measure is the direct result of the intended measurand. For example, if a valid measure of the changes in the length of a wood specimen caused by differences in humidity is sought, all other variables, such as temperature, must be controlled.

Consideration for external validity of the system must be given after the system's internal validity has been established. This consideration should include the relevance of the measurements to the implications for settings other than the controlled environment in which the project was conducted. External validity addresses the subject, populations, settings, experimental variables and measurement variables to which the findings can be generalized. (Van Dalen, p. 269)

Although internal and external validity are the common statistical measures of validity, technical research must also consider the validity of the instrumentation and procedures. In any technical research activity, instrumentation and procedure validity will take the form of a standard. Standards are formulated when an organized group agrees to a common definition or procedure for an identified activity or phenomenon. Any such recognized group then becomes a standardizing agency. Some of these recognized groups include the American National Standards Institute (ANSI), Society of Automotive Engineers (SAE), American Petroleum Institute (API), American Society for Testing and Materials (ASTM) and International Organization of Standardization (ISO). (Davis, Troxell, & Hauck, p 12-15). The validity of technical research will depend on the ability of an identified instrument or procedure to measure an activity or phenomenon using an accepted standard.

Error-free results are the goal of any measurement procedure. No instrument or device is perfect. Error will creep into the readings and/or interpretations of any procedure. It is important to understand the measuring techniques being used and the type and magnitude of potential errors associated with these techniques.

There are two types of errors associated with research, (1) variable errors and (2) constant errors. Variable errors tend to decrease in significance as the number of measures increases. For example, if a researcher flips a coin 10 times, the laws of probability indicate that the number of heads and tails will be the same. However, experience has shown that this is not always true. As the number of measures increases (coins flipped) the ratio between heads and tails tends to more closely conform to the laws of probability.

Constant errors are not affected by an increase in the number of measures taken. If a constant error is present in any of the systems variables, it will affect each series of measures. Examples of constant error could include errors in (1) detector/transducer/recorder calibration or design, (2) failure to consider all behaviors or conditions and (3) failure to report or record all appropriate data. Suppose a coin in the previous example was out-of-round. No amount of repetition would improve or eliminate the constant error (Tarrants, pp. 17-20).

The final characteristics of an effective measurement system are *efficiency and understandability*. The primary goal of an efficient measure system is ease of data collection with minimal disruption to the environment surrounding the person/s, object/s or phenomena being measured. Understandability is important because individuals who will be required to approve and/or use the results of the technical research study must be able to comprehend them. Too often these characteristics are taken for granted or are not considered carefully during the systems planning process. Then instrumentation and procedures that are inappropriate or too costly for the information gathered may have been used.

Data Collection by Observation

Collecting data by observation is a common technique used to measure the characteristics of and/or interaction among people, materials, processes, machines, energy, information, products and services. Studies which survey and measure attitudes, motives, opinions and work typically use observation methods. Observation methods include interviews, projective and expressive techniques and the use of detectors and comparators.

Technical observation techniques are typically referred to as visual inspection processes. Visual inspections are used to detect and/or record the presence of surface flaws or defects, surface roughness or make surface comparisons. Selected visual (optical) measuring and inspection devices include visual inspection with the assistance of illuminated magnifiers, microscopes, optical flats, optical comparators, alignment telescopes, autocollimators, penetrant tests, television, photography and photoelasticity. These techniques can be and are used to perform technical research. Many of them are referred to as nondestructive tests.

When selecting and using observation data collection methods, their dependency on imprecise human judgments, which is a major drawback, must be considered.

Data Collection by Instrumentation

An instrument or transducer is a device which can be calibrated to measure a variable or interaction among variables. Measuring devices, sensors and/or transducers are the sensory components of a measuring system that are part of the broad field or technology called instrumentation. The process of selecting, using instruments and evaluating collected data is referred to as measurement engineering.

Instrumentation is a significant element of our modern technological world. Instrumentation improves the researcher's ability to cope with extreme environments, develop new forms of energy, reduce pollution, improve automobile mileage ratings and develop faster, safer, quieter and more efficient processes, (Seippel, pp. 1-7).

Automobiles and other products are now partially assembled by computer-directed robots using instrumented feedback control systems. The automobile's instruments and computers automatically sense and adjust systems for optimum performance. Similar instrumentation systems are used to control energy exploration and refining processes, launch and guide space probes, monitor machine operations and operate automatic cameras. These systems use mechanical, electric, magnetic, fluid, optical, chemical, thermal, atomic or a combination of instruments and sensors. These sensors deflect, vibrate, resonate, interact, conduct sound, detect stress and strain and transfer force and motion. Instruments also behave differently at low, medium and high frequencies, manifesting different modes of behavior. It is the interaction between, or the fluctuations in, energy levels of instruments that provides measurable system outputs, (Seippel, pp. 3-7). Table 8-2 identifies common investigated properties, applicable measurands and typical measuring instruments used in industrial technical research.

Property Under Investigation	Measurand	Typical Measuring Instruments
Motion (Mechanical)	Force Distance Speed Attitude Direction Vibration Etc.	Altimeter, unit scales odometers, acceleration levels, seismographs, tachometer, vibrometers, accelerometers, dynamometers, A/D converters, potentiometers, transducers (comparators, displacement, location, position), strain, gauges, gyros, etc.

129

Property Under Investigation	Measurand	Typical Measuring Instruments
Motion (Fluid)	Rate of flow Volume Pressure Viscosity Level Etc.	Hydrophones, microswitches piezoelectric crystals, penetrometers, viscometer, indicators (cloud point, flash point, volatility), flow gauges, transducers, (pressure, level, radiation), magnetic flow meters, rotameter, etc.
Thermal	Specific heat Thermo expansion Thermo conductivity Thermo electric Etc.	Temperature scales, resistance and temperature detectors, thermistors, thermocouples, bimetal strips or transducers, gas thermometer, heating valves, bolometers liquid expansion and vapor pressure thermometers, etc.
Light	Wavelength (Optics) Saturation Hue Intensity Transmission Reflectivity Absorption Transparency Refractivity Luminescence Photoelectric Photoelasticity Etc.	Interferometer, photodiodes, color photodetectors, photo-conductors, photovoltaic cells, phototransisters photomultipliers, pyrometers, photoemissives, photoelectro-magnetic devices, etc.
Electrical	Voltage (Electro-magnetic) Power Phase Frequency bridges, etc. Conductivity Magnetic permeablility Dielectric properties Galvanic action Etc.	Oscilloscopes, moving coil current meters, wave analyzers, resistance digital metering, recorders, voltage potentiometers, Wheatstone bridges, impedance
Radio-activity	Ionizing Nonionizing Etc.	Ionizing transduction, photoelectric transduction, proportional counters, Geiger counter, etc.

Property Under Investigation	Measurand	Typical Measuring Instruments
Time	Length Duration Elapse Etc.	Counters, analyzers recorder, etc.
Mechanical	Tension Compression Shear Stiffness Elasticity Plasticity Ductility Brittleness Hardness Creep Fatigue Torsion Flexure Endurance Etc.	Scleroscope, impact tester, hardness testers (Vickers, Brinell, Rockwell), universal testing machine, brittle coatings tester, creep tester, extensometer compression tester, torsion tester, mirror scales, indicators, multiplying levers, stiffness testers, scratch testers, fatigue testers, transducers (displacement, location, position), load cells, etc.
Physical	Dimension Density Specific Porosity Moisture Macrostructure Microstructure Permeability Weight Surface Absorption Etc.	Scales, vernier calipers, micrometers, microscopes, gravity optical devices, electrical transducers, optical content comparator, strain gauges, radiographic devices, electromagnetic devices, electric resistance moisture testers, ultrasonic testers, texture load cells, etc.
Chemical	Acidity or alkalinity Corrosion Toxidity Oxidation Environmental attack Electronchemical action Absorption Reactivity Etc.	Electrical transducers and detectors, chemical tests and comparison, etc.
Acoustical	Transmission Reflection Absorption Etc.	Underwater detectors, piezoelectric transducers, electrodynamic generators, sound level meters, spectrum analyzers, noise analyzers, etc.

Property Under Investigation	Measurand	Typical Measuring Instruments
Physio-Chemical	Water absorption Water repellence Shrinkage Swelling Etc.	Dimension and weight detectors and transducers water analysis devices, moisture content testers, etc.
Processing	Ability to convert, transmit, and/or transport: Materials Energy Information	Combination of instruments identified in other areas
Environmental	Ability to resist: Abrasion Chemical attack Changes in temperature Weathering Insects Etc.	Hygrometers, psychrometers dewpoint meters, humidity indicators, etc.
Service Requirement	Integrity of shape Strength Integrity of structure Service life Function Environmental	Combination of instruments identified in other areas
Machine Performance	Effectiveness in changing inputs to outputs Materials Energy Information	Combination of instruments identified in other areas

Table 8-2: Data Collected by Instrumentation

The energy transfer resulting from an interaction between objects is transduction and is the principle upon which transducers work. Transducers rely on energy transfer, effort and motion to sense and communicate information. Transducers cannot measure a quantity (measurand) without changes occurring.

Since a transducer must extract energy from an object to function, it not only changes the quantity being measured but the object or process being evaluated. These changes and the validity of the measurement can be checked by using a different transducer and observing the effects on the results. The change in energy caused by transduction is often ignored or assumed in the design of the study, except when extremely accurate measurements are desired.

Instruments are generally classified according to the property under investigation, measurand being evaluated, type of sensor and the behavior of the property. For example, an instrument might be labeled a quartz piezoelectric stress-gage force transducer for measuring dynamic forces relative to an initial or average level, (Seippel, p. 5).

Instruments interact with or are sensitive to outside inputs such as pressure, force, physical-chemical, motion, environmental, strain, sound, temperature, radiation, electric and magnetic fields. To be effective, instruments are designed for sensitivity to one variable while being relatively insensitive to others.

The accuracy of an instrument is determined by the preciseness of its calibration and the distortion, delay, and degradation of the energy signal used. Calibration of instruments involves comparing the output to a known standard. Most standards are traceable to a measure at the National Bureau of Standards. Measurements taken in conditions differing from those used to calibrate the instrument will invalidate the measurement to some extent.

Table 8-2 identified a large number of instruments used to measure selected properties. The list of instruments is extensive but far from being complete. Three diverse examples will illustrate the use of instruments in technical measurement systems.

Temperature Sensitive Instrument Example

A chemical firm requires constant temperature data on a toxic and highly corrosive chemical produced by a continuous flow system similar to petroleum distillation. A thermocouple was selected because continuous, fast, responsive and accurate measurements were needed. More specifically, a thermowell-thermocouple was selected because it will function properly for the specified period of time and is protected (isolated) from vibration, corrosion, erosion and extremely high pressures and temperatures. The thermocouple was interfaced with an electronic self-balancing potentiometer to provide the required fast, constant and accurate temperature readings. Permanent recording of the data could be provided by interfacing the potentiometer with a chart recorder or direct recording onto magnetic tape or disc (Whitaker, pp. 34-56). See Figure 8-2.

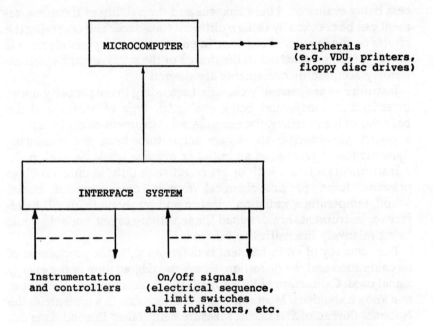

Figure 8-2: Temperature Sensitive Instrument System (Holland)

Pressure Sensitive Instrument Example

Pressure is measured by detecting the amount of force exerted by a fluid's motion and is usually measured in force per unit/area. It can be used to determine the operating pressure in a vessel or the amount of work done by pumps and compressors. Pressure measurements are important because of their effect on liquid boiling and condensing points. Pressure measurement is often used instead of temperature to monitor processes because changes in pressure are more rapidly sensed than changes in temperature.

A pharmaceutical firm must maintain the pressure of liquid within the range of 0 to 10 psi. The measurements must be taken and interpreted in close proximity to the process. The process requires only periodic checks and no data recording function is necessary. A metallic, diaphragm type gauge was selected because diaphragms are superior to bellows and Bourdon tubes at this range. This type of gauge is resistant to fatigue, permanently set and is adaptable to the process and mounting requirements (Whitaker pp. 57-66). See Figure 8-3.

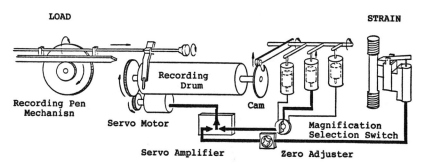

Figure 8-3: Pressure Sensitive Instrument System

Stress-Strain Instrument Example

The primary purpose of a tensile test is to detect, measure and evaluate the material's behavior under load (stress-strain). Stress is the force per unit of area (measured in pounds per square inch (psi)). Strain is the change in original size of a specimen due to applied stress (measured in inches or millimeters of change of the original dimension) (Kazanas, Klein, and Lindbeck, pp. 283-289).

An aerospace company needs to evaluate standard .505 inch threaded metallic specimens to determine their ultimate strength, total elongation, yield strength, proportional limit and module of elasticity. This test required a testing machine that met industry and government standards. Thus, a highly accurate universal testing machine with a stress-strain magnification chart recorder was selected.

The data were collected using an extensometer which was compatible with the specimen and results required. The knife edge of the extensometer moved as the specimen elongated and produced a voltage and directional signal. This signal was amplified and caused the chart recorder to graph the stress-strain data. See Figure 8-4.

HUMAN AND MECHANISM MEASUREMENT

The measurement process exists on a continuum from human-centered (direct) to mechanism-centered (indirect). These measurement systems all involve sensors. See Figure 8-5 which shows a human-centered measurement system. The human senses transfer environmental stimuli into electrical signals which are carried to the brain by

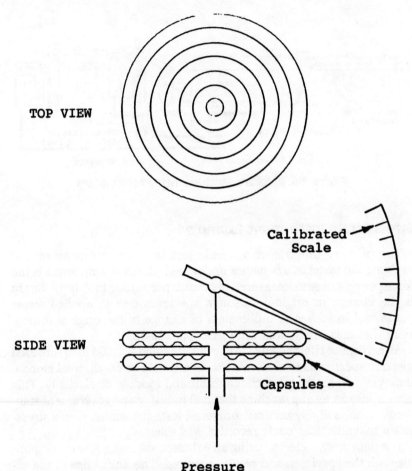

Figure 8-4: Metallic Diaphragm Schematic

nerves. The brain forms a picture or image of the sensed phenomena in the environment. The feedback process is completed when the sensed phenomena is compared with an established, expected and standard stored in the memory. Corrective or controlling action is taken as the result of comparing the difference between sensed and expected units or values (Seippel, pp. 36-38). Likewise, mechanism centered systems have sensors, transmission pathway, information analyzers and information loops.

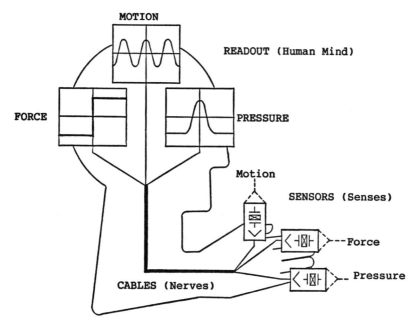

Figure 8-5: Sensor Systems (Courtesy, PCB Piezotronics, Inc.)

In a human-centered measurement system, the process of measurement relies heavily on the judgment and skill of the individual using the system. For example, when a human measures the thickness of a specimen with a standard rule, he/she must possess a certain degree of skill in placing the rule on the specimen and making a judgment about the specimen's alignment to units on the scale.

On the other end of the continuum are mechanism-centered measurement processes. In a mechanism-centered system, a device, sensor or transducer detects or measures a measurand. It then converts the energy in the system into an output which must be interpretable by a human or in a usable form for another mechanism. For example, in the production of paper the thickness of the paper is controlled by the distance between two rollers. During the process the distance (thickness of the paper) must be regulated. One method for controlling this thickness is to develop a controlled or closed loop system (See Figure 8-6). As the paper leaves the rollers it can be sensed by an actuator. This actuator could be electrical, pneumatic or hydraulic (Johnson, pp. 267-268). As the actuator senses the paper's thickness it automatically sends a

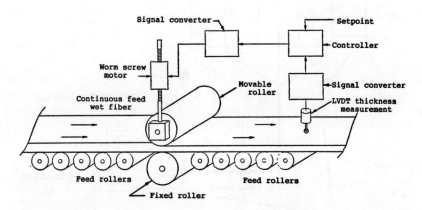

Figure 8-6: A Continuous Paper Thickness Measurement and Controlling System. (Johnson)

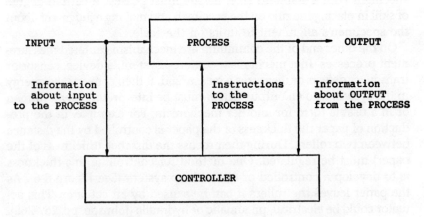

Figure 8-7: Modified Measurement System (Cassell)

signal to the mechanisms that adjust the roller separation. At the same instant, constant data is being sent to a microprocessor which records and plots information regarding paper thickness, quantities produced and adjustments made. In this instance the human will not see the measure until the data is extracted from the microprocessor. The measure will be given in precise units requiring little or no interpretation by the human.

The use of contemporary measurement systems makes modern industrial practices possible. All measurement systems, whether human- or mechanism-centered, have common design and application principles.

The first principle requires the measurement process to be a total system containing three parts: (1) input, (2) process and (3) output. The system can be used in its basic form or can be modified adding one or more elements to the basic parts. Figure 8-7 illustrates a modified system with an added control element. The process component of basic and modified measurement systems are able to (1) detect-transduce, (2) modify, and (3) control, indicate and record input and output signals. See Figure 8-8.

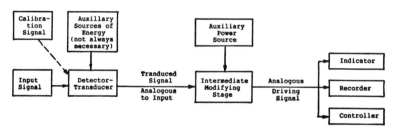

Figure 8-8: Modified Process Stage of a Measurement System. (Beckwith & Buck).

Measurements are taken during the process stage of the system. However, these measures have little or no value unless the second application principle is considered. This second principle is standards. The standards provide the basis for determining amounts, drawing comparisons or making adjustments on the system. Standards are used to measure such factors as conditions, accuracy, error and repeatability of the measurement system. Established standards are the basis for (1) device/detector selection, (2) measurement and assessment, (3) process or system adjustment and (4) measurement system design.

The third principle of application is the ability to read, analyze and interpret the measurement system. This ability is facilitated by *immediate feedback*, such as the speed of an automobile indicated on the speedometer or *postponed feedback* resulting from analytical evaluation of data collected. Whatever the form, all data must be understandable by the user. Chapter 9 will address assessing and interpreting data gathered by a measured system.

INSTRUMENTATION SIGNAL INPUTS AND OUTPUTS

Information is transmitted in the form of an input or output signal during the measuring, monitoring or control of a property, characteristic or phenomenon. This signal is often fed directly to an indicator. The drive for this indicator can be electrical, pneumatic, mechanical or hydraulic. This signal is often amplified or conditioned for (1) signal and data processing or (2) driving remote indicators, recorders, controllers or computer interfaces. Standard signal input and output ranges have been identified to allow equipment to be directly interfaced. These standards have been developed for electrical analog signals and pneumatic instruments.

Instruments often convert various forms of energy into electrical signals. These signals are analog (continuous) or digital (on/off). Digital input signals are easier to use in a measurement system because the signal is either on or off. Common devices transmitting digital input signals include relay contacts, pushbuttons, limit switches, cams and transistor drives. Digital outputs on the other hand are commonly used for activating indicators and alarms, numerical displays, relays and transistor drives (Holland, pp. 52-72).

Monitoring and Recording

The monitoring and recording data from detectors/transducers can be divided into two categories, real-time and delayed. Real-time monitoring and recording systems measure, evaluate and display data almost simultaneously. Real-time monitors and recorders include meters, gauges, plotters, counters, film and video.

Delayed time storage and retrieval devices handle analog and digital inputs and outputs. These devices monitor and store input signals from instruments for later retrieval, processing and/or interpretation. Selected storage devices include floppy discs, hard discs, magnetic tape, magnetic drums, bubble memory, printers and graph plotters. These delayed time storage devices can be interfaced with retrieval units to print out or display the data for interpretation. Selected retrieval units include printers, monitors and visual display units (VDU).

SUMMARY

The act of conducting a technical research is primarily a process of measurement. The measurement process is the monitoring, measuring and recording of characteristics and interactions among people, materials, processes, machines, energy, information, products and services. The measurement system consists of five main elements: (1) the measurand, (2) detector/transducer, (3) output, (4) the display/readout and (5) data interpretation.

During the technical research activity measurements must be constantly taken and evaluated. For this process to be productive and efficient, the standards for measurement must be established before the activity begins. Once the measurand is measured, the data gathered must be compared with these standards. Data output or feedback in the system allows for interpretation or adjustments to the system's input. Chapter 9 will emphasize the common analytical techniques and tools for organizing and interpreting data gathered by a measuring system.

BIBLIOGRAPHY

Allocca, J. A. *Transducers: Theory and Applications.* Reston, Virgina: Reston Pub. Co., 1984.

Beckwith, T. G., & Buck, N. L. *Mechanical Measurements.* 2nd ed. Reading, Massachusetts: Addison-Wesley Pub. Co., 1973.

Cassell, D. A. *Microcomputers and Modern Control Engineering.* Reston, Virgina: Reston Pub. Co., 1983.

Davis, H. E., Troxell, . E., & Hauck, G. F. W. *The Testing of Engineering Materials.* 4th ed. New York: McGraw-Hill, 1982.

Duckworth, W. E., Gera, A. E. & Lockett, A. G. *A Guide to Operational Research.* 3rd. ed. New York: John Wiley & Son, 1977.

Gingrich, H. W. *Electrical Machinery, Transformers, and Control.* Englewood Cliff, New Jersey: Prentice Hall, 1979.

Holland, R. C. *Microcomputers for Process Control.* New York: Pergamon Press, 1983.

Johnson, C. D. *Process Control Instrumentation Technology.* 2nd ed. New York: John Wiley & Sons, 1982.

Karger, D. W., & Murdick, R. G. *Managing Engineering and Research.* 3rd ed. New York: Industrial Press, 1980.

Kazanas, H. C., Klein, R. S., & Lindbeck, J. R. *Technology of Industrial Materials*. 2nd ed. Peoria, Illinois: Bennett and McKnight Pub. Co., 1979.

Kennedy, C. W., & Andrews, D. E. *Inspection and Gaging*. 4th ed. New York: Industrial Press, 1967.

Kochhar, A. K., & Burns, N. D. *Microprocessors and their Manufacturing Applications*. London: Edward Arnold, 1983.

Mann, C. K., Vickers, T. J., & Gulick, W. M. *Basic Concepts in Electronic Instrumentation*. New York: Harper & Row, 1974.

Norton, H. N. *Handbook of Transducers for Electronic Measuring Systems*. Englewood Cliff, New Jersey: Prentice Hall, 1969.

Roberts, E. B. *The Dynamics of Research and Developments*. New York: Harper & Row, 1974.

Safford, E. L., Jr. *The Complete Handbook of Robotics*. Blue Ridge Summit, Pennsylvania: TAB Books, 1978.

Seippel, R. G. *Transducers, Sensors, and Detectors*. Reston, Virgina: Reston Pub. Co., 1983.

Soisson, H. E. *Instrumentation in Industry*. New York: John Wiley & Sons, 1975.

Tarrants, W. E. *The Measurement of Safety Performance*. New York: Garland STPM Press, 1980.

Tull, D. S., & Hawkins, D. L. *Marketing Research: Measurement and Method: A Text with Cases*. 2nd. ed. New York: Macmillan, 1980.

Van Dalen, D. B. *Understanding Educational Research: An Introduction*. New York: McGraw-Hill, 1973.

Vaughn, R. C. *Quality Control*. Ames, Iowa: The Iowa State University Press, 1974.

Warren, J. E. *Control Instrument Mechanisms*. Indianapolis: Howard W. Sams, 1967.

Weber, L. J., & Mclean, D. L. *Electrical Measurement Systems for Biological and Physical Scientists*. Reading, Massachusetts: Addison-Wesley, 1975.

Whitaker, N. R. *Process Instrumentation Primer*. Tulsa, Oklahoma: Petroleum, Pub. Co., 1980.

Zoss, L. M., & Delahooke, B.C. *The Theory and Applications of Industrial Process Control*. Albany, New York: Delmar, 1961.

Tinius Olsen Testing Machine Company. *Tinius Olsen Super "L" Universal Testing Machines*. Bulletin 64. Willow Grove, Pennsylvania, 1961.

CHAPTER 9

ASSESSING THE RESULTS

by Ron J. Kovac

Sub-Topics:

- Goals, Purposes and Types of Analysis
- Common Technical Methods of Analysis
- The Computer as an Analytical Tool
- Interpretation and Synthesis of the Information
- Summary

During the data gathering phase of the research project raw data was amassed. The next task, and the topic of this chapter, is the manipulation and treatment of this raw data into a form amenable to decision making.

The manipulation and treatment of raw data is defined as the assessment or analysis phase of technical research. The input is raw, unorganized information which provides the foundation for analysis. Analysis unifies the data into compact, organized information, which serves as the basis for decisions concerning the project goals and research problem.

Analysis can be applied to a number of fields requiring insight into complex system behavior including philosophy, finance, chemistry and engineering. The differences among types of analysis result more from the subject matter being analyzed than from the processes being employed. The elements and logic for any application of analytical technique are similar, but technical research employs some unique elements and techniques. These unique elements and techniques will be highlighted in this chapter.

This chapter will be divided into four parts: (1) the goals, purposes and various types of analysis used in technical research, (2) the common technical methods of analysis with emphasis on visual and statistical techniques, (3) the computer as an analytical tool and (4) the synthesis and interpretation of the analyzed data.

143

GOALS, PURPOSES AND TYPES OF ANALYSIS

In research, assessment of data usually infers analysis of data. The distinction between these two terms can be drawn from their definitions. Assessment is a global term that involves an estimated evaluation of data. Analysis is a specific term that describes organizing raw data into constituent elements and component parts so that systematic interrelationships among the data elements become apparent.

By definition, analysis is confined to organizing data into elements and parts but in common practice the term refers to both (1) organizing data and (2) synthesizing and interpreting the organized data. The analysis/synthesis combination is a valuable tool used by every science or branch of study to provide insight into problems and phenomena. In this chapter the term analysis will imply both organizing and synthesizing data.

Assumptions of Analysis

The foundational elements of analysis should be understood before any discussion of tools of analysis is undertaken. An understanding of the basic elements is critical in selecting proper analysis techniques and in the resultant accuracy and validity of the analysis. Figure 9-1 provides a schematic representation of analysis and these basic elements.

Analysis is performed on raw data which must be gathered or measured in one of the ways discussed in the preceding chapter. The researcher must integrate the measurement and analysis phase closely because the output of measurement affects the selected technique of analysis. For example, if non-parametric data (ordinal or nominal) is gathered, the analysis techniques available would be limited. Similarly, the measurement technique affects analysis. Random sampling of parts, to assess quality control, allows a more credible analysis technique than a non-random scheme.

The measurements are gathered from representative models. Models are physical or conceptual representations of the actions of a complex system or situation. In physical form, measurements can be gathered from simulations, scaled models or population samples. In conceptual form, mathematical models can be used. For example, scaled airplane models are used in wind tunnel tests to measure the aerodynamic qualities of the craft. Also population samples are selected to represent the behavior of the whole population for testing a specific performance.

Models represent the parameters and elements of complex systems and the accuracy of the analysis is determined by how well the model simulates the full system's behavior.

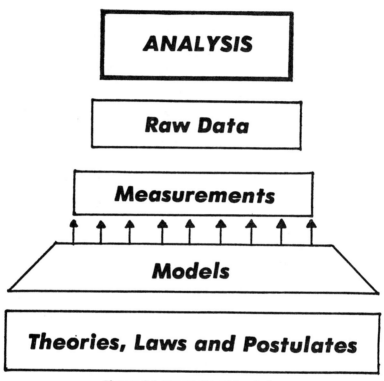

Figure 9-1: Elements of Analysis

The creation of models and modeling involves the complex understanding of numerous fields. The concerned reader is referred to Rivett (1980) for a complete treatment of models for decision making.

The models used, whether physical or conceptual, are always based upon underlying theories, laws or postulates. Mathematical models derived from differential and integral calculus are used in statistical treatments. The laws of statistical inference and probability are used to select random samples for product quality assessment. In applied technical research, a given theory or postulate is accepted as true. A model and analysis technique is then selected and used. This is one fundamental difference between basic and applied technical research.

Basic research questions the premises and accuracy of the underlying theories whereas applied technical research accepts them as true.

Figure 9-1 shows analysis as an open-loop system. An open-loop system is one in which the elements are dependent upon environmental factors and upon the input and output. This feature insures fluidity and strength in the analytical treatment by providing a model open to constant review and revision. For example, if empirical data derived from a technical research activity differed drastically from what would be suspected, the model and underlying theories would be questioned. Possibly a variable was unaccounted for, overlooked or poorly weighted. The advantage of the open-loop system is that as the research base grows, the accuracy of the model and underlying theory are improved. More accurate models result in more valid measurements, analyses and predictions. It must be remembered that it is not the purpose of applied technical research to question or verify the models, but unexpected insights sometimes arise as a result of the research. The open-loop system keeps the theories and models current and therefore provides more accurate representations, measurements, analyses and decisions for future research.

The Purpose of Analysis

The purpose of analysis is to provide detailed information so the researcher can derive an accurate answer to the original question. Analysis provides a fundamental understanding of a problem through isolating explanatory variables and therefore provides a basis for decision making.

Technical research does not always meet its specified goal. In the search for answers to question "A," unexpected insights might arise for an unasked question "B." These insights, although not originally sought, provide a basis for spin-off projects or further research.

The Placement of Analysis In Technical Research

The linear placement of chapters in this Yearbook suggests that analysis follows measurement. This is not always the case in technical research. Analysis can occur (1) at the beginning of and during the measurement stage of a research project or (2) following a planned intervention or manipulation of variables. Normally, analysis occurs after a manipulation of variables, observations or experiments. The interpretations based on this type of analysis provide a direct response to the research question. In some cases analysis occurs at the inception of a research project, immediately following problem identification. This "parameter analysis" would be a search for a technically feasible solution to a given problem by reducing the problem to its root elements and configurations. Parameter analysis methodology is more of a mental method of research than a physical one involving measurement. Parameter analysis is becoming more popular because it involves the independent mental work of a researcher rather than costly and time consuming experimental research.

Analytical Techniques

Analytical technique refers to the approach, or methodology, used in handling and analyzing the data. Analysis technique should not be confused with the tools of analysis. The former refers to the philosophic approach of the researcher while the latter is the definitive tool or instrument used to analyze the data. Both technique and tool are interrelated because the selection of one guides the selection of the other.

Many different analysis techniques exist but they all exhibit some common features. The first of these is the style of analysis which would range on a continuum from pure qualitative to pure quantitative thinking.

Quantitative analysis is a formal, logical analytical technique used to process numeric data into its fundamental parts. Quantitative analysis relies on quantifiable numeric data and gains its strength from the mathematical models and integral calculus underlying its approach. This style forms a large part of technical research analysis.

Qualitative analysis is informal and sometimes intuitive in nature. It uses critical thinking to derive the thrust of the data and is not typically found in a structured research setting. Qualitative analysis methodology is considered a primary technique by independent inventors, design entrepreneurs and intrapreneurs. Unlike the quantitative method which approaches items in isolation, the qualitative method takes into account the integral parts or organized systems. It approaches the whole as more than a sum of its parts.

Each strategy has its advantages and limitations and its appropriate place. Quantitative thinking is employed during the early stages of analysis with qualitative techniques called for when quantitative thinking fails (Beveridge, 1981).

Another dimension of analysis technique is data gathering methodology. The methods can be classified as either empirical or theoretical and can form one axis on an analysis matrix (See Figure 9-2).

147

The second axis contains the quantitative and qualitative methodologies or styles previously discussed.

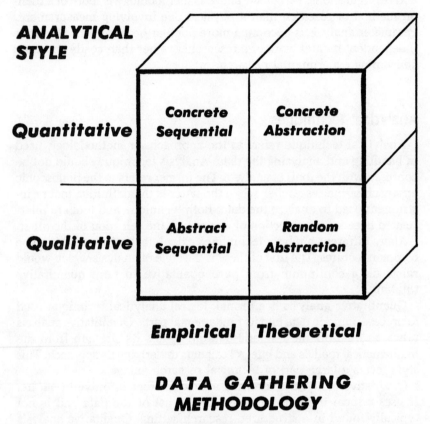

Figure 9-2: Analysis Matrix

Empirical techniques gather data from concrete, repeatable and verifiable observations by the researcher. Empirical data is usually gathered by an accurately calibrated measurement device. Empirical data gathering techniques could involve physical measurement, frequency measurement, density observations or airflow pressure measurements.

Theoretical techniques are based on speculation of future action. Theoretical data gathering techniques can be derived from computer simulation, intuition, or speculation of future actions.

The matrix provides four quadrants into which analysis techniques can be grouped: Abstract Sequential, Concrete-Sequential, Random-Abstract and Concrete-Abstract.

Abstract-Sequential: This quadrant uses a qualitative style of analysis on empirical evidence. Many managerial decisions fall into this category of analysis. As an example, a manager is faced with the decision of continuing or terminating a research project. Preliminary results look good and the probability of success is encouraging. The decision calls on conventional wisdom, personal knowledge of the research staff, a feel for upper-management's flexibility and an integration of empirical evidence. Although a small empirical base exists on which the manager can rely, a large part of the decision is qualitative in nature.

Random-Abstraction: This quadrant of analysis uses an aspect of thinking called intuition. Random abstraction involves subjective, non-consciously directed thought to seek solutions to a problem. Random-abstraction seeks relationships, analogies, similarities and differences through association thinking. Rowan stated, "The Eureka factor... involves using the cumulative knowledge, experience, taste and sensation that lies buried in the subconscious." (STAFF, 1986). This analysis technique can be used in the early stages of technical research because it is based on "what can" or "what should be" and not on "what is." In parameter analysis, this technique often forms the starting point of a research project.

Concrete-Sequential: The concrete-sequential quadrant involves analysis of empirical data coupled with a critical mode of thinking. The analysis follows logical paths and inhibits thoughts that are not based on known facts, data or accepted theory. Thinking is linear and systematic and is epitomized by rational scientific thought. The concrete sequential approach provides an unbiased, verifiable technique of problem definition. Deductive and inductive logic are used extensively to come to breakthroughs and insights in thinking.

Concrete-Abstraction: Analysis in the concrete-abstract quadrant could be described as an educated guess. The system uses linear systematic thinking, but the data upon which the decisions are based is mostly theoretical. The researcher may use a computer to analyze speculative data. Developing "what if" scenarios of aircraft design would provide an example of this technique.

The quadrants are not mutually exclusive but the matrix provides a means of categorizing analysis techniques. No single technique can be used to solve every problem and the researcher who is best equipped with the greatest variety of methods is most likely to succeed.

COMMON TECHNICAL METHODS OF ANALYSIS

The number of analytical tools is large, but two stand out as common in their use for technical research applications. These are visual analysis and statistical analysis.

Visual Analysis

Visual or photographic analysis is an important analysis tool in technical research. Photographic analysis plays a vital role in many areas such as component failure and system operation. Visual analysis provides an easily interpreted hard-copy record of the problem as contrasted with information provided by numeric analysis techiques which requires skilled interpretation.

The greatest advantage of visual analysis can be summed up in the cliche: "One picture is worth a thousand words." The visual language is cross-cultural since it is graphic and pictorial rather than symbolic.

Another advantage of visual analysis is its quick access and low cost. For example, a technical research problem arises to increase tool-bit life by decreasing tool-bit degradation. It was hypothesized that changing the coolant composition would increase tool-bit life. After experimentation with various coolants, the bits were analyzed using microphotographic techniques and the bit with the least wear was noted. The coolant composition used with this bit was selected for inplant use.

Photographic or electronic recording devices are often coupled with visual analysis. A camera used to record stress contours on film would provide an example of the former, while an electron microscope delineating fracture surfaces would be an example of the latter.

Photographic equipment can enlarge objects, record events where the environment is harmful to humans (space exploration) and see characteristics unseen by the human eye (infrared analysis of heat loss). Photographic analysis also is appropriate where the dimension of time must be varied. High speed analysis techniques allow the operation of a complex system to be recorded. Time-lapse photography can offer the researcher the opportunity to analyze events that occur very slowly, such as the growth of crystals.

Photographic techniques can also be used to study stress and fracture analysis to determine the strength and character of materials. (Acharia, 1985).

Statistical Analysis

Statistical tools are used today in almost every endeavor of human enterprise. In any technical research activity there is an underlying core of uncertainty which must be dealt with in an objective and scientific manner. This is true with predicting or assessing the weather, the effects of medical drugs, the future use of the computer, the evaluation of new products or the forecasting of population growth. Statistics provide the capability of dealing with uncertainty objectively and scientifically.

Statistics is a mathematical study of probability. With technical research, statistics is different from other fields because the questions under investigation are different. The questions asked may be: Is this manufacturing process under control?. . . Are the parts selected for testing representative of the total output?. . . Are the variations present in the incoming material significant and will they affect the final product?. . . What material will best fit the design need?. . . All these questions contain a certain level of uncertainty. Statistical argument can be used to objectively handle the uncertainty and improve the chance for a better decision.

This chapter will not examine all the specific tools that are available for statistical analysts. There are many excellent statistical sources which contain such descriptions. This chapter will introduce the area of statistical analysis, indicate how these techniques fit in the overall scheme of the research and suggest some of the statistical tools that may be applied to technical research. The following specific topics will be addressed:

1. Which statistical tools are most often applied?
2. When is it valid to apply certain tools?
3. How are the outputs interpreted and inferences drawn?

It is assumed the researcher has available an institutional mainframe computer or a mini- or micro-computer and appropriate statistical software. This assumption allows the subject to be presented in a non-mathematical approach. This tack limits the detailed instruction in the techniques of analysis and emphasizes the synthesis of results.

Descriptive statistics: As the name implies, they describe the derived data in a simplistic manner. Technical research activities often generate too many pieces of data for the mind to handle. Statistical methodology is employed to condense and describe the character and essence of the data. Descriptive statistics allow a quick insight into a series of individual observations and permit comparison of values.

151

Three types of descriptive statistics are commonly used in technical research projects: central tendency, variability, and visual data patterns. Each of these methods describes (1) a different character of the data and (2) provides a summary of the data.

Central tendency, which is sometimes called an average, describes the thrust or direction of a data group as a whole. There are five common measures of central tendency. The selection of the appropriate measure would depend upon the type of data derived and the desired results. Table 9-1 summarizes each measure of central tendency and provides a brief description of its purpose.

Variability, or dispersion, is another method of describing data distributions. Variability describes the tendency of individual values or observations of a variable to cluster or scatter about the average. While central tendency defines the central value, variability describes how all the values, as a group, cluster around the central value. The three common measures of variability are range, variance and standard deviation. In the above order, each measure of variation provides an increased accuracy of description with an increased complexity of computation. Range provides a quick, superficial indication of dispersion whereas standard deviation provides an accurate means of comparing and evaluating variability. Variance falls in the continuum between standard deviation and range and is generally used in the calculation of standard deviation. With the availabilty of electronic calculation, standard deviation is the most useful and widely employed index of variation.

Type	Definition	Purpose
Mean	Sum of all data values divided by the number of values.	To show the arithematic center of a distribution.
Median	Middle value of an ordered data set.	An average which is not heavily weighted by extreme high or low scores.
Mode	Most frequently occurring value.	The most typical data value.
Geometric Mean	The Nth root of the product of N values.	Describes true rate of change.
Harmonic Mean	An average of the reciprocals of the values of the variables and finding the reciprocal of this average.	Average rates that need weighting adjustments for their calculation.

Table 9-1: Measures of Central Tendency

A third method used to describe large amounts of data is visual graphing which includes graphs, histograms, line charts and other graphic methods. The data patterns can provide the reader with a high impact condensation of the data and be more informative than numeric calculations to the untrained eye. Visual displays, found on many software programs, are useful and powerful in showing trends or comparisons of data. However, the inherent loss of mathematical accuracy can be detrimental to properly evaluating the data.

Commonly used graphic procedures as shown in Figure 9-3 are:

Line Graph — Best used to illustrate changes or trends over time.

Histogram — Best displays the frequency of occurrence of a value.

Pictogram — A specialized chart that uses symbols to illustrate magnitude of frequency of an event or device.

Pie Graph — Similar to a pictogram, it is used to illustrate magnitude in a general manner.

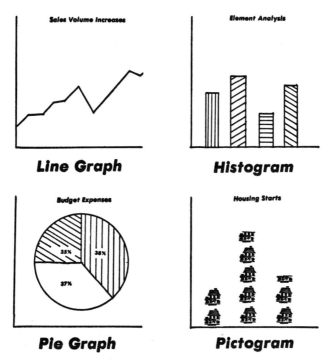

Figure 9-3: Graphic Procedures

Assessing the Results

Descriptive statistics have widespread use in the area of quality control. One of the best ways to describe the level of quality for a process is with a control chart. Among the most versatile and sensitive control charts are the average (mean) and the range (R) charts which are commonly used together.

For example, management is concerned with the quality control of widgets. The attribute under concern is widget weight. It is discovered that the weight is varying excessively and causing problems with packaging, shipping and material waste. The specified weight of the widget is 1.10 gram. Five random samples are taken off the assembly line every hour and weighed. The results of this technical research are shown in Table 9-2. At the end of the day the researcher determines the mean and range of each sample. Two graphic control charts are plotted for these values. The use of descriptive statistics (means, variability and visual data patterns) has described the widget production for the day and will give management a basis for decisions (See Figure 9-4).

Hour				Sample #		Mean	Range
	1	2	3	4	5		
1	1.00	1.01	1.02	1.03	.99	1.01	.04
2	.99	.98	.97	1.01	1.02	1.00	.03
3	1.00	1.10	1.05	1.15	1.20	1.10	.20
4	1.08	1.16	1.00	1.10	1.06	1.08	.10
5	.90	1.00	1.10	1.20	1.30	1.10	.40
6	1.04	1.14	1.14	1.14	1.24	1.14	.20
7	1.20	1.20	1.00	1.20	1.40	1.20	.20
8	1.01	1.21	1.31	1.41	1.11	1.21	.40
9	1.20	1.15	1.30	1.45	1.40	1.30	.25
10	1.25	1.25	1.35	1.15	1.25	1.25	.20
11	1.26	1.26	1.26	1.26	1.26	1.26	.00
12	1.30	1.00	1.60	1.50	1.10	1.30	.60

Table 9-2: Mean and Range of Widget Weights

The data pattern shows a trend occurring in the manufacture of widgets. The upward trend must be corrected in order to control the weight of the widgets. Gathering data daily and comparing the data can benefit management in controlling the manufacturing process and lowering company expenditures and waste.

Inferential Statistics: In the previous section the discussion dealt with the use of statistics to describe a large amount of data. In most cases the data are assumed to be a complete record of a population or event so the statistics are accurate descriptions of the whole. When compiled from the whole population, descriptive measures can be used directly for decision making. Unfortunately the availability of a whole population for observation is uncommon. Take for example a problem dealing with statistical quality control. It would be time consuming and

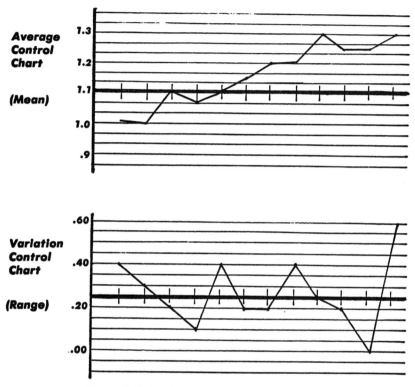

Figure 9-4: Control Charts for Mean + Range

expensive to test every product manufactured. Likewise, it would be ludicrous to test dispensable products, such as bullets, since the test is destructive in nature. In these cases, a sample (a few bullets) of the whole population (factory output) would be selected for testing and evaluation. Based upon this sample, an estimate of population performance would be made. Inferential statistics are used to make decisions upon partial information.

Statistical inference allows, with a certain calculated measure of uncertainty, an estimate of population performance based upon a small sample of the whole. The concept is used frequently and informally in everyday life. For example, a person may look out a window, with its limited view, to determine weather conditions. A taste of a dish may be used to determine if it pleases the palate, or another person's actions may be judged by moments of conversation. In essence, we infer from one part what the whole is like.

There are many underlying concepts and rules governing statistical inference. For the above examples, would any teaspoon sized sample of a whole dish of food prove it is appealing or, would looking out a basement window provide an accurate description of the weather? Probability, sampling techniques and distributions are all topics fundamental to statistical inference, but beyond the scope of this chapter.

This discussion will focus on selected inferential tools and present a limited explanation of their proper selection and use. Specific emphasis will be placed on the tests of means using analysis of variance and chi-square techniques. These tools are common analytical tools for technical research projects and for specific use in quality control and production forecasting.

A word of caution must be given for the analysis of variance as it is a parametric statistic. Parametric statistics assume a normally distributed parent population and a population with equal variances. Powerful statistics as they are, when used improperly or with a false assumption on the researcher's part, they will lead to incorrect judgments. When the stringent assumptions about the distribution of the parent population cannot be met non-parametric or distribution-free statistics should be employed. Distribution-free statistics require a less restricting assumption, often require less arithmetic computation and can be suitable for analyzing ranked data.

Analysis of variance, or ANOVA, is a technique that allows the researcher to compare the variations of more than two population means. In doing so, the variations or causative agents associated with each mean may be isolated and estimated. An example will clarify its use. A researcher is concerned with the effects of temperature on the hardness of a material. It is speculated that the length of time the peak temperature is held and the rate of temperature drop during cooling might affect the hardness of the material. An experiment can be set up with temperature, length of time at the peak temperature and rate of temperature drop as the three critical (independent) variables, and the resulting material hardness as the dependent variable. Analysis of variance allows the researcher to study the effects of these three variables upon the material and determine the magnitude of variation attributed to each variable. Through this procedure the researcher can determine which specific variable or combination of variables affects product hardness the most.

An analysis of variance routine will provide two critical indices: the F statistic and the significance level. Both of these indices indicate the impact, or statistical significance, of each variable on the dependent variable.

Analysis of variance is a powerful technique that judges the effect of input variables (independent variables) upon an output (dependent) variable. Since ANOVA is a parametric statistic, it must be qualified by three assumptions: (1) a random sampling of products, (2) a normal distribution of data and (3) homogeneity of variances.

Chi-square is a test of statistical significance that determines whether a systematic relationship exists among variables. In the analysis, Chi-square provides an estimate of whether the observed results are significantly different from the expected results. It also indicates whether the difference is due to a statistically significant relationship among the variables or is due to sampling errors.

As an example, management is sensitive to general complaints about different communication equipment available for employees use. It appears the dissatisfaction will result in monies being placed into developmental research projects aimed at improving the system. Management questions whether the dissatisfaction is directed toward any one type of equipment or is across the board. Data is gathered from users of the system and is shown in Table 9-3 part A.

The Chi-Square statistic compares the data in Part A with data that would be expected if there was total independence between the "Technology" and the "Level of Dissatisfaction" (Table 9-3, Part B).

A.	Observed Level of Dissatisfaction	Telephone	Technology Facsimile	Video
	High	15	25	5
	Medium	5	10	5
	Low	25	5	5
B.	Expected Level of Dissatisfaction	Telephone	Technology Facsimile	Video
	High	20	18	7
	Medium	9	8	3
	Low	16	9	5

Table 9-3: Chi-Square Assessment

Chi-Square compares the gathered results with the expected results and provides a basis for determining whether the variables were independent, and the observed difference due to chance, or if the variables

157

were interrelated. If independence is found, management can use the monies across the board to improve the various technologies. If on the other hand an interrelationship was found, monies would be directed to a specific technology.

Table 9-3, Part A, identifies a matrix of nine cells. For example, one cell is 'High/Telephone.' Each cell corresponds to the number of respondents under the criteria by row and column. Table 9-3, Part B, having a similar number of cells, is the expected number of respondents in each cell. The expected frequency, using probability, is calculated mathematically based on the number of respondents in each row and column. If a die were rolled numerous times, one would expect each digit (one through six) to occur an equal number of times. Chi-square compares the number or responses in the expected category and derives a variance for each cell. These cell variances are summed and compared against a mathematical expected at a given significance level. Calculating a higher than expected chi-square value would indicate that the respondents were "technology specific" in their level of dissatisfaction and management should consider directing funds toward a specific technology.

Chi-square draws a lot of its power from its classification as a non-parametric or distribution free test. Non-parametric tests are ones that do not require knowledge of population parameters and is therefore free from assumptions.

Correlational Statistics: Technical research projects often assess the relationship between two independent variables or among explanatory variables. Observations used to assess these relationships are derived from either pairs of observations or multiple measurements of a single variable. The researcher would like to know how the action of one variable is related to a second variable. Once a relationship is established it becomes possible to use the relationship for future decision making. Some typical questions that exemplify this idea include:

1) Are the temperature and pressure of a gas related?

2) Is volume of sales related to the amount of television advertisement?

3) Is the time of year important in the purchasing trends of a particular product?

4) Does emission output vary with octane rating?

To answer these and similar questions, a measure of correlation is made to quantify the degree, or magnitude of relationship between two or more variables. This relationship is expressed as a coefficient of correlation which is a numerical measure of the relationship between two series of numbers representing factors. It is not a measure of the actual factors themselves, but of a series of numbers representing these factors. The coefficient of correlation, represented by r, always has a value between −1 and +1.

$$-1 \ \{r\} \ +1$$

When two variables, A and B, have a perfect relationship, the coefficient of correlation, or value of r, would be either +1 or −1. When r is +1 and A increases, B will predictably increase. For example, increasing the revolutions-per-minute of a shaft will have a high positive correlation with frictional heat generated. When r is −1 and A increases, B will predictably decrease. For example, the relationship between the weight of a vehicle and its gas mileage has a very high negative r value. As the road weight of a vehicle increases, with all other factors held constant, the resultant gas mileage will decrease.

When no relationship exists between two variables, the coefficient of correlation would be 0. An example of two very poorly related variables would be weight and color of a material. The obvious extension of these extreme examples would place values of r anywhere on a continuum between −1 and +1. The closer to the extremes, the better the correlation between variables. The lack of relationship between variables becomes apparent as the value of r approaches 0.

Correlation statistics can also be used to help assess validity and reliability. These topics have been discussed in other chapters of this yearbook. As an example, correlation can be used to assess the construct validity of a given instrument. If the correlation is high between data derived from an instrument and outside observable behavior, it can be inferred that the instrument is valid in construct. Similarly, correlation can also be used to assess the reliability between two sets of data. If an instrument is reliable and valid, high correlations will exist internally within the instrument's data and externally with outside behavior.

Many statistical tools exist that can be selected to determine the coefficient of correlation for paired or bivariate data. The decision of which to employ, with a specific set of data, would depend on the following factors:

1. The scale of measurement (nominal, ordinal, interval or ratio data).
2. The assumed nature of the underlying distribution (continuous or discrete).

3. The characteristic of the distribution of scores (linear or nonlinear).

Three statistical tools are the most commonly employed in technical research and can be implemented for the vast majority of correlational problems. These tools are scattergrams, Pearson Product-Moment Correlation and Spearmen Rho.

Scattergrams: These were first used by Sir Frances Galton in the mid 19th century to study the relationship between intellect and family upbringing. Scattergrams offer a visual insight into the relationship between two variables after one variable is plotted on the X axis and the other on the Y axis. Each paired measurement, such as X = 1 and Y = 2, is plotted as a single point. The alignment of the points displays the degree of relationship between the variables. Figure 9-5 provides examples of scattergrams displaying: (a) near perfect positive correlation (r = +1), (b) very low correlation (r = 0) and (c) near perfect negative correlation (r = -1).

Scattergrams do not offer the mathematical precision necessary for correlation analysis, but they do provide a visual interpretation of the relationship. This visual interpretation can show the linearity, or nonlinearity, of the relationship. Knowledge of the linearity of a relationship, which is the ability to plot a straight line through the center of the series of points, is essential for the selection of a statistical tool to produce a mathematically precise coefficient of correlation. For this reason, scattergrams should be produced as a preliminary correlational analysis to determine linearity and provide the researcher a "feel" for the data.

Pearson Product-Moment Coefficient of Correlation: The Pearson r is the most powerful correlational tool available. Its ease of use and availability make it the most commonly used correlational procedure. Two assumptions must be met before the Pearson formula would be appropriately used. The data must be at least interval quality and there must be a linear relationship between the variables.

Spearman Rho: When the strict assumptions of the Pearson r formula cannot be met, the Spearman Rho formula can be used. The Spearman formula is a non-parametric statistic that (1) involves no assumptions about population parameters, (2) can be used when the shape of the distribution is in question and (3) relies on ordinal or ranked data. Because the Spearman formula assumes less about the nature of the data, it can be used in more situations although its general applicability is offset by a loss of statistical power.

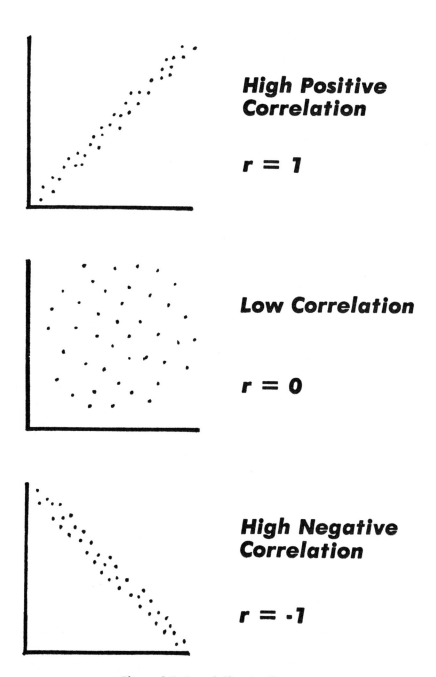

Figure 9-5: Correlation Scattergrams

Since Spearman can be used with ranked data, correlations between characteristics that cannot easily be expressed quantifiably can be analyzed. For example, ranked data such as: the perceived importance of staff members, the value of decision criteria or the personality of supervisors may be subjected to the Spearman formula.

There are certain precautions that should be taken in using correlation. Of all the statistical tools available, correlation is the one most subject to misinterpretation. The researchers should take certain precautions in the presumption of cause and effect, closeness of relationship and significance of correlation.

Cause and Effect: The most common error is NON CAUSA PRO CAUSA, or false cause. There is a strong impulse to assume a cause and effect relationship exists between two variables that are highly correlated. This is a dangerous assumption because the coefficient of correlation shows only the degree of relationship between a series of numbers representing certain factors and not the factors themselves. This imperfect representation of the actual factors leads to potential misinterpretation of correlation. Correlation does not show cause and effect. It can only estimate the mathematical degree of relationship between the data. Past knowledge and an intuitive feel for the researched problem must be taken into account before any inference about cause-effect can be made.

Closeness of Relationship: In a non-perfect relationship, variation in one variable cannot be totally explained by variation in the other variable. For an example, if the coefficient of correlation between sales volume and type of advertisement used was r = .80, a non-perfect relationship would be noted. Other factors besides type of advertisement would be impinging on the volume of sales. The question arises, how strong a relationship does this type of advertising have to sales volume? The coefficient of determination, which is expressed as a percentage, tends to be more informative and provides a better explanation of identified variation than does the coefficient of correlation.

The coefficient of determination is equal to the value of r squared.

$$r = \text{Coefficient of Correlation}$$

$$r^2 = \text{Coefficient of Determination}$$

For our hypothetical example, $r^2 = .80 \times .80 = .64$ or 64%. The interpretation is relatively simple. Sixty-four percent of the variation in sales volume is related to the type of advertising used. The remaining percentage (100 - 64 = 36%) is related to other unexplained variables.

Most computer packages provide both r and r² values. These are both meaningful in analysis and interpretation. Table 9-4 provides relevant information for interpretation of either r or r² values.

Coefficient of Correlation	Coefficient of Determination	Interpretation of Results
1.0	1.00	Perfect
.9	.81	Excellent
.8	.64	Very Good
.7	.49	Good
.6	.36	Fair
.5	.25	Borderline
.4 to 0	.16 to 0	Little/None

Table 9-4: Significance of r and r² values

<u>Significance of Correlation</u>: Since the r value obtained is usually derived from sample data and not from population parameters, the question arises as to the significance of the relationship. Simply worded, is the r value obtained due to a real correlation between the variables or is the relationship produced by chance alone? Although the estimate of significance is a highly complex study, a simplified version will show the variable involved.

The estimate of significance is determined by knowing three elements: (a) the number of observations, (b) the number of variables involved and (c) the confidence level desired. For example, a correlation is sought between two variables. A sample of 100 observations is taken (N = 100) and the confidence level desired is equal to 95% (95 times out of a 100 the relationship exists between the variables). Referring to any statistical text, a "critical value of r" table will provide a threshold number for significance. For our example, with 100 observations and a risk factor of .05, the threshold number of .195 is obtained. An r value of over this threshold would indicate that the correlation is significant and therefore not due to chance alone. The sample is regarded to be significant at the .05 level (less than a 5% chance that we are rejecting a true hypothesis).

The larger the sample size, the lower the coefficient of correlation necessary for significance. Any given value of correlation is more significant with a larger number of observations. The value of a large sample must be weighted against the cost of obtaining the additional data.

Statistical Forecasting

Building upon simple correlation, regression statistics allow the researcher to forecast future events. Forecasting technological events has held great importance for the researcher and the technologist. Forecasting involves the prediction of the characteristics of machines and techniques still to come. Mathematically, these predictions are possible by using regression equations. Regression analysis uses the relationship known among variables to estimate an unknown, related variable.

For example, a researcher is concerned with the growth of microchip sales in the next five years so that research on new designs and configurations can be justified. Historic data is collected on chip sales over the previous years. Figure 9-6 provides the scattergram for the fictitious data. A strong positive correlation between two variables is readily apparent. Using regression, a mathematical model of the current existing relationship can be developed and used to predict chip sales. In this example chip sales will predictably increase over the next three years.

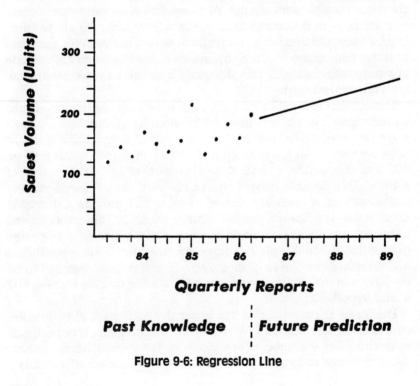

Figure 9-6: Regression Line

The preceding example is limited because it fails to take into account many other variables that affect sales, such as seasonal fluctuations, demands of key industries and raw materials costs. Multiple regression techniques, readily available on most computer packages, can consider the effects of numerous other variables and therefore provide a more accurate prediction. Similarly, multiple correlation techniques involve the correlation of more than two variables.

THE COMPUTER AS AN ANALYTICAL TOOL

Technological advances have brought changes in industrial processes and procedures and have produced concurrent changes in methods for approaching and solving technical problems. The power of electronics, via the computer, has been brought to bear on data analysis and technical research. The advent of microprocessing technology brought first the mainframe computer and more recently the microcomputer.

These technological advances have been timely. As technology became more complex, technical research based upon complex models became unmanageable for the human mind. The computer offered relief by providing a precise, fast, accurate and reliable method of analyzing an almost unlimited number of variables and equations simultaneously. The computer can readily handle models that were once simplified to meet human abilities. This allows the researcher to focus on the results of the analysis rather than the mathematical manipulation of data. Time once spent on execution can now be spent on conceptualization of the research and interpretation of the results.

Constraints of the System

Contemporary computer analysis requires that the computer's power be tempered by a recognition of its limitations. Two general problems arise when the computer is used in technical research. The first problem is seeking research methods amenable to numerical solutions by digital computers. Computers deal with quantifiable, numeric data and require this input from the measurement phase. Occasionally the researcher changes the focus of the project by quantifying a research variable that would best be handled in other ways. The method of analysis is often chosen for its ease of use and not its applicability to the problem.

A second potential problem lies in the credibility associated with computer generated analysis. Potentially this is a false sense of security.

Assessing the Results

Using the computer's speed to search for any significant relationship, coupled with human data entry errors, provides two potentials for arriving at faulty or invalid conclusion.

The researcher must develop an understanding of the computer's limitations. Following is an abridged list of questions that should be asked before using computer analysis.

Hardware Constraints: Does the mainframe or microcomputer selected for analysis have any memory or architectural limitations that would hinder or falsify the analysis? Is the memory capable of handling the amount of data fields in their proper format?

Input/output Constraints: Are the input and output modes appropriate for the research project? For example, does the printer/interface combination have the capabilities of producing needed graphs and charts? Can measurements be recorded directly from a sensor into the computer, thereby bypassing potential human error?

Software Assumptions: What assumptions does the programmer make about the analysis technique and/or the type of data provided? For example, does the program require interval data when the project will generate only ordinal data?

Program Limitations: Is the program limited, either by design parameters or by the capabilities of the system, in its solution to the problem?

Program Purpose and Definition: How does the program define a task and execute these tasks? An understanding of the program's purpose and definition is essential for intelligent use.

Software Routines and Their Uses

Many software programs are available to aid in technical research. In more recent years, the number and complexity of programs has risen while the difficulty of their use has declined. These changes have led to the increased acceptance of the computer in technical research.

Most computer analysis programs, although developed by various manufacturers, are essentially similar. The program's logic, options available, graphic capabilities, speed and ease of use may vary but the formulas, or models, upon which they are based are fairly constant. Listed below are some of the major categories of software programs and a brief description of their benefits.

Management Analysis: As discussed in Chapter 7, the management of technical research is an essential element of the project. Computers provide versatility and efficiency in management by offering programs for PERT, CPM and other analysis techniques.

Finite Point/Stress Analysis: Provided proper data, the computer will calculate the load effect or stress on any particular point or element of a complex system. The programs are used in product design and in predicting part fatigue and failure. The analyses obtained from these programs are becoming increasingly accurate as feedback from empirical observations is used to modify models.

Computer Simulation: Simulation is a process that is becoming increasingly used with the advent of the computer. Computer simulations are used when (1) the discrepancies and inaccuracies present in experimental situations are present and (2) the cost and complexity of empirical analysis is prohibitive, (3) the experimental analysis is impossible. For example, simulation is useful when costs prohibit running a realistic experiment which requires destructive testing of the product or when the experiment subjects humans to excessive danger.

Statistical Analysis: Use of statistical analysis has grown tremendously in the last 20 years due to the advent of the computer. Listed in Table 9-5 are the commonly used software programs available for mainframe computers. These programs will each support the statistical tools discussed in the previous section.

INTERPRETATION AND SYNTHESIS
OF THE INFORMATION

The research model and the analyzed data form the basis for decision making. The first step after analyses is to interpret or synthesize the data in the context of the original research objective. Synthesis can be defined as the search for a solution to the research problem. The elements and their interrelationships found during analysis form the basic building blocks for an acceptable solution to the problem.

Software Programs	Description
MiniTab	An easy to operate, with a modicum of instruction, interactive statistical package. Help facilities and documentation provided make the program extremely user-friendly. Only detriment to the program is lack of computational power and limited number of statistical on-line tools. Designed specifically for researchers with no previous experience with computers.
SAS	The most complete and versatile system for analysis available today. The language used, in and of itself, permits the researcher to edit any analysis technique and to write user-specific programs for graphics and formatting. The power of the system is only thwarted by its difficulty of use.

SPSS-X	Originally designed as a package specifically for the social sciences, it now has become one of the most used statistical packages available. Extreme power and excellent documentation are available although beginning researchers are often stymied by the program's complexity.
Lindo	A moderately powerful package designed specifically to calculate linear quadratic equations.
SCSS	The interactive (vs. Batch) version of SPSS-X. A bit more user-friendly than SPSS-X but also a bit less computational power.
BMDP	A program designed specifically for bio-medical mathematics by the University of California. It provides methods ranging from simple descriptive displays to exotic statistical techniques such as cocnonical correlation, stepwise discrimination and Boulian factor analysis.

Table 9-5: Statistical Analysis Packages

A situation to avoid after analysis is "analysis paralysis" which occurs after all the variables have been identified and inspected and the researcher is looking so closely at every block that he/she fails to see the whole problem. One useful way of avoiding analysis paralysis is to represent the problem visually, in a functional block diagram. (See Figure 9-7). The block diagram shows each input variable, the system of operation and the outputs.

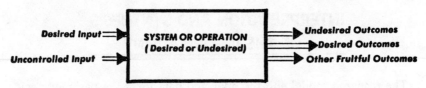

Figure 9-7: Information Synthesis

Notice that the figure shows uncontrolled input and undesired outputs that usually accompany the goal. It is these undesired components that must be identified and dealt with in forming an acceptable solution.

In synthesizing the data, the original purposes as represented by the desired output, must be met. But a context of practical and theoretical significance must temper the solution. Theoretical significance implies integration with accepted physical laws and current theories as discovered through past research or current undertakings. Practical significance deals with environmental, economic, technical and human constraints. For example, the tool-bit degradation problem discussed earlier was answered, however, the implementation plan may not be warranted. Suppose the experimental coolant compound was corrosive or caustic. Would implementation justify the probable corrosive action on the equipment? Human and physical environmental concerns must become variables in the synthesis. Could humans work safely in contact with the compound?

Sometimes the analyzed and synthesized data may not provide a practical solution to a given problem. Three alternatives must be considered.

1. Drop the project as unfeasible.

2. Discover, develop or invent a device to solve the problem.

3. Change the project's objectives.

Recommendations are made after (1) the data are interpreted and synthesized and (2) conclusions are drawn. The recommendations provide direction for further research based upon previous research findings and the completed study. The researcher must be able to objectively defend the logic used to derive the recommendations.

Structured research models and procedures are essential for valid research programs, but these components may be modified as preliminary research findings become available or company goals change.

SUMMARY

Assessment of data, through analyses and syntheses, provides the researcher with a better posture in which to engage a given problem. Basic to this task are the processes of measurement, modeling and conceptualization of the underlying theories, laws and postulates.

Analysis involves the appropriate selection of technique and tool with which to address the raw data. These selections must be based upon an understanding of the research problem as well as knowledge of each stage of the research project (design, measurement etc.).

The computer and its software can be a valuable tool for the researcher. The computer provides an expeditious, reliable and accurate method of handling many data elements and numerous variables. The power of the computer must be tempered with a knowledge of its capabilities and its limitations.

Synthesis involves the restructuring of the data elements into a form amenable to decision making. Synthesizing involves representing, assembling, identifying and directing all the research variables into a cohesive direction.

BIBLIOGRAPHY

Abe, R. *Statistical Mechanics*. Tokyo, Japan: University of Tokyo Press, 1975.

Acharia, K. M. "Lighting Transparent Acrylic Specimens for Surface Detail." *Functional Photography*, Vol. 20, No. 6, Nov./ Dec. 1984.

Angeletti, G. and Bjorseth, A. (Eds). *Analysis of Organic Micropollutants in Water*. Boston: Reidel Publishing Co., 1984.

Balsley, H. L. and Clover, V. T. *Business Research Methods*. 2nd ed., Columbus, Ohio: Grid Publishing Inc., 1979.

Besterfield, D. H. *Quality Control, A Practical Approach*. Englewood Cliffs, New Jersey: Prentice-Hall, 1979.

Beveridge, W. I. *The Seeds of Discovery*. New York: W. W. Norton & Co., 1980.

Blank, L. *Statistical Procedures for Engineering, Management, and Science*. New York: McGraw-Hill, 1980.

Cole, J. P. and King, C. M. *Quantitative Geography*. New York: John Wiley & Sons, 1968.

Davies, O. L. *The Design and Analysis of Industrial Experiments*. New York: Hafner Publishing Co., 1971.

Dennery, P. *An Introduction to Statistical Mechanics*. London: George Allen & Unwin, LTD, 1972.

Enrick, N. L. *Decision-Oriented Statistics*. New York: Brandon Systems Press, Inc., 1970.

Gantt, H. L. *Gantt on Management*. New York: American Management, 1961.

Heyel, Carl *Handbook of Industrial Research Management*. New York: Reinhold Publishing Corp., 1968.

Hodge, B. K. *Analysis and Design of Energy Systems*. Englewood Cliffs, New Jersey: Printice-Hall, Inc., 1985

Layton, C. *Ten Innovations*. New York: Crane, Russak and Company, Inc., 1972.

Li, Y. T. *Technological Innovation in Education and Industry*. New York: Van Nostrand Reinhold Company, 1980.

Logsdon, J. M., Ed. *The Research System in the 1980's - Public Policy Issues*. Philadelphia: Franklin Institute Press, 1982.

Luftig, J. T. and Norton, W. P. "Technological Forecasting with a Multiple Regression Analysis Approach." *Journal of Epsilon Pi Tau*, Vol. VII (2), Fall, 1981.

Megeath, J. D. *How to Use Statistics*. San Francisco: Canfield Press, 1975.

Noether, G. *Introduction to Statistics - A Fresh Approach*. New York: Houghton-Mifflin, 1971.

Rivett, P. *Model Building for Decision Analysis*. New York: John Wiley & Sons, 1980.

Robinson, E. A. *Statistical Reasoning and Decision Making*. Houston: Goose Pond Press, 1981.

STAFF, "The Best Managers Play Hunches." Roy Rowan. *US News and World Report*, Vol XIV, No.2, May 12, 1980.

Stockton, J. R. and Clark, C. T., *Introduction to Business and Economic Statistics*. Pakaito, California: South-Western Publishing Co., 1975.

Vaughn, R. C. *Quality Control*. Ames, Iowa: Iowa State University Press, 1974.

Watters, G. A. *Modern Analysis and Control of Unsteady Flow in Pipelines*. Ann Arbor, Michgan: Ann Arbor Science, 1979.

Wilson, I. G. and Wilson, M. E. *Management, Innovation and System Design*. New York: Averbach Publishers, 1971.

CHAPTER 10

Reporting the Results

by Wayne D. Andrews

Sub-Topics:

- Organizing the Results
- The Written Research Report
- The Oral Report
- Summary

Reporting the results of technical research is tremendously important. This information is used by management in the decision making process. Decisions related to product development, production and marketing are frequently supported by technical research. The information may be used to (1) present research findings to professional societies, (2) provide technical information in litigation proceedings or (3) document a product or process as part of the patent process. Regardless of its ultimate use, the information gathered during technical research must be collected, organized and recorded in a way that preserves the integrity of the process. The purpose of this chapter is to present an overview of a process for reporting the results of technical research. The topics that will be covered include organizing the results of the research, writing a technical research report and giving an oral presentation of the research findings.

ORGANIZING THE RESULTS

The basic purpose of conducting technical research is to gain information. The technical research process usually results in great quantities of data being collected. Raw data must be analyzed, organized and presented in a meaningful way to make it informative. This process is a very systematic one. During the initial phases of problem identification, a research strategy is developed. This strategy includes the identification of data collection methods and the analysis procedures.

Once the data have been analyzed it may be organized and arranged in informative and visually pleasing ways to enhance the written and oral presentations.

There are a number of acceptable ways of organizing and recording data to make it informative and visually pleasing. Table 10-1 presents a summary of common devices used in organizing and presenting data. The table is organized so that each device is presented along with a summary of features and uses common to each. The major devices discussed are tables, charts, graphs, diagrams, photographs and samples.

Device	Feature	Use
Table	Data arranged in vertical columns under headings	Display numeric or non-numeric data
Chart	Display of relationships plotted on other than a coordinate system (pie or flow chart)	Representation of data showing cause and effect relationships
Graph	Data arranged by plotting a set of points on a coordinate system (bar or line graph)	Representation of the relationship between two variables usually shows a comparison, trend or change over time
Diagram	Sketches or drawings of parts of an item or the steps in a process	Used to represent mechanical parts, exploded views, procedures or schematics
Photograph	Documents actual device	Provides an overall view or a close up
Sample	The real thing	To display the actual object under consideration

Table 10-1: Summary of Devices as Compared by Feature and Use

Tables are systematic arrangements of data, usually in vertical columns under headings. Tables are used to display numeric or non-numeric data. Table 1 is an example of a non-numeric table. This format facilitates ready reference and allows for a condensed presentation of information. Data presented in a tabular format allows the reader to see relationships not easily viewed in text form. Tables are appropriately used to supplement text but are always labelled so that they stand alone. They may be simple or complex but tables generally have the following features: (1) a title which identifies the information presented, (2) headings that identify sub-divisions of data, and (3) data divided into parts so that it can be easily separated. Table 10-2 is an example of a table displaying numeric data.

Alloy	Tensile Strength in psi
1020 CRS	62,500
1030 CRS	73,650
1045 CRS	85,000
1050 CRS	91,500
1060 CRS	99,450

Table 10-2: Tensile Data for Various Alloys of Steel Tested under Standard Laboratory Conditions

Charts are often similar to tables in appearance and use. A chart is a visual display of data showing cause and effect relationships. The terms chart and graph are frequently used interchangeably. A chart may be thought of as a device used to show relationships but not plotted on a coordinate system. Two examples of charts are the pie chart and the flow chart. A pie chart depicts the relationship of the whole to all of its parts. This is normally done by dividing a circle proportionally according to the percentage of the data presented. Figure 10-1 is an example of a pie chart. Notice that it has a caption that explains what it is and labels that explain all parts clearly.

Another common type of chart used to organize information is the flow chart. A flow chart illustrates a process from beginning to end and moves or flows from event to event. This helps to represent the progressive nature of a process. Figure 10-2 is an example of a flow chart. Notice that the figure caption explains fully what is being represented and that all components are clearly labeled.

Other charts, like the organization chart, are very important but they are outside of the present discussion.

A graph is a more complex form of a chart in that data are plotted against a set of points on a coordinate system. A graph depicts relationships between two or more variables. Graphs usually show comparisons, trends or change over time and may take different forms. Two common ones are the bar graph (Figure 10-3) and the line graph

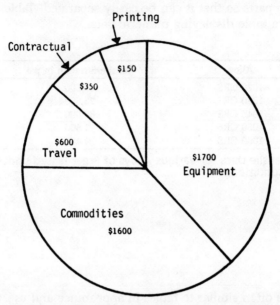

Figure 10-1: Research and Development Costs for Project Mole by Budget Line Item, 1986.

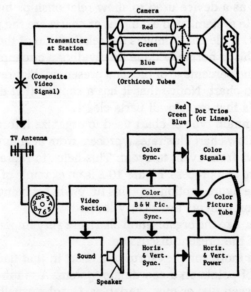

Figure 10-2: How a Color Television Works from John M. Lannon, *Technical Writing*, 3rd Ed., Figure 13-10, p. 270. Copyright @ by John M. Lannon. Reprinted by permission of Little Brown and Co.

(Figure 10-4). They are similar in that they both (1) have a particular scale and (2) are labeled appropriately.

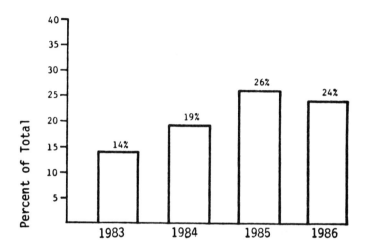

Figure 10-3: Incidence of Component Failure as a Percentage of the Total by Year.

Frequently during technical research, numeric data are supplemented with diagrams, photographs and samples. Each has the potential to enhance a presentation by focusing visual attention. The old adage that, "a picture is worth a thousand words" applies in this case. Whenever possible, sketches, drawings and photographs should be used to document the research process. Quantitative data is often enhanced with diagrammatic or photographic information. This is particularly true when one wishes to show evolutionary change, catastrophic failure, or document a series of developments that have been tried. Photography may be particularly useful to assist in the interpretation of results. The photographs taken during the space shuttle Challenger's lift-off and subsequent disaster caused scientists to investigate the right booster rocket seal.

Diagrams are sketches or drawings of parts of an item or the steps in a process. A diagram might depict an exploded view of a complex mechanical part such as the one depicted in Figure 10-5. A diagram

175

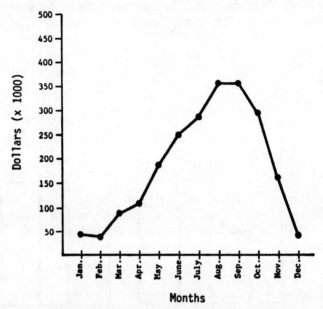

Figure 10-4: Projection of Research Expenditures by Month for 1987.

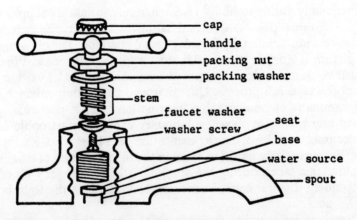

Figure 10-5: A Typical Faucet in Exploded View from John M. Lannon. *Technical Writing*, 3rd Ed., Figure 13-11, p. 271. Copyright @ by John M. Lannon. Reprinted by permission of Little Brown and Co.

may also illustrate complex circuitry through the use of an electrical schematic.

Photographs are sometimes used to document a process. They are particularly well suited to provide the "big picture" or a close-up view of some smaller element. In failure analysis, photographs are essential for documenting the overall appearance of certain parts and the close-up view of certain others.

Samples are frequently used to show new products, materials and components. They can easily be passed around, displayed or attached to a report.

The overall purpose of this section has been to describe how data collected during technical research can be organized. The major organizational devices discussed were tables, charts, graphs, diagrams, photographs and samples.

The discussion has focused on compilation systems that might be used in technical research. It is important also to understand the necessity of documenting the information collection process. This documentation can take many forms including notebooks or logs. The research notebook is a complete anecdotal record of the research process. It may be an outline of activities and events or a written narrative detailing the step-by-step process used. It frequently contains notes from texts and other reports that have been examined. The significance of documentation cannot be overstressed. Maintenance of good documentation insures integrity in a process that is ever changing. Once data have been compiled and documented, a written research report can be prepared.

THE WRITTEN RESEARCH REPORT

The ability to communicate effectively is an essential skill necessary for all technical personnel. Olsen notes that:

> Scientists and engineers may be technically brillant, and creative, but unless they can convince coworkers and supervisors of their worth, the technical skills will be unnoticed, unappreciated, and unused. In a word, if technical people cannot communicate to others what they are doing and why it is important, it is they and their excellent technical skills that will be superfluous. From this perspective, communications skills are not just handy; they are critical tools for success, even survival, in "real-world" environments (Olsen, p 3).

Olsen also describes the skills needed in technical communication. He states that, "communicators should understand the situation, uses, and audiences for a given communication and write for those audiences and uses; that they should have clear organization and logical reasoning; that they should write clear and concise sentences; and that they should follow the standard conventions for grammar, punctuation, and other mechanics" (p 9).

The written research report must be directed toward the intended audience with specific goals in mind. Three audiences that will be discussed are: (1) the researchers within the company, (2) the corporate management within an organization, and (3) external technical organizations and societies. Regardless of the audience, several common themes will be present. The extent of presentation, or emphasis, will be determined by the audience to be addressed. The common themes are (1) statement of and need for the problem, (2) expected outcomes or goals, (3) review of research procedures, (4) presentation of findings, (5) summary and conclusions, (6) bibliography and (7) appendices. An overview of each possible audience will be presented. Table 10-3 presents a summary of emphasis and goal by audience.

Audience	Emphasis of Presentation	Goal
Company Researchers	Findings, summary, conclusion and implications	Keep colleagues appraised of research effort. Stimulate further investigation
Company Management	Summary and implications	Inform or persuade. Present the "bottom line"
Professional Associations	Overall process, strengths and weaknesses, implications for further study	Stimulate further research, knowledge sharing

Table 10-3: Summary of Target Audiences Contrasting Emphasis of Presentation and Goals

Report to Company Researchers

The most common technical report is written for distribution to other researchers in the company. Most corporations engage in technical research to enhance their profitability. Research results are generally proprietary information not intended for distribution outside the corporation. As such, these reports tend to be written according to a company or corporate standard. The purpose of this report is to keep all researchers appraised of the details of ongoing projects. Emphasis in this type of report is on (1) the nature of the problem under investigation, (2) the variables controlled and manipulated and (3) the research questions addressed, and (4) the findings, summary and conclusions. The report also contains an outline of the procedures followed, including a description of the population, instruments used, data collection devices and data analysis techniques. Only essential documents and a brief list of pertinent references are included.

Report to Company Management

The second audience for a technical research report is corporate management. This group is not usually interested in the intimate details of how the research was conducted. The information presented would focus on findings, summary and conclusions. Corporate management is interested in the "bottom line" because they must consider the research findings and determine the appropriateness of further study and/or product development. In this light, the written report presented to the management group should present data objectively. If the project has positive implications for the company, a persuasive tone should be used to present the written report.

Reporting to Technical Organizations and Societies

The third audience is members of national or international research and technical societies. This audience is generally reached through reports and scientific journals which conform to acceptable scholarly standards. Journals have published guidelines for authors that include substantive information on form, style and content. The components of a typical journal report are:

1. A problem statement with its associated components.
2. An identification of the variables being controlled and manipulated.
3. The research questions or outcomes being examined.
4. An explanation for the need of the study placing it in the context of national or international arena.
5. A list of assumptions and limitations.
6. Definitions for terms not generally known.
7. A description of the research procedures used including the delineation of population and subjects.
8. An explanation of the research design selected.

9. A listing of specialized instrumentation.

10. An explanation of the data collection devices and procedures.

11. A discussion of the data analysis processes used.

In the preparation of the written research report, several stylistic conventions are frequently followed regardless of the audience. One such convention is to write in the third person which means the writer never uses "I" or "we" in the report. Phrases like, "the author discovered", or "the group concluded" are used.

Another convention is to write reports in the past tense. One frequent problem in technical reports is the mixing of tenses. Consistency should be maintained throughout the report.

A third convention requires using an "objective" presentation of the information. The report should be presented as if written by an impartial third party observer. The only place in the technical research report for subjective comment is in the conclusions and summary. Even then, the conclusions should be related directly to the findings deduced from the data presented.

Once a research report is written, dissemination may be appropriate. The dissemination of information related to technical research is generally governed by company policy. These policies are based upon a "need to know." In other words, if a person has a need to know certain information to function more effectively in his or her job, then it would be possible to obtain the report. Because of tremendous competition in industry today, the vast majority of corporate technical research information is not shared outside of the corporation and its availability within the company is restricted. In fact, industrial espionage is a multi-billion dollar business in the world today. Corporations usually control information dissemination very carefully and a breach of this confidence is considered a very serious matter.

THE ORAL REPORT

The written report is frequently accompanied by a formal presentation to management. A formal presentation might also be presented to a group external to the corporation, such as a scholarly society. Regardless of the target group, the verbal presentation is a very powerful medium to explain the technical research results. The verbal report may have different purposes. Two of the most common purposes are to inform and to persuade. The former is aimed at creating a level of understanding relative to the topic in question. It is generally succinct and highly objective. The latter, persuasion, is perhaps the more common purpose. Objective persuasion is presenting the findings of the research in such a way as to encourage further study, apply the findings in a certain area, interest others in further development or encourage the commercialization of a product. Further elaboration on each of the aforementioned topics is provided as this is a very powerful medium frequently used in companies and corporations.

One use of persuasion in a verbal presentation is to encourage further research. This type of presentation is a "progress report." The presentation is aimed at convincing management that progress has been made, that results are inconclusive and further study is necessary. Since management is always cost conscious, the benefits of continued study will be enumerated. Another use of the verbal persuasion presentation is to convince management that the findings of the technical research should be applied. This might take the form of building a prototype or using the information in a production environment. A third use of verbal presentation is to encourage further development work. Finally, the persuasive presentation is used to convince management that some development warrants commercial attention. This could be in the area of patent development and application or the formalization of a new product idea. The verbal presentation is a powerful medium for informing and persuading management relative to the findings resulting from technical research.

Once the purpose of the report has been identified, as either information or persuasion, development may begin. The first step in developing the report is to determine the nature of the audience to be addressed. Another way to think of this step is to ask the question, "Who will the presentation be informing or persuading?" Asking the question may seem trite, but many good ideas have fallen by the wayside due to ineffective communication with the audience. Next, develop a list of the specific objectives and points that will be addressed in the verbal presentation. Are the objectives and points identified in keeping with the overall purpose of the presentation? Will the audience relate to the points addressed? If the answer to these questions is yes, proceed. If not, then revise the points to be presented. A word of caution is offered at this point. Minimize the number of objectives to three or four. Remember, the overall purpose of the presentation is information or persuasion. If too much information is presented, confusion may reign. After carefully considering these issues, the development of the presentation may begin in earnest.

Any good presentation, written or oral, should have three essential components: an introduction, a body and a conclusion. Another way to conceptualize these components is that the introduction is where one, "tells the audience what you are going to tell them", the body is where "one tells them" and the conclusion is where one "tells them what one told them." Authors vary in their approach to preparing the introduction, followed by the body or text and then the conclusion. Others prefer to begin with the body or text and then write the introduction and conclusion afterwards. The process followed by the author does not matter so long as the major components are addressed. A brief elaboration of each of the three major components follows.

The introduction should provide an overview of the entire presentation. This should include the overall purpose of the presentation and the objectives to be addressed. The scope of the presentation should be delimited. It is helpful to tell the audience what the presentation will not address. Finally, if the presentation involves multiple speakers, movement from one place to another, or special media or hand-out materials, alert the audience to these things in the introduction.

The text or body is the "heart" of the presentation. This is where the speaker operationalizes the objectives to be presented. In the development of the body or text consider the following: (1) sequencing of objectives, (2) number of points related to each objective, (3) interrelationship among objectives and (4) the allocation of time. In the sequencing of objectives there may be a logical arrangement or progression from one to another. It may be that some component is particularly familiar to the audience and that presenting it first helps to fix the audience's attention. Limit the number of points discussed per objective to a maximum of four and summarize frequently so that the audience will be able to follow the presentation. Do not assume that the audience will automatically see relationships among points being made. Finally, consider time carefully. Time is of the essence and the speaker has the opportunity to use time to emphasize the points of greatest significance.

Once the body is developed, the summary or conclusion may be written. The summary is extremely important and its significance is frequently overlooked in the development of a presentation. Remember, recency, frequency and intensity are key variables in people remembering what they hear. The summary will be the last part of the presentation heard by the audience (recency). If the summary is a reiteration of the text then the audience will have heard it before (frequency). The manner in which the major points are summarized, for example use of voice and special effects, can impact remembering (intensity). In planning the summary, be sure to " tell them what you told them" but emphasize the significant elements that should be in the forefront of their thinking.

Rarely would one prepare an entire presentation and then ask, "What visual aids and media are needed to enhance the presentation?" Normally one would be thinking about media as the presentation was being developed. However, for the purpose of this paper it will be dealt with separately. Remember, the overall purpose of the presentation is to inform or persuade. Use whatever means are at your disposal to accomplish the mission. Merely talking to people is not an effective means of communications. The greater the sensory involvement, the greater the opportunities for learning. Talk to them? Yes, but reinforce the presentation with visually stimulating information as well. Visual aids work in several ways to improve the oral report. They:

1. Increase the reader's interest and focus attention.
2. Provide a means of setting off significant data.
3. Condense information.
4. Simplify the interpretation of data.

For example, summarize key points on an overhead transparency and refer to it as each point is discussed. Use charts, graphs, slides, photographs and objects to reinforce the points being discussed. The key idea to remember is "appeal to as many senses as possible."

SUMMARY

The overall purpose of this chapter was to describe the manner in which the results of technical research are reported. This discussion involved the organization of the results, the written report and presenting the oral report. The key elements of each were discussed. However, several common themes persist throughout. First, understand your purpose. Second, know your audience. Third, be well prepared.

The manner in which technical research is reported may be critical to the overall success of a project. Research well done but poorly reported will rarely attract attention.

BIBLIOGRAPHY

Anderson, P., Brockman, J. and Miller, C. *New Essays in Technical and Scientific Communications and Practices.* Farmingdale, New York: Baywood Pub. Co., 1983.

Reporting the Results

Brusaw, C., Alred, G. and Oliu, W. *Handbook of Technical Writing*. New York: St. Martin's Press, 1982.

Houp, K. W. and Pearsall, T. E. *Reporting Technical Information*. New York: Glencoe Press, 1973.

Lannon, J. M. *Technical Writing*. 3rd ed. Boston: Little Brown, 1985.

Mathes, J. C. and Stevenson, D. D. *Designing Technical Reports*. Indianapolis: Bobbs-Merrill, 1976.

Morgan, M. and Journet, D., Eds. *Research in Technical Communication: A Bibliographical Source Book*. Westpoint, Connecticut: Greenwood Press, 1985.

Odell, L. and Goswami, D. *Writing in Nonacademic Settings*. New York: Guilford, 1985.

Olsen, L. A. & Huckin, T. N. *Principles of Communication for Science and Technology*. New York: McGraw Hill, 1983.

Turner, M. T. *Technical Writing: A Practical Approach*. Reston, Virgina: Reston Publishing Co., 1984.

VanTil, W. *Writing for Professional Publications*. Boston: Allyn and Bacon, Inc., 1981.

CHAPTER 11

Evaluating and Applying the Results

by Max E. Kanagy

Sub-Topics:
- Evaluating Research for Development
- Applying the Results
- Summary

The previous chapters focused on technical research. The authors have defined, placed in perspective, modeled, identified and explained the components for conducting technical research. This chapter presents the factors that management should consider in using the results of the research. They may use the findings to (1) develop a marketable product, (2) postpone a decision or (3) terminate further work on a given project. When the decision is to develop a project, the development will include all the activities necessary to convert the research results into a marketable product. These activities include product engineering, reliability testing, production and process planning, test marketing, and organizing for production, marketing and servicing.

Corporate management is responsible for (1) planning a specific set of actions to implement the research findings, (2) postponing a definitive action or (3)canceling any further work. The criteria for making these decisions must be related to the corporate goals, existing technology resources available and marketing projections.

The technical research report becomes very significant in this setting. This report is the primary written information on which many managers base their product development decisions. These managers use the technical research report to review the goals of the project, accomplishments, potential impact on the corporation, strengths and weaknesses or unresolved topics.

The evaluation of the technical research project should consider its primary goal which can be invention, discovery or innovation. The definition for these terms, as given in Chapter 1, Creativity in the Technologies, will be repeated here.

Invention: a creative mental process through which knowledge and experience are combined over time to produce something which did not exist before and which is represented by some *physical* form, *social* form or *mental* concept.

Discovery: the process of observation and recognition of phenomena which were inherent in the nature of things but unknown before.

Innovation: the process of refining and improving that which is already created and/or established.

The results of these types of research are inputs to the development process which is defined as:

Development: the process of using known methods and procedures of creating new methods and procedures for the purpose of evolving an invention or innovation from *initial concept to commercial application*.

Technical research directed toward invention creates a more complex set of problems during the development phase than innovation research. Inventive research is often referred to as "technology driven" while innovative research is regarded as "market driven." The inventive or technology driven research is focused on connecting experience and knowledge to advance the technology. It has little relationship to a market. It may be a technical success and a marketing failure (Finkin, p. 39).

The inventive process and associated development does not move in a linear path from research, to development, to production and finally marketing. Instead, the inventive path is circuitous as modeled in Figure 11-1 by Kline (pp. 37-38). There is direct linkage between research and invention and research and marketing. Current knowledge is affected by research findings and in turn has an effect on market findings, invention, design, production and marketing. Each of the five functions link with each other in a well modeled development process.

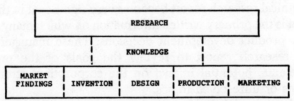

Figure 11-1: Kline's Chain Linked Model Showing the Relationships of Research, Invention, Innovation and Production (Kline, pp. 37-39).

Inventions are on the cutting edge of technology. They create a supply which results in creating a demand. The ability to estimate expenses required to solve technical problems is limited. Similarly, predicting production problems for an invention are very difficult.

Innovative or market-driven research is often smaller in scope than inventive research. Even if the research is fairly complex, the refinement nature of the research is defined specifically with fewer unforeseen difficulties than inventive research. Innovative research is often "market-based" or generated by communication between marketing personnel and customers. Marketing managers have a better prediction of the impact of the research and development because the impetus for the project came from marketing activities.

The successful transaction of the technical research results in a product, process or service. It is based on the management of the project and the solving of technical problems. Management problems focus on raw materials and equipment costs, production costs, development and production space, skills by production people, scheduling and finances. Technical problems include the design of the product, engineering, projected life cycle, process selection or design and material selection (Finkin, pp. 42-43).

EVALUATING RESEARCH FOR DEVELOPMENT

The research report requires action by management to consider developing the findings into a product, postponing a decision or canceling any further work. When management elects to use the research results to develop a marketable product, process or service, they must consider the technical, economic and marketing factors that impinge upon the decision.

Management Considerations

Management considerations are fundamental in developing a product. These considerations are a result of a company's internal strengths and weaknesses and its external environment. The corporate goals, fiscal condition and ability to develop products are significant internal factors. Externally, the nature of government regulations, marketing issues, competitor actions, suppliers' capabilities, alternative products, potential products and marketing position are all significant factors (Bedell, pp. 32-35).

Internal Factors

The corporate goals and strategy for reaching those goals should impact managers' decisions regarding the development of technical research findings. The nature of the goals is extremely significant. A corporation may decide to diversify into new product lines (electric shavers to electric chain saws). Another company may capture a larger share of the market through product line extension (four styles of vacuum sweepers - upright, self-propelled upright, tank, and broom - rather than two: upright and tank). The criteria for selecting projects for development would be affected in a very significant manner if the first company had wanted to manufacture only electric shavers, or if the second company had wanted to have a wider range of products for use around the home (Balachandra and Raelin, p. 33).

Most corporations desire some diversification in products. The development of products that are too dissimilar in manufacturing process or customer base is often outside the corporate goals and capabilities. The electric shaver/electric chain saw example illustrates products that are dissimilar in size and function. They are similar with respect to using universal electric motors.

A change in corporate goals to diversify resulted in a decision by Celanese Research Company to revive a project in the 1980's that they had previously abandoned. In 1972, the company decided not to continue the development of polybibenginaidazola (PBI), a plastic material with high thermal heat stability and low heat transfer. In 1980, the company saw the need to diversify. This along with additional markets for PBI and the availability of key raw materials resulted in the company having a PBI production plant on-line by 1983 (Sprague, pp. 26-29).

Corporate growth projections and their demands on capital are other considerations. A company in a period of expansion may have other demands on its capital and may not want to fund product development. However, if cash flow is extremely positive, funding new product development may be appropriate. If company sales or market share are shrinking, it may be time to develop new products to regain a portion of the market or a share of a different market.

The fiscal condition of a corporation may make development of a given product impossible because it does not have the financial resources. The product development process may take up to ten years, which makes the financial requirements large. For example, in the 1970's, Lear spent millions of dollars in an unsuccessful attempt to develop a steam-driven automobile.

A corporation may still decide not to undertake a development project because there is limited demand for the product or the demand for a product may be high but for a very short period of time. The corporation must cover the developmental costs through product sales within the company's established payback period (Bedell, p. 34). This was a major decision in the original Celanese Research Company's decision not to produce PBI.

The impact of the new product on existing products and product lines needs to be identified. Will the new product complement, compete with or displace established products? When a new product displaces an existing one, the new product must produce the same or greater profit. Products which complement existing products should fill gaps in the company's product line. Products which compete with the existing products of the company should be developed when they will strongly compete with competitors' products. Most of the sales of the product should come from the competitors' market share.

A corporation's ability to market a new product is still another consideration. An excellent product without marketing does not generate sales. A new product line representing a major diversification will present a major marketing challenge to the corporation. The existing marketing organization may be inadequate to the task and additional personnel or distributors, or a new marketing division, may be needed. A manufacturer of automotive test equipment faced this type of decision when they broadened their product line. They had been a major supplier of automotive test equipment marketed directly to automotive dealerships, independent garages and vocational schools. They decided to produce a line of test equipment for the do-it-yourself mechanic. This new line was marketed through retail stores and sales catalogs, resulting in creating a new marketing strategy and division (Finkin, pp. 44-46).

Servicing a new product is another relevant issue in developing new products. Training service personnel for new products adds costs to the developmental process. These costs, whether paid for by the company or the distributors, become part of the retail price of the product.

It is common for development projects to compete for limited financial resources within a corporation. The projects that survive this competition usually meet the internal factors or criteria for evaluating technical research (Bedell, p. 34).

External Factors

External factors which impinge on economic considerations are growth patterns in the economy, government regulations and policies, the potential market, resource availability, competitor áctions and patents. These factors should be considered before embarking on a product development project.

The ability of a corporation to plan for the future is limited, especially when influencing forces come from outside the organization. It is important for the corporation to identify the most critical external forces that will affect the company for the next three to five years. These influences could include interest rates, new products or marketing strategies by the competition and government embargoes. The corporation should identify the significant external forces that are projected to increase, decrease or stay the same over the next three- to five-year period (Bedell, pp. 32-35).

Government regulations have a major affect on product development. Specific areas of the economy are more controlled than others. The Federal Aviation Administration (FAA), Federal Communications Commission (FCC) and the Food and Drug Administration (FDA) are three important agencies that influence the economy. In 1986, changes in FDA regulations regarding over-the-counter sales of medicines in capsules affected several companies adversely, even though most of them had no specific problems with their capsules. Another example is the Environmental Protection Agency's (EPA) automotive emission regulations (Bedell, pp. 34-35).

The costs for product development must be weighed against the potential market demand. There may be a great need for a product, but, because of a low market demand, most corporations are not willing to fund the research and development costs. The demand for most invented (entirely new or technology-based) products will have to be developed. The level of this demand is extremely difficult to predict. For example, xerography and digital computers had extremely low market projections. These are classic examples of the difficulty in projecting market needs for inventions. The market for these products had to be created, and it was created with great success (Finkin, p. 39).

Innovative research (market demand) is the opposite of the inventive form. The buyer is aware of the want or need. The more relevant question is if the manufacturer can produce the product at a price that the consumer will pay. As production of a product rises, the selling price to the customer tends to decrease. Examples of this phenomenon include pocket calculators, xerography equipment, video cassette recorders and personal computers. This phenomenon has been especially true with integrated circuit-based equipment (Finkin, p. 40).

The availability of raw materials and standard parts is another constraint. Domestic-produced materials will generally be available unless the only source is a competitor. A more serious problem occurs when the source for given material lies outside the sphere of control or influence of the United States. Availability of many materials, such as industrial diamonds, tin, nickel and petroleum are influenced by foreign nations. Vendors for toxic materials may also be difficult to find. Another important consideration is the availability of personnel to manufacture a product or deliver a service. The personnel must possess requisite knowledge and skills or be willing to participate in training programs. Both raw materials and personnel must be available to produce the product once it is developed.

Competition in certain industries is a significant factor to consider. A corporation must be aware of its competitors' plans and its ability to retain or improve its share of the market. New competitors in an existing market can change the relationships among the original manufacturers. IBM's entry into the personal computer field had a major impact on a number of microcomputer companies (Roehrich, pp. 63-65).

The relationship of a potential development project to the patent process is of prime concern. The patent must be broad enough to protect the originality of the product from competitors. Concern should be given to the extent to which the competitors can circumvent the patent. The patent process should be started early to allow time for market testing.

The use of balanced judgment is essential. Corporate officials will never have all the data suggested in these criteria. The various managers will have to use their experience and "feel" in making certain decisions. Each manager must be careful not to let his/her specialty overly influence the final decision. For example, an accountant should not place disproportionate emphasis on payback forecasts. Likewise, the production manager cannot ignore the return on investment. Exercising balanced judgment is a significant responsibility.

Technical Considerations

The technical nature of a product is significant to the company when development activities are considered. Products have a life cycle with some similarity to that of living organisms. Computers are now in their fifth generation of hardware. Bicycles, automobiles and airplanes are middle-aged. The manned space program was in its infancy in the sixties and robotics in the seventies. Mature industries tend to show a spurt of innovative research and development just before they are replaced. Sailing ships showed such a spurt just as they were being replaced by steam-driven vessels. A product sales life cycle includes four major phases: establishment, growth, maturation and decline (Bedell, pp. 30-31). See Figure 11-2.

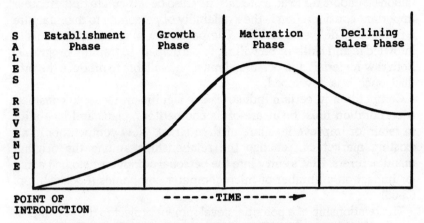

Figure 11-2: Product Sales Life (Cleland and King, p. 239).

The establishment phase has components of technical research, development and introduction of the product into the market. The development component includes engineering, reliability testing, production planning and test marketing. The actual time values for establishment, growth, maturation and decline phases vary considerably with different products. Some fad products pass through all phases in less than a year. Pet rocks and topical posters are examples. Citizen band (CB) radio market matured quickly in comparison to many products. Other products require more than a decade to pass through the cycle. A few products such as Monopoly® and the bicycle nearly defy the cycle. As development costs increase and product life cycles decrease, development risks increase.

A fundamental goal for management is developing a successful product, process or service which involves solving technical problems. If these problems are in technologies that are understood, the probability for success is high. This is especially true for companies that have a limited engineering staff. The chances of success in development are improved if the technical problems can be clearly identified and defined. Serious technical problems in a project should be red flagged, especially when the technical problems are not clearly defined or are in technologies that are not understood.

192

A common concern of management in evaluating projects for development is discerning when project proponents (project champions) have a *personal* interest in seeing a project developed in contrast to a project champion who has a *professional* interest. The personal interest that is closely linked to one's ego, survival or promotion often reduces objectivity and recognition of technical problems and their severity. The professional project champion is often appointed to guide a project through the development component because of his or her support, objectivity and recognition of the technical obstacles that still need to be conquered.

During this establishment phase, product designs are often in transition and engineering changes are common. Companies have found that CAD/CAM have provided real benefits and a competitive edge as they respond to the need for product changes. CAD makes it easier to modify designs while CAM allows many manufacturing processes to be quickly changed.

Materials, personnel, facilities and equipment resources required for production are all technical considerations strongly related to the product development decision. These production-oriented technical questions need to be answered. They relate to the physical space required to develop and produce the product. The type and cost of equipment should be a major concern. The production equipment and its maintenance may be a severe financial burden. A shortage of trained production personnel may be an additional problem. Serious problems with materials, personnel, facilities or equipment availability may be reason enough to abandon a development project (Drucker, p. 12).

When the physical space, equipment and personnel to produce a newly-approved product do not exist, lead time is needed to construct facilities, purchase equipment and hire or train personnel. The lead time and costs for these activities must be considered before establishing product availability dates.

Managerial and technical factors that were significant to the success or failure of previous development projects should be analyzed. When management is aware of the reasons for past successes and failures, they will be able to make better decisions about current product development proposals (Finkin, pp. 41-43).

APPLYING THE RESULTS

The management decision to develop a product is not the last decision to be made. A decision of major importance is how the corporation should be organized to enhance the development process. Time is of significance in getting a product to the marketplace. The timing for the entire product development project could be upset if one department moves more slowly than the others. The organization strategy will affect the potential impact of the product on the company. Proper organization is a key to insure that all departments meet stated deadlines. Four common organizational approaches for a development project are: (1) project director, (2) task force, (3) laissez-faire system or a (4) combination of these.

Project Director

The director, who may be the project champion, has a great deal of authority and reports to the president of the corporation. He or she is the planning, coordinating, and communicating center for the research, engineering, production, marketing, and finance divisions. He or she has an overall viewpoint of the corporation, its potential and its capabilities.

Task Force

The task force is a group representing the various divisions and may include the originator of the idea. The task force is the focal point for planning, coordination and communication. The task force is responsible for guiding the developmental project through its stages. Since the task force members represent specific divisions, they have legitimate authority with their groups. The task force typically solves problems with persuasion, but often has authority to direct an activity within the budgetary limits. It is common to have the developmental task forces report to the president. When the originator of the idea is a member of the task force, he or she brings his or her enthusiasm to the group and acts as the project champion.

Laissez-Faire System

The laissez-faire system is in direct contrast to the director or task force approach. In this system, each group performs its function without

194

special leadership or input from a particular group or individual. Each division shares its information with the other divisions. It is often difficult to find a project champion in this organization style unless an individual appoints himself or herself.

Combination Approach

The combination method uses components of all three systems to administer project development. In this system (1) a task force screens projects and sets policy, (2) coordinators guide the project and (3) the various departments complete their tasks with considerable autonomy (Field, pp. 48-53).

The different methods fit different companies with different formal and informal operating procedures. In all of these organizational structures, the departments must openly share information and cooperate with each other. The personnel in each department must command respect from the other departments. Teamwork is the key. People make organizations work effectively. The organizational structure can only help or hinder the process (Finkin, p. 42).

SUMMARY

The information gathered during a technical research project must be evaluated and applied. This information is often presented to management through a technical report. The information in this report becomes the basis for the management and technical parameters of the development activity. Once the development project has been approved, based upon these parameters, an organization structure appropriate for the product and company must be established.

BIBLIOGRAPHY

Balachandra, R. and Raelin, J. "When to Kill That R&D Project." *Research Management*, July-August, 1984, 27, pp. 30-33.

Bedell, R. J. "Terminating R&D Projects Prematurely." *Research Management*, July-August 1983, 26, pp. 32-35.

Cleland, D. I. and King, W. R. *Systems Analysis and Project Management*. New York: McGraw-Hill Book Company, 1983.

Cooper, R. "New Product Performance and Product Innovation Strategies." *Research Management*, May-June 1986, 29, pp. 17-25.

Drucker, P. F., "Principles of Successful Innovation." *Research Management*, September-October 1985, 28, pp. 10-15.

Evaluating and Applying the Results

Field, J. A. "'Techniques for Utilizing Research." *Achieving Full Value from R&D Dollars.* New York: American Management Association, Inc., 1962.

Finkin, E. F., "Developing & Managing New Products." *Journal of Business Strategy*, Spring 1983, 3, (4), pp. 38-46.

Kline, S. J., "Innovation Is Not a Linear Process." *Research Management*, July-August 1985, 28, (4), pp. 36-45.

Roehrich, R. L., "The Relationship Between Technological and Business Innovation." *Journal of Business Strategy*, Fall 1984, 5, pp. 60-73.

Sprague S. "An Industrial Innovation that Was Nearly Shelved." *Research Management*, May-June 1986, 29, pp. 26-29.

CHAPTER 12

Creativity in the Technologies a Search for Insight — Inventors and Inventions

by Paul W. DeVore

Sub-Topics:

- Observations by Inventors and Innovators on the Technical Research Process
- Observations by Managers on the Technical Research Process
- Selected Inventions and Innovations
- Summary

There is much confusion and controversy about creativity in the technologies. One of the reasons is the extremely broad spectrum of activities ranging across basic research and invention to product design, technical research and day-to-day research related to product production and operation. Comprehending the essence of technical research is further clouded by the fact that many of the day-to-day operations in the design and development of products and systems utilize information and techniques that are already known. There is still the myth that new technical means, inventions, innovations and products evolve from science. Many believe that there is a linear progression starting with a scientific theory and progressing through a number of orderly steps, ending in a new device, product or procedure. There is no evidence to support this view. There is considerable evidence that the creative process lacks order, in the sense that the creative process is linear and descends from science.

This is the reason why we should be concerned about technical research and the creative process in the technologies. It is a complex multifaceted process. More knowledge about the behavior of the process will enable us to enhance the process.

Research about the technical research process has become more important today than ever before. Today we live in a complex, interrelated and constantly industrializing world. Those industries and businesses that desire to compete effectively in the global marketplace must invest in research and product development. Concurrently, those countries that desire to remain economically and politically strong must create environments that enhance creativity in the technologies. They must provide for a continual accumulation of the all-important reservoir of knowledge and people from which new technical means are born. The sustainability of social orders is linked to change, not stagnation. Technical research is an important variable in the health of a society and an understanding of the factors that enhance research and creativity is essential.

The purpose of this chapter is to investigate the technical research process from three perspectives: (1) the individual inventor or researcher, (2) the manager of the research process and (3) selected inventions in several fields of technology. The search will be for those factors that are necessary for technical research to be successful or for an invention or new product design to come about.

Today the problem is more complex than ever before. In years past technical research involved such well known items as: James Watt's separate condenser for the steam engine; Joseph Nicephore Niepce's contributions to photography; Christopher L. Sholes' typewriter; Nicolas Otto and the four-stroke cycle internal combustion engine; the Wright Brothers and the aeroplane; Charles Kettering's self-starter for the automobile; Rudolph Diesel and the compression ignition engine; Wallace Carothers and neoprene; Chester Carlson's xerography; and Johannes Croning and shell molding. Other examples are H. F. Hobbs' automobile transmission; the gyrocompass from the work of A. Kaempfe, E. A. Sperry and S. G. Brown; the frequency modulation (FM) radio by Edwin Armstrong; John Harwood and the self-winding wristwatch; mercury dry-cell by Samuel Ruben; Edwin Land and the polaroid camera; the ballpoint pen from the work of Ladislao and Georg Biro; and tungsten carbide by Karl Schroeter. These and hundreds of other inventions have made significant contributions to the evolution of civilization as we know it and many people are intimately acquainted with these technical developments.

Today the nature of the new technical means is of a different order. Although there appears to be ready acceptance of new technical means, the level of understanding of the way the new technical mean's works or functions is lower. The "working parts" of the technical means of today are less visible, the behavior of the devices or products is more involved and the level of comprehension of the users is less.

The esoteric nature of the current technical means can be illustrated by example. Each year, the editors of *Research and Development* publish a special report which details 100 of the award-winning products, processes, materials and software that came to the market during the preceding year. The award winners are chosen from more than 10,000 entries. Some examples of award winners for 1985 are: Fourier transformer infrared spectrometer; time-resolved imaging X-ray spectrometer; pulsed helium ionization detector electronics system; high performance liquid chromatography system; high voltage, high frequency power static induction transistors; geometric arithmetic parallel processor; error compensation system for computerized numerically controlled machine tools; electric discharge machine; lead-iron phosphate process for high-level radioactive waste disposal; advanced thermoplastic composites; image-processing system (fluorescent microthermography); pyroelectrochemical extraction process; real-time acoustic robot vision system; magnetic wire position transducer; and high-current monochromatic electron gun, among others (*Research and Development*, October 1985).

The above commercial products came from a wide range of research and development (R & D) laboratories which are private, governmental and university. Some are well known laboratories, while others are less well known. Examples are Argonne National Laboratory; Beckman Instruments; Corning Glass Works; Dowell-Schlumberger, Inc.; GTE Laboratories; Isco, Inc.; University of Michigan; National Bureau of Standards; Skantels Corporation; Union Carbide and Zeiss, Carl, Inc.

The products, materials and processes created in the R & D laboratories listed above are the outcomes, the manifestations, of the creative potential of the human mind. Some laboratories and some researchers have been more successful than others. What are the factors that make a difference? There are several ways to pursue this question. One way is to find out what creative people say about the process and to examine given inventions and innovations in detail. Another way is to find out what managers of the process believe to be critical factors. In the sections which follow, the process will be examined from the perspective of the (1) inventors and innovators, (2) managers of technical research and (3) specific inventions and innovations.

OBSERVATIONS BY INVENTORS AND INNOVATORS
ON THE TECHNICAL RESEARCH PROCESS

One of the most significant technical developments that provides the base for the current communication and information evolution was the creation, by Jack St. Clair Kilby of Texas Instruments, of the integrated circuit, patent number 3,138,743— Miniaturized Electronic Circuits. Kilby, in reflecting on himself and his research, volunteered "that is basically what I have always wanted to do, to solve technical problems. It is quite satisfying, extremely satisfying, to go through the process and find a solution that works" (Reid, p. 34). Reid, in his review of Kilby's work, noted also that Kilby learned exactly how the realities of the manufacturing process restricted the complexity of transistorized circuitry (Reid, p. 34).

Richard R. Walton (1985), independent inventor and researcher of Boston, Massachusetts, pioneered the creation of shrinkage control processes for the textile industry. He believes that corporate researchers often play it safe and try for small improvements in their company's existing products rather than risk the creation of a new solution (Walton, personal correspondence). Walton has been highly successful in meeting the needs of the textile industries by coming up with new solutions, by going at risk, and by seeing things differently. By doing so he has researched and created an automatic cloth pick-up and feeder to sewing machines, a device for feeding flat goods in laundries, a portable washing machine for developing countries, improved agitators for washing machines, a device for increasing the absorbency of non-wovens and imparting drape, and machines for creping and elasticizing paper. Walton believes that involvement, intensity and the subconscious are critical to problem solving associated with technical research. Many researchers mention the importance of getting away from the problem and letting the subconscious work.

John V. Atanasoff credits his subconscious as being critical in his work. This resulted in the development of the regenerative memory which made a significant contribution to the development of the ENIAC computer by J. Presper Eckert and John W. Manchly. Atanasoff's work at the University of Iowa required an improved calculating instrument to solve linear operational equations, including partial differential system and integral equations. His search was for a "practical solution to practical problems" (Gardner, p. 12).

Walton and Atanasoff each stressed the importance in technical research of identifying the true problem and staying with it. Persistence is the hallmark of success in technical research. Walton (1985) believes that "continuity and determination are more important than anything else." He also stresses the need for the inventor to "isolate everything from his mind except the current project." Walton believes that "almost by definition the independent researcher,innovator or inventor has little regard for social and textbook rules; you can't schedule ideas and something about a large company militates against creativity" (Walton, personal correspondence).

Samuel Ruben, the inventor of the mercuric oxide cell and major contributor to numerous electrochemical developments, found in his research that "the systematic use of existing knowledge is used to solve the unknown" and that "the development of concepts is built upon previous insights in a step-by-step process." For Ruben, his motivation and drive were derived from the realization of industrial needs as was the case with Austin Elmore who said: "Everything I invented was created because it was needed" (Associated Press, 1985). Ruben also believes that an inner sense of direction, together with imaginative thinking, is necessary for the actualization of a concept. Self-motivation is also a necessary factor to catalyze the generation of imaginative concepts. Ruben believes the researcher is motivated by the intellectual excitement of the thought process and will resist adverse premature opinions of others who lack imaginative thinking (Ruben, 1981).

The researchers, the problem solvers and the innovators have a number of characteristics as does the process they use. In a special issue of *Varian Associates Magazine* in 1979, the Corporate Communications staff interviewed a number of technical researchers working for Varian in an attempt to gain insight into the process (Himmelman, 1979). One of the primary findings in most research about technical research is stated clearly by Curt Ward of Varian. "Conformists don't invent." From his experience, non-productive researchers or innovators are trapped by "the way it's already been done." The primary problem, though, is the problem. Ward has found that "unless you can define the problem, you'll never get an answer or an invention" (Himmelman, 1979).

Ward and Anderson support the concept of the gestation period mentioned previously. There seems to be an "act of insight." Solutions to problems, according to Ward, "almost always just pop up." Anderson supports this view by saying that "many times the solution just suddenly appears" (Himmelman, 1979).

Mars Hablanian believes that each successful researcher or inventor has a basic ingredient of personality that produces a kind of intellectual delight in solving problems similar to the way Jack Kilby perceived himself. This problem solving interest melds with another characteristic, that of dissatisfaction with doing something the way it has been conventionally done. Al Scott of Varian emphasized the importance of nonconformist, non-conventional factors.

> "In searching for the solution, you see that it won't be solved in conventional ways and look for an unconventional solution. . . . Then, as a result of some other work we were doing, we realized that if we stopped thinking like tube engineers and started thinking like microwave solid state engineers, we might find the answer. It suddenly occurred to us that if we could print an absorber or resonator on a little ceramic substrate, it would be small enough to fit inside the tube. The resonators would absorb all the power at the oscillation frequency and not interfere with the operating band of the tube." (p. 3)

Other researchers at Varian Associates stressed the importance of motivation, immersion in the problem, the intuitive thought process and, perhaps the most critical variable of all, the realization that there is a problem to be solved.

According to Hablanian, those who are successful researchers are people who usually have a tendency for disorganized thinking. He feels that "there is really no systematic way of stimulating the inventive process" (p. 6), a view held by those who do the research and create the innovations.

There are other views held by those responsible for managing research projects which bring to light one of the central issues concerning technical research in a business and industry. How do you create an environment that enhances the productivity of creative minds?

OBSERVATIONS BY MANAGERS ON THE TECHNICAL RESEARCH PROCESS

The search for a magic solution to managing and controlling the technical research process continues almost universally throughout business and industry that invest in research. Managers without technical research experience, often believe that research can be reduced to a sequential, rational process which, if organized properly, would provide a greater return on investment. Those who have investigated the process of technical research, product development and successful product marketing have found the process to be less than orderly. This is particularly true at the innovation/invention end of the technical research spectrum.

The problem is a critical one for business and industry in a highly competitive international market economy. Various estimates place the contribution of technical change at 50 to 65 percent of U.S. economic growth (Alexander, 1982; Ross, 1986). Yet it has been concluded by numerous authorities that the United States is lagging in research and development.

The President's Commission on Industrial Competitiveness stressed a number of factors believed to be important in enhancing the ability of business and industry in the United States to compete. Among the factors stressed were (1) capital resources, (2) human resources and (3) improved international trade and investment policy. Even though these were important elements,

> ... the Commission concluded that the area of *technology* is where we have a current competitive advantage , and where there is the opportunity not only to sustain that advantage but to grow in our leadership (Ross, 1986).

This relationship between creativity in the technologies and economic competitiveness among firms or nations is not new. It is often overlooked by chief executive officers and managers devoid of background and experience in the technologies. There is a tendency to believe that financial management is the panacea and that organization is the secret. There is the belief that if one could just find the "right" organizational structure, the technical research and new product problem would be solved. The reality is that the problem is much more complex. There are many patterns of organization and they vary with the nature of the goals, mission and tasks of technical research. In addition, there are critical interfaces between technical research, product development operations, marketing and sales. Companies such as 3M have recognized the critical nature of these interfaces and have structured their operations to assure linkages among them in what they call a Business Development Unit Organization, BDU (Pearson, 1983).

Roland Schmitt in his analysis of the problems of corporate level research and development believes that the categorization of research into basic versus applied, and market-driven versus technology-driven, have outlived their usefulness. He concluded that "there is no single model appropriate for doing first-rate corporate level R & D," but that there is a way of thinking that makes the different approaches, and their implications, clear (Schmitt, 1985).

Schmitt contrasts two forms of corporate research and development, *generic* and *targeted*. He concludes that:

203

The success of a corporate R & D program becomes visible only in the light of its mission and purpose. If the choice is to adopt a *generic*,* loosely market-coupled approach, then organization requires a strong discipline orientation and close attention to the number and excellence of contributions to the technical literature. If the choice is to adopt a *targeted*,* tightly market-coupled approach, then organization needs a project orientation and must link its reward to ultimate business success (Schmitt, 1985).

Patrick E. Haggerty of Texas Instruments, in one of his lectures at the Salzburg Seminar of Multinational Enterprise, stressed the importance of perceiving innovation in a multi-national company as ranging from basic research, what Schmitt calls generic research, to research in the *make* and *market* functions. Haggerty ascribes Texas Instruments' success to their long-range planning system which is TI's system for managing innovation (Haggerty, 1977). In carrying out the long-range planning system Haggerty recognized the importance of the human factor and,

> "set policies in human terms to motivate employees, to permit them to understand, as much as possible , what the company was attempting to do and why, and to establish as closely as possible parallelism between individual and corporate goals" (Fagenbaum, 1980).

There are those who question the formal product planning process. Thomas J. Peters', *In Search of Excellence*, and Brian Quinn of Dartmouth's Amos Tuch School of Business Administration, maintain that "not a single major product has come from the formal product planning process" (Peters, Summer 1983). Peters, in his study of the innovation process, has concluded that:

> The course of innovation—idea generation, prototype development, contact with initial user, breakthrough to final market—is highly uncertain, to say the least. Moreover, it always will be messy, sloppy, and unpredictable, and this is the important point. It's important because we must learn to design organizations that take into account, explicitly, the irreducible sloppiness of the process and take advantage of it rather than attempt to fight it (Peters, Fall 1983).

Some of the variables in the innovation process that Peters and others have discovered to be important and that challenge conventional wisdom are:

1. New ideas either find champions or they die.

2. Perseverance, not great leaps of insight, is the norm.

---

*Italics, author's.

204

3. Placing cooperation and teamwork above all other desirable traits eliminates the product champions, the ones that have the potential to give a company success.

4. Failure is a normal part of the innovation, product development process.

5. Most advances are incremental and cumulative (Peters, Fall 1983).

The focus of R & D efforts is often directed toward the wrong factors. Too often the belief is that structure and organization will bring results and that people are the problem. Too often the product or research focus is forgotten in blind attempts to make the process work by appointing more committees and reorganizing the departments or divisions. The latter only distances those responsible for the management of the process from the real problems and the real people. Peters has concluded that "American management suffers from an excess of the administrative mentality" (U. S. New and World Report, July 15, 1985).

The "administrative mentality", Peters challenges, surfaced after World War II. He notes that many large enterprises became managed by administrator finance-oriented people. He feels that in business schools, courses on manufacturing and selling were dropped and replaced by courses in finance, accounting and decision science. In many cases, those who are making decisions about products, product design, manufacturing and marketing have never been involved in these central processes of the business enterprise (U.S. News and World Report, July 15, 1985).

Another way of viewing the complex world of technical research is from Freeman's "degree of uncertainty" approach. Freeman proposes that there are qualitative degrees of uncertainty for various types or categories of technical research. Figure 12-1 contains an overview of Freeman's analysis (Freeman, 1974). In reviewing the degrees of uncertainty, it is possible to gain some understanding of the complexity of the technical research paradigm and the many interrelations. Caution is in order since linearity of the process should not be concluded. An interrelated network is more appropriate where there are relationships. Where there are no relationships among any categories of uncertainty, the technical research effort may stand alone at that point in time.

1. True uncertainty	Fundamental research
	Fundamental invention
2. Very high degree of uncertainty	Radical product innovations
	Radical process innovations outside firm
3. High degree of uncertainty	Major product innovations
	Radical process innovations in own establishment or system
4. Moderate uncertainty	New "generations" of established products
5. Little uncertainty	Licensed innovation
	Imitation of product innovations
	Early adoption of established process
6. Very little uncertainty	New "model"
	Product differentiation
	Agency for established product innovation
	Late adoption of established process innovation in own establishment
	Minor technical improvements

Figure 12-1: Degree of Uncertainty Associate with Various Types of Innovation. C. Freeman, *The Economics of Industrial Innovation*, p. 226.

In any analysis of technical research it is critical to clearly state exactly what type of research is being discussed. It may be (1) incremental product performance improvements, (2) the creation of new solutions to existing problems or (3) the creation of wholly new approaches to meeting basic human and social needs.

SELECTED INVENTIONS AND INNOVATIONS

In addition to gaining insight into the creative process of technical research from the perspectives of the researchers and managers, it is possible to obtain an understanding by an analysis of the outcomes of the process: the inventions and products of the creative mind. The nature of the invention or product provides information about the uniqueness and/or complexity of the solution.

The inventions and innovations selected for the purpose of illustrating creativity will represent several fields of technological endeavor. It is not possible to provide a complete case study of each invention or innovation and all the variables related to the "act of insight." This includes the social-cultural environment at the time of the act, the inventor's or researcher's background, education and personality, relation to other preceding research and economic support. All of these variables are important. However, the focus will be on a brief description of each invention or innovation with the interpretation and analysis left to each reader.

Category: Manufacturing

Invention or Innovation — Flush Riveting

Inventor or Innovator — Charles Ward Hall
                               Buffalo, New York, 1935

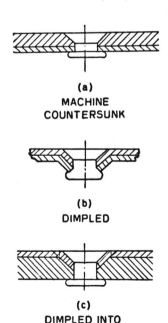

(a)
MACHINE
COUNTERSUNK

(b)
DIMPLED

(c)
DIMPLED INTO
MACHINE COUNTERSUNK

Figure 12-2: Three Basic Types of Flush Riveting from G. Rechton. *Aircraft Riveting Manual*, Addendum I: Riveting Methods, Douglas Aircraft Company, pp. 7, 21 and 26.

Creativity in the Technologies

The development of flush riveting took place primarily in the aircraft industry. As the speed of aircraft increased, the aerodynamic drag of protruding rivets was detrimental to performance of stressed skin aircraft. The obvious answer was to make the rivets flush. As simple as the answer was, it took a long development effort over a considerable period of time. The original work was done by Charles Ward Hall at his Hall Aluminum Aircraft Corporation in Buffalo, New York, in the early 1920's to the 1950's.

The basic stage of development occurred during the second half of the 1930's. Three types of riveting emerged, depending on the sheet thicknesses being riveted: (1) the machine countersunk, (2) the dimpled and (3) the dimpled into machine countersunk. During the early stages of development each aircraft company pursued the problems associated with flush riveting independently. Later standards were adopted and the 100° angle for rivet heads was adopted (Vincenti, 1984).

Category: Communication and Information Systems

Invention or Innovation — Sealed alkaline battery structure embodying mercuric oxide and other depolarizers in primary and secondary cells.

Inventor — Samuel Ruben
Portland, Oregon, 1943

THEORY OF ZINC / MERCURIC OXIDE SYSTEM

Material: Zn / KOH, ZnO, H_2O / HgO.
After solution: Zn / KOH, K_2ZnO_2, H_2O / HgO.
Ionization product of electrolyte: $K^+ + OH^-$, $2K^+ + ZnO_2^{--}$, $H^+ + OH^-$.

	ANODE	CATHODE
Reactions when producing electricity:	$Zn - 2e^- \rightarrow Zn^{++}$	$HgO + H_2O \rightarrow Hg(OH)_2 \rightarrow Hg^{++} + 2OH^-$
	$Zn^{++} + 2OH^- \rightarrow Zn(OH)_2$	$Hg^{++} + 2e^- \rightarrow Hg$ $2OH^- + 2H^+ \rightarrow 2H_2O$
Since electrolyte is saturated with ZnO: $Zn(OH)_2 \rightarrow ZnO + H_2O$		
Electrode end products:	ZnO	Hg

Since the basic electrode reactions are the oxidation of the $Zn - 2e^- \rightarrow Zn^{++}$ and the reduction of the $Hg^{++} + 2e^- \rightarrow Hg^0$ at the cathode, and since water appears at both electrodes, there is no significant change in KOH or H_2O concentration. The over-all chemical reaction for producing 2 Faradays per gram mol of anodic zinc and gram mol of cathodic mercuric oxide is: $Zn + HgO \rightarrow ZnO + Hg$.

Figure 12-3: Theory of Zinc/Mercuric Oxide System, from Samuel Ruben's Lectur for the Metropolitan Section of the *American Electrochemical Society.* February 15, 1966, p. 7.

In 1941, the only commercially available dry cell system for portable communication equipment was the Le Clauche zinc/carbon cell. During World War II, there was an urgent need for transceiver batteries capable of maintaining their voltage on loads, retaining their transmission range and not deteriorating in tropical climates. The solution to the problem was the result of research done by Samuel Ruben. He developed a chemical battery embodying (1) an amalgamated zinc anode, (2) zincated potassium hydroxide electrolyte in an absorbent spacer, (3) a barrier in contact with a consolidate depolarizing mercuric oxide and (4) a graphite cathode. All of these elements were assembled and sealed in a steel container. This development enabled the production of miniature cells for electric watches, implanted cardiac pacemakers, hearing aids and hand-held calculators. (Ruben, 1976).

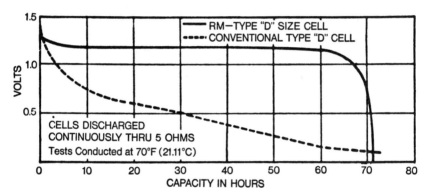

Figure 12-4: Comparison of RM-Type "D" Size Cell to Conventional Type "D" Cell Illustrating Maintenance of a Constant Closed Circuit Potential During Discharge, from Samuel Ruben's Lecture for the Metropolitan Section of the *American Electrochemical Society*. February 15, 1966, p. 8.

Category: Communication and Information Systems

Invention or Innovation — Photographic Product comprising a Rupturable Container Carrying a Photographic Processing Liquid.

Inventor or Innovator — Edwin H. Land
Cambridge, Massachusetts, 1951

The photographic process developed by Edwin H. Land is commonly known as the Polaroid process. It is a product that consists of at least two layers, a photosensitive layer and a base layer for a transfer image and a container that holds a liquid photographic developer. The container is so constructed that it can be ruptured and release its liquid content between the two layers and partially permeate the superimposed base layer and photosensitive layer capable of forming a latent image upon photoexposure and subsequently a visible image upon development.

Land's research was on providing a photographic product comprised of a rupturable, disposable container carrying a photographic processing liquid or solvent. It was constructed to release the liquid content and distribute it uniformly over a photosensitive material to process the exposed photosensitive layer and produce a positive print (Land, Patent No. 2,543,181, 1951).

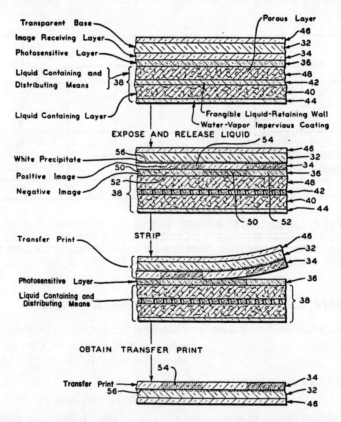

Figure 12-5: Patent Drawing of Rupturable, Disposable Container Carrying a Photographic Processing Liquid that is Released and Distributed Uniformly to Process Exposed Photosensitive Material. Patent Number 2,543,181, February 27, 1951.

Category:Transportation and Communication and Information Systems

Invention or Innovation — Localizer Antenna System

Inventor or Innovator — Andrew Alford
Cambridge, Massachusetts, 1954

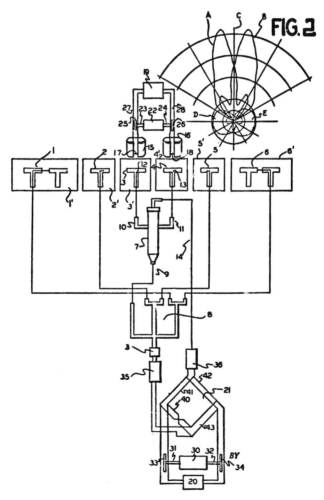

Figure 12-6: Localizer Antenna System Design. Patent Application of Andrew Alford, filed June 22, 1951.

The problem which Andrew Alford's invention solved was the instability of the instrument landing system for aircraft and the interference from airport structures. The ground based localizer provides an electronic signal which instruments on the plane receive. The signal is transferred to a visual reference which the pilot uses to guide the plane to the runway in low visibility weather.

The system was developed by Alford at ITT under contract with the Federal Aviation agency. The primary claim of the invention by Alford was:

> "A localizer signaling system for guiding a craft along a course, means for radiating at a main carrier frequency two beam patterns overlapping along the line of the course symmetrically, means for radiating two comparatively broad intersecting lobe patterns slightly off the main carrier having a comparatively lower magnitude of radiation in the direction of the beams than the beam radiations, the beam and the broad lobe radiation on one side of the course having the same modulating frequency and the beam and broad lobe radiations on the other side of the course also having the same modulation frequency but differing from the first modulation frequency" (U.S. Patent No. 2,683,050).

Invention or Innovation — Transistor Radio developed by
Texas Instruments and Regency Radio

Inventors or Innovators — Roger Webster, Paul Davis, Jim Nygaard,
Art Evans and Mark Shepherd,
Dallas, Texas, 1954

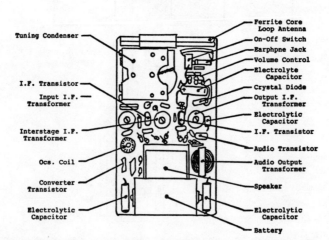

Figure 12-7: The Texas Instruments-Regency Radio of 1954

The transistor radio was based on the 1947 development of the transistor by Walter Brattain, John Bardeen and William Shockley of Bell Laboratories. Texas Instruments (TI) obtained a license to produce transistors in 1951. Gordon Teal of TI developed a reliable mass produced transistor that would sell for $2.50 which became the base for the four germanium transistor Regency radio. The TI research group faced many challenges ranging from reducing the design from eight to four transistors and obtaining miniaturized parts such as a speaker supplied by Jensen sound laboratories (Harris, 1980).

Category: Manufacturing-Materials

Invention or Innovation — Lucalox

Inventor or Innovator — General Electric Research and Development Center Schenectady, New York, 1959

Lucalox is a form of sintered alumina used principally as an envelope in high efficiency discharge lamps that provide a large share of the world's outdoor and factory lighting. The project that led to its invention began in 1954, as the General Electric (GE) R & D Center decided to enlarge its research effort in ceramics by using a more scientific approach to a field that had previously progressed by trial-and-error. Two researchers chose to concentrate on understanding the process of sintering (causing ceramic particles to stick together). They worked with alumina because they could obtain it in reasonably pure form. By 1956, they had developed a way to remove pores from sintered alumina, which greatly improved its ability to transmit light. A representative of GE's Lamp Division who saw a sample of this material became interested in it as an envelope material capable of sustaining the high temperatures of a high temperature discharge lamp. Up to that time such lamps used quartz, which is less temperature resistant than alumina. Single crystals of alumina had been used in experimental lamps but were too expensive for commercial use.

GE introduced the material as a product in 1959. Meanwhile, engineers in the company's Lighting Group were developing a new sodium vapor discharge lamp that took advantage of Lucalox's excellent heat resistance and translucence. The new lamp was announced in December 1962, but sealing and manufacturing problems delayed its introduction until 1965. It has now attained sales of about $120 million a year (Stewart, 1985).

Category: Communication and Information Systems

Invention or Innovation — Ruby Laser Systems
Inventor or Innovator — Theodore H. Maiman
Los Angeles, California, 1961

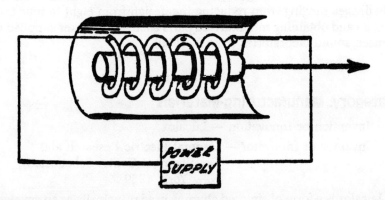

Figure 12-8: Schematic Diagram Illustrating the Embodiment of a Ruby Laser System which Utilizes a Helical Gas-filled Flash Tube for Optical Pumping of the Laser Material.

Laser is an acronym for light amplification by stimulated emission of radiation. It is a device capable of generating or amplifying coherent light.

Considerable effort was expended to develop a means of generating or amplifying coherent light. This source of light would open up a vast new region of the electromagnetic spectrum for a multitude of purposes, including communication, measurement and medical procedures.

There are gaseous and solid state lasers. The solid state lasers are superior because they are less complex. The design of a typical ruby laser consists of a cylindrical ruby (Al_2O_3 doped with CR_2O_3) rod with a reflective coating at each end. This rod is placed coaxially in a helical flash lamp. The green and blue components of the white light are absorbed by the ruby. The red light is emitted and coupled out of the system through a hole in the reflective coating at one end of the rod.

The ruby laser is mechanically stable and can be operated at room temperature without complex vacuum or vapor pressure techniques. It provides light which can be focused with extreme precision (Maiman, 1961).

Category: Communication and Information Systems

Invention or Innovation — Integrated Circuit

Inventor or Innovator — Jack S. Kilby
Dallas, Texas, 1964

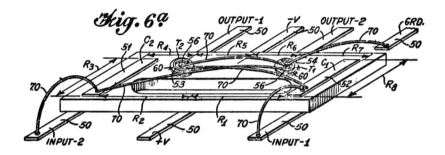

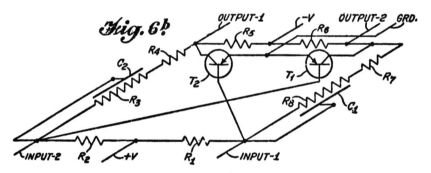

Figure 12-9: Drawing from Patent Application of J. S. Kilby filed February 6, 1959 for Miniaturized Electronic Circuits.

On June 23, 1964, J. S. Kilby was granted patent number 3,138,743 for Miniaturized Electronic Circuits. The integrated circuit is the base of the microelectronics revolution which made possible digital stereo, robotics and long range navigation systems. The integrated circuit solved the problem of the tyranny of numbers in large complex electronic circuits involving hundreds of thousands of components.

Kilby's research was based on the idea of G. W. A. Dummer of Great Britain who suggested in 1952 that "it seems now possible to envisage electronic equipment in a solid block with no connecting wires." Kilby

215

knew that various electronic components like transistors, capacitors, resistors and diodes could be made out of silicon. The idea that revolutionized electronics was "if you could make all the essential parts of a circuit out of one material, you could probably manufacture all of them all at once in a single block" (Reid, 1982).

On July 24, 1958, Kilby sketched in his notebook the idea of an integrated circuit on a single chip and on September 12, 1958, proved the idea valid in a laboratory at Texas Instruments. His idea broke with conventional wisdom and enabled the manufacture of a "novel miniaturized electronic circuit fabricated from a body of semiconductor material containing a different P-N junction wherein all components of the electronic circuit are completely integrated into the body of the semiconductor material" (U.S. Patent No. 3,138,743).

Category: Transportation Systems

Invention or Innovation — Stored energy (Flywheel) propulsion
for rapid rail cars

Developer — Garrett AiResearch Corporation, 1974

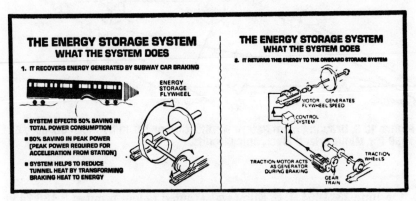

Figure 12-10: The Stored Energy Flywheel System.

The use of the stored energy flywheel in a rapid transit environment was researched by the Garrett AiResearch Corporation using New York City Transit Authority lines. This development has the potential of significantly reducing power consumption, operating costs and the amount of heat released in subway tunnels during the braking cycle.

216

During the braking process the energy normally dissipated as heat through the resistor grids is used by a motor/generator to increase the speed of the flywheels. During acceleration, the spinning flywheels produce electricity through the motor/generator to assist in driving the traction motors. A DC chopper system is the core of the solid control system.

Category: Construction Systems

Invention or Innovation — Tension Arch Structure

Inventor or Innovator — Samuel G. Bonasso
Morgantown, West Virgina, 1984

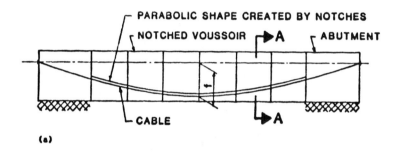

(a)

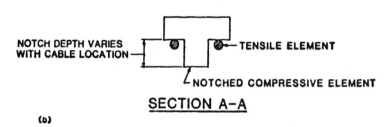

SECTION A-A

(b)

Figure 12-11: Patent Drawing of Tension Arch Structure Illustrating the Relation of the Cables (21) Stretched and Anchored Between End Supports and the Lateral Compressive Elements Placed Over the Cables with Grooves Across the Bottom of the Elements. Patent No. 4,464,803, August 14, 1984.

The tension arch is a structural system for use in bridges, buildings and other structures. The system supports part of its load by tension action and part by arch action. The tension arch represents a unique combination of two elements, the compressive member or arch and the tensile element or suspension structure. The tension arch concept minimizes the use of material at higher overall stress levels. In spans greater than 80' to 100', the system has the potential of achieving system-wide weight reduction of 20 percent or more. It is a structure whose geometry is relatively insensitive to a variety of support movements along all three axes (Bonasso, 1984).

Category: Transportation Systems

Invention or Innovation — Oscillatory Motion Apparatus

Inventors or Innovators — Alfred H. Stiller and James E. Smith
Morgantown, West Virginia, 1985

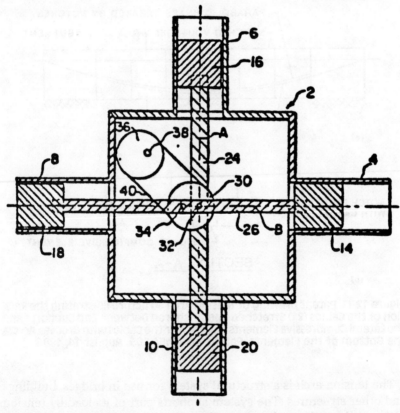

Figure 12-12: Patent Drawing of Oscillatory Motion Apparatus Used as Basis for a New Engine Design Called the Stiller-Smith Engine. European Patent No. 0167149, February 1985.

The Stiller-Smith engine design is based on an oscillatory motion apparatus that has one reciprocating rod oriented perpendicularly to a second reciprocating rod. A first trammel gear (30) is pivotally secured to the first and second rods, A and B. Reciprocation of the rods produces responsive rotation of the trammel gear. This oscillating design may be used in an engine block with two or more pairs of opposed cylinders, each containing pistons adapted for reciprocation.

The engine is compact, 12 inches square and 8 inches deep, and weighs less than 100 pounds. It has a one and one-half to one power to weight ratio. A prototype one liter engine produced 140 plus HP (Nadler, 1985; Stiller and Smith, 1985).

* * * * * *

The foregoing brief overview of selected inventions and innovations illustrates the potential that detailed studies of these have for gaining insight into the technical research process. Personal interviews with people who carried out the research can provide an understanding of the human side of the creative venture, including preparation, background and personality factors. Study of the social and cultural context in which the research took place provides information about factors that affect the creative process. The preparation of lineage studies can assist the comprehension of the linkages between and among various technical developments.

The list of technical developments which follows is presented as a resource to those who want to study the technical research process in greater detail.

____ Variable geometry aircraft
____ Tetrafluorethylene polymers
____ Nitinol
____ Cellophane
____ LEXAN®
____ Wood flour
____ NORYL®
____ Medical magnetic resonance
____ Computer aided design
____ Lytegem high-intensity lamp
____ Tungsten carbide
____ Litton pocket socket wrench
____ Bell Tourlite bicycle helmet
____ Turbocharge

____ Storm scope
____ Stored program concept—
computers
____ Pen recorder
____ Polaroid Camera
____ Pitot tube
____ Medical magnetic resonance
____ Tungsten inert gas welding
____ Super aluminum TM
____ MCS linear tracking
turntable
____ Compact disc player
____ Kodak disc camera
____ Supercharger

Creativity in the Technologies

_____ Magnetohydrodynamics

_____ Integrated circuits

_____ Electrical discharge machining

_____ Electrochemical machining

_____ Explosive forming

_____ High strength concrete

_____ Plywood

_____ Tower crane

_____ Light emitting diodes

_____ Linear induction motors

_____ Electronic ignition

_____ Vinyl chloride

_____ Inertial guidance

_____ Surface effect vehicles

_____ Altimeter—radar

_____ Barbed wire manufacture

_____ Contact lens

_____ Dynamometer

_____ Basic oxygen process
         for steel making

_____ Video tape cassette

_____ Automatic pilot

_____ Thermite welding

_____ Fibre optics

_____ Tufting

_____ Fresnel lens

_____ Heart pacemaker

_____ Holography

_____ Microphone

_____ Crease-resisting fabrics

_____ Telephone

_____ Cable television

_____ Turbine engine

_____ Superheterodyne radio circuit

_____ Potentiometer

_____ Power steering

_____ Quartz clock

_____ Tachometer

_____ Xerography

_____ Citizens band radio

_____ Bakelite

_____ Power metallurgy

_____ Radial tires

_____ Nonwoven fabrics

_____ VelCro

_____ Chemical milling

_____ Stretch forming

_____ Prestressed concrete

_____ Particle board

_____ Transponders

_____ Thermionic power

_____ Fuel injection

_____ Supercritical wing

_____ Video tape cassettes

_____ Polaroid camera

_____ Achromatic lens

_____ Aqualung

_____ Bathyscaphe

_____ Derailleur gear

_____ Float glass

_____ Magnetic tape recording

_____ Optical readers

_____ Shell moulding

_____ Laser

_____ Escalator

_____ Flight recorder

_____ Flight simulation

_____ Fuel cell

_____ Heat pump

_____ Hydrofoil

_____ Thermionic power

_____ Fluorescent lighting

_____ Telegraph

_____ Gyrocompass

_____ Refrigeration

_____ Parachute

_____ Power brakes

_____ Pressure cooker

_____ Stirling engine

_____ Wankel engine

_____ Electrostatic machine

_____ Automatic transmission

_____ Ballpoint pen

_____ Continous casting of steel

____ Tufting   ____ Transistor
____ Numerical control   ____ Fuel cells

SUMMARY

Creativity in technologies is directly affected by the personal traits and abilities of the researcher/inventor and the social and environment in which the creative activity takes place.

Various individuals have identified the following personal traits as typical of successful researchers:

( ) challenged intellectually by problem situations
( ) self motivated
( ) non-conforming to organizational rules
( ) willing to take risks
( ) see things differently or unconventionally
( ) focus on identifying the "true" problem
( ) little regard for social and textbook rules
( ) recognize and respond to societal needs
( ) disassociate themselves from the problem and let their sub-conscious operate
( ) engage in disorganized thinking
( ) use existing knowledge systematically
( ) resist adverse premature opinions of others
( ) intense and focused when working on the problem
( ) are persistent and stay with a problem once the problem is identified

These traits are best fostered by companies interested in innovation. Companies that have been most successful recognize the need to:

1. Foster champions of product ideas.
2. Emphasize long-term growth over short-term profits.
3. Focus on individuals and their unique abilities.
4. Emphasize the research mission based on the goals of the company.
5. Emphasize technological leadership as opposed to market domination.
6. Willingly accept uncertainty in product and process research and development projects.

When a majority of these personal and company traits are present, the likelihood of a continuing flow of new products and improved processes is enhanced.

BIBLIOGRAPHY

Alexander, Tom. "The Right Remedy for R & D Lag." *Fortune*, January 25, 1982.

Associated Press. "Prolific Inventor Continues His Creative Work at Age 86." *Dominion Post*, Wednesday, August 28, 1985.

"Basement Tinkerer Scoops the Pros." *Business Week*, March 16, 1968.

Bonasso, Samuel G. The Tension Arch Concept. Paper Number 1BC-84-13 deliverd to International Bridge Conference, Pittsburgh, Pennsylvania, June 1984.

Brumley, Cal. "Affluent Inventor." *The Wall Street Journal*, Friday, August 31, 1962, p. 1.

Compton, Dale W. (ed.). The Interaction of Science and Technology. Urbana: University of Illinois Press, 1969.

Editors. "R & D Magazine Selects 100 Most Significant Technological Advances." *Research and Development*, October 1985.

Fagenbaum, Joel. "Patrick E. Haggerty: Engineer and Visionary." *IEEE Spectrum*, December 1980.

Freeman, C. The Economics of Industrial Innovation. London: Penguin Books, 1974.

Gardner, W. David. "The Independent Inventor." *Datamation*, September 21, 1982, pp. 12-22.

Haggerty, Patrick E. Three Lectures at the Salzburg Seminar on Multinational Enterprise. Dallas, Texas, 1977.

Harris, S. T. "Marketing the Product." Twenty-fifth Anniversary Observance—Transistor Radio and Silicon Transistor. Dallas, Texas: Texas Instruments, Inc., 1980.

Himmelman, Laurie (ed.). "Recipe for Invention: A Pound of Perspiration + a Dash of Inspiration = Flash." *Varian Associate Magazine*, Vol. 24, No. 7., August 1979.

Jewkes, John; Sawers, David and Stillerman, Richard. The Sources of Invention, New York: St. Martin's Press, 1979.

Kay, Neil M. The Innovating Firm: A Behavioral Theory of Corporate R & D. New York: St. Martin's Press, 1979.

Kline, Stephen J. "An Appropriate Model for Industrial Innovation." *Science, Technology and Society*, No. 49, September 1985.

Kroll, W. J. "How Commercial Titanium and Zirconium Were Born." *Journal of the Franklin Institute*, September 1955.

Land, Edwin H. Photographic Product Comprising a Rupturable Container Carrying a Photographic Processing Liquid. U.S. Patent No. 2,543,181. February 27, 1951

Langrish, L. et al. Wealth From Knowledge. New York: John Wiley and Sons, 1972.

Maiman, Theodore H. Ruby Laser System. U.S. Patent No. 3,353,115. November 29, 1965.

Nadler, Elsa (ed.). "Something from a 'Do-Nothing.'" *Inquiry*, Morgantown, WV: West Virginia University Office of Sponsored Programs, Spring 1985.

Pearson, John W. "Organizing the R & D-Manufacturing-Marketing Interface." *Chemtech*, 1983, pp. 470-475.

Peters, Thomas. "The Mythology of Innovation, or a Skunkworks Tale, Part I." *The Standford Magazine*, Summer 1983.

Peters, Thomas. "The Mythology of Innovation, or a Skunkworks Tale, Part II." *The Standford Magazine*, Fall 1983.

Reid, T. R. "The Chip." *Science 85*, February 1985, pp. 32-41.

Reid, T. R. "The Texas Edison." *Texas Monthly*, July 1982.

Ross, Ian M. "Successful R & D Management: Catalyst for Competitive Advantage." *Vital Speeches of the Day*, April 1, 1986, pp.374-378.

Ruben, Samuel. Inventions in Chemistry. Proceedings of a Symposium, American Society of Engineering Education. University of Tennessee, Knoxville. June 17, 1976, pp. 29-41.

Ruben, Samuel. Inventions in Society—Response to Industrial Needs. 1981 Armstrong Memorial Lecture. Department of Electrical Engineering, Columbia University. April 17, 1981.

Sahal, Devendra. *Patterns of Technological Innovation* Reading: Addison-Wesley Publishing Company, Inc. 1981.

Schmitt, Patrick E. Three Lectures at the Salzburg Seminar on Multinational Enterprise. Dallas, Texas. 1977.

Stewart, P. J. Correspondence with P.W. DeVore. 1985.

Stiller, Alfred H. and Smith, James E. Oscillatory Motion Apparatus. European Patent No. 0167149. February 7, 1985.

Tornatzky, Louis G. et al. *The Process of Technological Innovation: Reviewing the Literature*. Washington, DC.: National Science Foundation, 1983.

U. S. Department of Commerce. *U. S. Industrial Outlook, 1986*. Washington, D.C.: U. S. Government Printing Office, 1986.

U. S. Department of Transportation. *Innovation in Public Transportation*. U. S. Government Printing Office, 1976.

"Something is Out of Whack in U. S. Business Management." *U.S. News and World Report*, July 15, 1985, pp. 53-56. Vincenti, Walter G. "Technological Knowledge Without Science: The Innovation of Flush Riveting in American Airplanes, ca. 1930- ca. 1950." *Technology and Culture*, Vol. 25, No. 3. July 1984.

Walton, R. R. Personal Correspondence and Discussion with P. W. DeVore, 1985.

Westney, D. Eleanor and Sakakibara, Kiyonori. "Designing the Designers: Computer R & D in the United States and Japan." *Technology Review*, April 1986, pp. 24-31.

Index

225